The BRS Reference Book

John Mollett

Copyright © 2018 J Mollett
Published by Huge Jam, England, 2018. All rights reserved.

ISBN: 1911249258
ISBN-13: 978-1-911249-25-2

CONTENTS

	Introduction	i
1	1950-1953 Group Codes	1
2	1953-1956 Denationalisation and Fleet Reduction	21
3	1956-1964 District Codes	40
4	1964-1972 Two-Letter Branch Codes	65
5	1972-1979 Two-Letter Codes – Regional Companies	88
6	1979-1983 Three-Letter Codes	110
7	1983-1991 Revised Regional Network	126
8	1991-1998 National Hub-and-Spoke Network	140
9	Parcels, 1955-1956	146
10	Parcels, 1956-1964	149
11	Parcels, 1964-1976	157
12	Roadline, NCL and SPS, 1976-1987	164
13	Lynx, 1987-2005	170
	Appendices	175
	Bibliography	228
	Addendum	229
	At a Glance: Milestones in BRS History	230

INTRODUCTION

Some twenty years have passed since the final portion of the once-familiar British Road Services (BRS) fleet became a matter of history, yet interest in the company's vehicles – especially those in recognisable liveries until white became the overall fleet colour in 1983 – remains as keen as ever. This is evidenced by the number of enthusiasts who still painstakingly restore rescued former BRS vehicles, or even replica vehicles put into BRS livery, and take them rallying; others who prepare their own model BRS lorries from die-cast kits, the sheer range of die-cast models produced by the likes of Corgi, EFE and Base-Toys in BRS liveries; and the clamour for photos of BRS vehicles at side stalls accompanying outdoor rallies.

A small band of dedicated enthusiasts, meanwhile, has painstakingly compiled written records (fleet lists) for as many vehicles that BRS had operated as possible ever since the earliest days, and right up to the end in 1998. The attraction of the fleet to be 'lorry spotter' was always the fleet-numbering system, an ingenious mix of letters and numbers that indicated whereabouts in the country each vehicle came from. This hobby did not go unnoticed and at the fleet's peak, during the 1950s – long before the present-day fascination for Eddie Stobart's fleet encouraged by their fan club – the Ian Allan organisation produced a series of booklets, 'The ABC of British Road Services', enabling fans to identify the fleet number codes in use and also to send their observations to their 'Lorry Spotters Club' for records to be compiled.

In all, six editions of this booklet were published, the last in 1963. By coincidence the very next year, 1964, saw yet another renumbering exercise, introducing the two-letter depot codes that remained in use, subject to numerous variations in successive years, virtually up to the end, yet to the best of our knowledge no publication has ever been produced identifying these various codes to the enthusiast. We are frequently asked

Introduction

what the fleet numbers on particular photographs mean and we believe there is a demand for a publication outlining these details.

In this publication we will, therefore, attempt to identify the various codes that have been in use during different periods of time. For completeness we will go right back to the beginning, as well as covering all the post-1964 two-letter codes. Although the 1950s and early 1960s were covered in the six aforementioned Ian Allan ABCs, not everyone has access to these (now scarce and much sought after) and while Ingram and Mustoe also included glossaries of the codes used during the 1950s in their book 'BRS – The Early Years', this too does not include some very early additional information unearthed at the Kew Reference Library, nor the many changes that occurred after de-nationalisation commenced at the end of 1953.

The various periods of fleet-number currency will be divided into sections as follows:

1950-1953: Division-District-Group structure. Ian Allan's first three ABCs cover the period 1951-1953; Ingram & Mustoe have back-tracked to late 1950 in addition but several other changes occurred earlier in 1950.

1954-1956: De-nationalisation. Many changes to fleet numbering occurred as the fleet contracted and vehicles left BRS service to find new owners.

1957-1963: Division-District structure (covered by three further Ian Allan ABCs). This was a relatively sterile time for enthusiasts as the numbers held by the much-reduced fleet now indicated only the District to which a vehicle belonged and not the fascinating variety of different Groups as they had previously. None of the ABCs, however, related the new District Codes to the previous codes, which will now be explained.

1964-1972: District & Branch structure with two-letter codes now identifying individual Branches once again. The mid-1960s were also the period of so-called 'back-door nationalisation', when a number of haulage businesses were acquired and added to the fleet.

1972-1979: Restructuring of BRS into seven regional limited companies, each with its own livery from 1973 onwards, still using the two-letter code system.

1979-1983: Introduction of 'Activity Letters' to Branch codes, resulting in the formation of three-letter codes.

1983-1991: Contraction of the six BRS companies in England and Wales to four, and adoption of a uniform livery for the entire fleet once again, now simply of white with red and blue decals, identical to the Truck Rental fleet introduced in 1974.

1991 onwards: Combination of all regional fleets into one national fleet once again, now administered from a head office at Milton Keynes. This brought about closure of all the former regional offices and, hence, lack of access to local information, so details are largely unclear for this period. It was made more difficult too as so few vehicles carried fleet numbers physically by this time.

We will also outline the codes used by the company BRS (Parcels) Ltd which was set up in 1955, duly becoming a separate entity and similarly adopted different Branch codes in subsequent years.

Pickfords

The Pickfords fleet does not concern this publication as it was numbered on a national basis; the capital letter 'M' used as a prefix to its fleet numbers was regarded as the company letter from 1957 onwards, as was 'X' for the Meat Haulage fleet until it was wound up in 1963. Prior to 1957, both these services and the fleet of Carter Paterson and Pickfords Joint Parcels Service, had all been numbered in the same series using a small letter 'm' as prefix, this identification having originally been introduced by Pickfords as far back as 1905 to signify 'motor vehicle' as opposed to the horse traction used formerly.

1

1950-1953

We are concerned in this publication with BRS Group codes which were not introduced until 1950. Historically, however, it is worth recording events prior to this. Initially each business acquired by the Road Haulage Executive (RHE) of the British Transport Commission (BTC) was termed a Unit and assigned a Unit number. At first, the Units were grouped into batches whereby related companies within transport families such as Hauliers Ltd, Holdsworth & Hanson, Bristol Industries, etc, were given related numbers. From August 1949, however, the Units were reorganised into eight regional Divisions offering general haulage and parcels, lettered A-H, and given numbers – e.g. A1, A2 onwards, within each Division. A ninth Division covering 'Special Traffics' was later added offering nationwide services through the Pickfords network.

As the numbers of businesses acquired increased, Units began to be merged and based upon a strategic network of retained premises which became BRS depots. During 1950 batches of such Units were combined to form Groups; sometimes the Units were linked geographically, in other cases they were combined because they operated similar services. In due course each of the eight Divisions comprised several Districts, each controlling a number of Groups and the Groups were responsible for raising the fleet numbers that came to the attention of enthusiasts.

Unit numbers continued to be assigned to each business acquired up to the conclusion of the compulsory takeover period in November 1951 even though the Groups had been set up from the mid-1950s onwards. It has been established that the Unit numbers raised attained approximately the following maxima: S. Eastern Division: A625; Scottish Division: B270; N. Western Division: C800; N. Eastern Division: D730; Midland Division: E750; S. Western Division: F280; Western Division: G240 and Eastern Division: H435.

At least 115 numbers were known to be voided which indicates a total allocation of Unit numbers of just over 4000, although there were many instances where, for one reason or another, an acquisition was deferred and later given a new number, or did not take place at all. In fact, it is on record that 3706 businesses joined the BTC during nationalisation and this included those in the Special Traffics Division, such as Pickfords, which, being numbered nationally, were not allocated Divisional Unit numbers. This total comprised an original 418 undertakings acquired voluntarily to October 1948 plus 3288 acquired under compulsory regulations.

As well as the Divisional letter another identifying feature for each Division was the background colour to the circular crest carrying the BTC 'lion over wheel' emblem on the cab doors. This later changed in format to a coloured ring surrounding a black centre on which the lion emblem was superimposed in 1952.

There follows a summary of the first allocation of Group codes; in this listing, alongside the name of each Group, is given the location of the Group's head office (usually the main depot) and its origin (i.e. Unit No and former operator).

SOUTH EASTERN DIVISION (HQ London)

Divisional letter A: BTC crest colour 'Royal Blue'. New vehicle registrations raised by Head Office in City Road, London EC1, usually in batches of 100, from 1950 onwards.

Initially this was divided into four geographical Districts covering general haulage and contract hire, while parcels work continued to be carried out by the original BTC Units, which remained ungrouped. The Group codes were:

South Eastern District

1A	East Kent	HQ Wincheap, Canterbury	A78. C & G Yeoman
2A	Mid Kent	Len House, Mill St, Maidstone	A27. Kent Carriers A28. Phillips Motors
3A	North West Kent	Woolwich, London SE18	A6. Browning & Hoar A30. C&C Tuff A31. Tuff & Hoar
4A	Medway	Priory Road, Strood, Kent	A14. Gamman & Dicker
5A	Blackwall Tunnel	King William Walk Greenwich SE10 Later Canon Beck, SE16	A102. Broad & Montague
6A	Bermondsey	24 Crucifix Lane, SE1	C17. Miller & Co, Liverpool C18. Motor Carriers (Liverpool) Ltd
7A	Camberwell	395 Albany Road, SE5	A79. Bowler & Mack
8A	Rother Valley	East Cross, Tenterden, Kent	A142. C Corke & Co
9A	Newington Butts	Searles Road, London SE1	A32. Tillings Transport

1950-1953 Group Codes

South Western District

20A	Brighton	Warwick Street, Brighton	A26. Southern Transport
21A	No record		
22A	No record		
23A	Croydon	155 Stafford Road, Croydon	A119. Gilchrist Road Services
24A	Kingston	205 Kingston Road, New Malden	A138. Adams Bros (Super Transport) Ltd
25A	Battersea	35 Battersea Bridge Road, SW11	A71. J R Munday
26A	Guildford	53 Epsom Road, Guildford	A120. H Rackliffe
27A	Lambeth	170 Westminster Bridge Road, SE1	A5. British Motor Wagon Co A12. H & G Dutfield Ltd
28A	Borough	3 Southwark Street, SE1	? Dawson

North Western District

40A	St Albans	229 Hatfield Road, St Albans	A89. H G Currell & Co
41A	High Wycombe	99 Richardson St, High Wycombe	A219. W H Mealing
42A	Shoreditch	87 Curtain Road, London EC2	A2. Henry Bayes & Son
43A	Islington	141 Kingsland Road, E2	A15. General Roadways
44A	Tottenham	98 Balls Pond Road, N1	A13. Bert Whiting & Son
45A	Brentford	52 London Road, Brentford	A70. Cliffords
46A	Slough	68 Alpha Street, Slough	A92. Johns Transport (Slough) Ltd. A93. C & B Transport
47A	City (?) *	89 Rivington Street, London EC2	A80. Joseph Eva
48A	Hayes	Springfield Road, Hayes	A103. H Burgoyne
49A	Finsbury	3 Bonhill Street, EC2	A23. McNamara
50A	Muswell Hill	Coppetts Road, N10	C33. Fisher Renwick (Manchester)
51A	Chiswick	Power Road, W4	A8. C D & T (Contracts) Ltd
52A	Perivale	Walmgate Road, Perivale	D59. NMU Ltd (York)
53A	West London	86a High Road, Chiswick W4	F7. Southern Roadways (Poole) F12. Geo Baker & Son (Southampton)

* *(unconfirmed – reported by Arthur Ingram and Gordon Mustoe only) – address later became HP of 42A Group*

North Eastern District

60A	Bow	7 Maverton Road, E3	A11. W Dowling A33. G W Transport
61A	Thurrock	London Road, Stanford-le-Hope	A7. E J Burrough & Sons
62A	Bishopgate	62 Quaker Street, E1	A18. Kneller & Chandler
63A	Hackney Marsh	Waterden Road, E15	A76. R J Weeks
64A	Monument	10 St Dunstans Hill, EC3	A72. J Reece
65A	Millwall	Klondyke Garage, W Ferry Rd E14	A127. N Eslick
66A	Stratford	2 Martin Street, E15	A192. Rockman Bros Ltd
67A	Plaistow (?)	Unconfirmed – early demise	
68A	No record		
69A	Poplar	166 High Street, E14	A104. R Davis Ltd
70A	Victoria Park	260 Cambridge Heath Road, E2	A9. Charles A Wells Ltd
71A	East Ham	62 High Street North, E6	A194. East Ham Haulage

72A	Stepney	10 Christian Street, E1	? T M Fairclough
73A	No record		
74A	Edmonton	6 Ferry Lane, N17	B5. H & R Duncan (Edin.)

Parcels Services

Unit A3	Bouts Tillotson	Waterden Road, E15
Unit A16	Holdsworth & Hanson	Seward Street, EC1
Unit A19	Suttons	72 Whitecross Street, EC1
Unit A34	Carter Paterson	128 Goswell Road, EC1

Amendments

Groups 47A (reported by Arthur Ingram and Gordon Mustoe), 67A (only one reference at Kew) and 69A (two references at Kew) were proposed but never became effective and were wound up before fleet numbering was introduced.

Groups 44A and 74A were transferred to Pickfords New Furniture Service, Special Traffics Division in February 1951 and absorbed into the Pickfords fleet.

There then followed a major reorganisation of the SE Division, proposed from April 1951, whereby all existing Groups were sub-divided into the type of service offered rather than their geographical location. This resulted in the foundation of four 'Services':

- 'Southern District' comprised Groups 1A, 2A, 4A, 8A, 20A, 26A, 40A, 46A and 61A
- 'Long Distance Services' comprised Groups 5A, 6A, 43A, 45A, 53A, 60A, 65A and 66A
- 'Short Distance Services' comprised Groups 3A, 7A, 23A, 24A, 25A, 27A, 48A, 62A, 64A, 71A and 72A
- 'Contracts Services' comprised Groups 9A, 42A, 49A, 51A, 52A, 63A and 70A
- 'Parcels Services' comprised Groups 28A & 50A which traded alongside the existing Units
- Group 41A was wound up and split three ways – between Pickfords New Furniture Service, 46A and 44G.

During this reorganisation depots were re-allocated between Groups resulting in the winding-up of Group 27A (split between 43A & 49A), Group 65A (split between 5A, 43A & 72A) and, later, Group 60A (split between 64A & 66A). Proposals to abolish four Groups were put into effect later in 1951; in July Group 40A was merged into 46A & renamed 'Slough & St Albans Group' as a result, and Group 24A was merged into 23A; then in November Group 48A was merged into 25A and Group 71A into 62A.

From January 1st 1952 all Groups in Kent and Surrey within the 'Southern District' were transferred to the South Western Division (F) which formed a new 'Home Counties District' with codes 60F-65F to accommodate them. This action was followed, in September 1952, by a further reorganisation of the remaining General Haulage Groups in SE Division to produce the following structure:

- 'Directional Services' (long distance) comprised Groups 5A, 6A, 43A, 45A, 53A and 66A
- 'General Services' (short distance) comprised Groups 3A, 7A, 23A, 25A, 62A and 72A plus 46A and 61A from the former Southern District.

Further Group mergers followed at the end of 1952 in which 7A absorbed 3A and was renamed 'South East London'; 25A absorbed 23A and was renamed 'South West London'; and 64A absorbed 72A to be renamed 'East London'.

Parcels Services meanwhile had finally been formed into a Group structure by introducing the following codes from the start of 1952:

33A	Smalls - Metropolitan Area	Ex Units A3 & A16, Groups 28A & 50A	HQ Waterden Road, E15
34A	Parcels – City Area	Ex Units A34 & A19	HQ Goswell Road, EC1
35A	Parcels – South of Thames Area	Ex Unit A34	HQ Willow Walk, Bermondsey
36A	Parcels – North of Thames Area	Ex Unit A34	HQ Harrow Road, Paddington
37A	Shipping, Trunk Pool & Cartage	Ex A34	HQ Central Street, EC1

No vehicles received fleet numbers in the 35A-37A series; all carried the 34A prefix.

A new service coded 99A was also set up late in 1952, administering work at Covent Garden and Spitalfields markets. It had no vehicle fleet at this time.

SCOTTISH DIVISION (HQ Glasgow)

Divisional letter B, BTC crest colour 'Traffic Blue'. New vehicle registrations were initially raised at Group level unit mid-1951. The premises at Linlithgow, formerly head office of West Lothian Group, were then reclassified as the Divisional Workshops, where all new vehicles were prepared for entering service and this site then became responsible for all new registrations from late 1951 onwards, from West Lothian CC (reg mark SX)

The Division was divided into four geographical Districts. Parcels work was carried out by one single Group based on the former services offered by Youngs Express Deliveries (Unit B18) and attached to the Glasgow District.

Aberdeen District

1B	Aberdeen General	HQ 31 Virginia Street, Aberdeen	B16. Wm Wisely & Son
			B50. John Barrie
2B	Old Ford Road	Old Ford Road, Aberdeen	B53. Charles Alexander
3B	Peterhead/Fraserburgh	Victoria Gge, St Peter St, Peterhead	B219. James Sutherland
4B	Buckie	2 Fishmart, Buckie	B32. D Taylor
5B	Inverness	61 Eastgate, Inverness	B17. Wordie & Co, Glasg.

Dundee District

20B	Dundee General	54 East Dock Street, Dundee	B1. David Barrie
21B	Angus	12 Roberts Street, Forfar	B31. David Callendar
22B	Perth	10 Mill Street, Perth	B17. Wordie & Co (Glasgow)
23B	North Fife	Glebefield Works, Levan	B58. C Adamson
24B	South Fife	29 Chapel Street, Dunfermline	B57. David West & Son
25B	Tay	98 Albert Street, Dundee	B69. David Horsburgh

Edinburgh District

40B	Edinburgh General	Lower Gilmore Place, Edinburgh 3	B5. H & R Duncan
41B	Leith	130 Leith Walk, Edinburgh 6 – later Marine Gardens, Portobello	B41. J R Carmichael
42B	Waverley	24 Market Street, Edinburgh 1	B19. Mutter Howey
43B	West Lothian	Stockbridge, Linlithgow – later Blackburn Road, Bathgate	B95. Wm Aitken & Sons
44B	East Lothian	Maitlandfield House, Haddington	B44. Geo Patterson & Son
45B	Borders	2 Sime Place, Galashiels	B52. John Arnott

Glasgow District

60B	Douglas	46 West George Street, Glasgow C2	B17. Wordie & Co
61B	Scottish Parcels	124 Portman Street, Glasgow S1	B18. Youngs Express Deliveries
62B	Clyde	33 Weir Street, Glasgow C5	B68. Frank Smillie & Son
63B	London Scottish	286 Clyde Street, Glasgow E1	B120. London Scottish Transport
64B	Wallace	54 George Square, Glasgow C2	B27. Cowan & Co (80 North Wallace Street)
65B	Taylor	2 Portree Street, Glasgow C4	B124. Alex Taylor & Sons
66B	Argyll	29 McFarlane street, Glasgow C4 – later 44 Warroch Street, Glasgow C3	B28. Brysons Motors
67B	Central Scotland	West Borland, Denny	B6. A & J Dunn Ltd

| 68B | Caledonian | Eastfield Road, Dumfries | B3. James Dickinson Tr. |
| | | | B4. Dumfries & Galloway Tr. |

Late in 1950 one further Group was added:

| 69B | Ayrshire | 25 Portland Road, Kilmarnock | B127. David McKinnon |

This was separated from 60B after the large Unit B36, which had previously been ungrouped, was added to Douglas Group's responsibilities in August 1950.

Amendments

The first Group to be wound up in the Scottish Division was 45B which was proposed for disbandment in April 1951. It was duly merged into 44B which was renamed 'East Lothian and Borders Group' as a result. To allow for this expansion two former 44B depots were transferred to the control of Group 42B. 4B, another loss-making Group, was another early failure, being broken up and split between 3B and 5B in 1952. 3B was renamed 'North East Scotland Group' following this adjustment.

Late in 1951 the decision was taken for each District to administer its own parcels activities. Adjustments to goods carried were made between depots in Dundee and Edinburgh before this proposal could take effect and, in October, 25B was renamed 'Dundee Parcels Group', followed by 41B which became 'Edinburgh Parcels Group'. Finally, in February 1952, a new Group (6B) was set up - Aberdeen Parcels Group – using one depot (349 King Street) and around 70 vehicles drawn from Old Ford Road Group (2B).

The title of 61B remained 'Scottish Parcels' and does not appear to have been altered to 'Glasgow Parcels' until after 1955.

NORTH WESTERN DIVISION (HQ Manchester)

Divisional letter 'C', BTC crest colour 'Sea Green'. Unusually all general haulage vehicle registrations were raised locally by individual Groups from the outset; however, contracts vehicles were registered from the Trafford Park office, using Lancashire CC. The Division was originally divided into four Districts but one – the Stoke District – was wound up as early as November 1950 and most of it transferred to the Midland Division.

Liverpool District

1C	North Liverpool	HQ Crosshall St, Liverpool 1	C35. Harding Bros Ltd
2C	Central Liverpool	19 Old Hall Street, Liverpool 3	C29. The Union Road Tpt Co Ltd
			C85. Bennetts Hlge & Warehousing

3C	South Liverpool	27 Water Street, Liverpool	C17. Miller & Co (Liverpool & London) Ltd
4C	East Liverpool	7 Tithebarn Street, Liverpool	C18. Motor Carriers (L'pool) Ltd
5C	Warrington	57 Knutsford Road, Warrington	C54. De Burgh (Warrington) Ltd
6C	St Helens & Widnes	Sherdley Road, St Helens	C86. R Heaton
7C	Wigan	92 Millgate, Wigan	C90. John Farr & Co Ltd
8C	North Wales	Premier Garage, Bretton, Chester	C50. Arthur Hughes (Carriers) Ltd C51. Shepherd & Hughes Ltd
9C	Liverpool Parcels	18 Wood Street, Liverpool	A19. Sutton & Co (London)

Lancaster District

20C	Lancaster Parcels	5 St James' Street, Burnley	C34. W V Greenwood
21C	Burnley	169 Accrington Road, Burnley	C31. Wesley Clegg C100. Burnley Reliance Transport
22C	Preston	65 Water Lane, Preston	C52. H Viney & Co Ltd
23C	Carlisle	83 Lowther Street, Carlisle	C180. Robsons Hlge (Carlisle) Ltd
24C	West Blackburn	Stansfield Street, Blackburn	C174. W H Bowker
25C	Morecambe Bay	25 Brock Street, Lancaster	C89. Fred Milner & Son
26C	Rossendale	Burnley Road, Accrington	C2. Ashworth Heys
27C	East Blackburn	Canterbury Street, Blackburn	C178. Kinder Bros

Stoke District

The District was wound up very early and no records survive to confirm its complete composition. The following has been established:

- 41C was Burslem - becoming the HQ of 28E, North Staffs Group, in November 1950
- 42C was Tunstall - becoming 29E
- 45C was Longton - becoming 31E

It is likely that 40C would have been Stoke itself as the main centre, becoming 30E and we suspect the remaining unidentified codes (43C/44C) could have been held by a 'Mid-Cheshire' which later became 11C (see below) and a 'South Cheshire', covering the area around Crewe, which became part of 28E, North Staffs Group.

There does not appear to have been sufficient parcels work to justify forming a specific Parcels Group in this District. In later years such work was carried out from Nottingham Parcels Group.

Manchester District

60C	Kearsley	Spindle Point, Kearsley, Farnworth	C158. Lawtons Transport Ltd
61C	North Manchester	33 Cecil Street, Greenheys, M'cr 15	C4. A H Barlow
62C	Manchester Contracts	Ashburton Road, Trafford Park	C53. Foulkes & Bailey
63C	Manchester Parcels	White City, Chester Road, M'cr 16	C33. Fisher Renwick

64C	Greenheys	Wentworth Street, Ardwick, M'cr 12	A3. Bouts Tillotson (London) E16. Holdsworth & Hanson (B'ham)
65C	Salford	12 East Ordsall Lane, Salford 3	C22. NWTS
66C	Central Manchester	York St, off Charles St, M'cr 1	C29. Springfield Carriers
67C	Trafford Park	Ashburton Road, Trafford Park	C27. G Smith & Co Ltd, Eccles
68C	Manchester Local	63 Corporation Street, Manchester 4	C19. Joseph Nall & Co
69C	Bolton & Bury	240 Blackburn Road, Bolton	C88. Melias Tpt (Bolton) Ltd C91. HFW Transport
70C	Oldham	Spencer St, Hollinwood, Oldham	C138. Samuel Cusick Ltd
71C	Cheetham	102 North Street, Manchester 8	C25. Lancashire Freight Services
72C	Rochdale	Holmes Road, Rochdale	C327. Clegg Tpt (Rochdale) Ltd
73C	South Manchester	Third Avenue, Trafford Park	C109. Wilfred Allen
74C	Cornbrook	326 Chester Road, Manchester	B27. Cowan & Co (Glasgow)

Amendments

A new Group 11C, Mid Cheshire (HQ Newcastle Road, Sandbach; origin unclear – principal constituent Unit 119. P L & G S Harris of Lostock Gralam) was added to Liverpool District in November 1950 from the former Stoke District. The rest of Stoke District was transferred to Midland Division after boundary revisions.

There followed the addition of the new Group 10C, Merseyside (HQ Leece St, Liverpool) in February 1951, which combined the Liverpool Branches of the Metropolitan Transport Co (ex S E Division) and Pickfords' local contract and general haulage services.

Observers have always been puzzled by the order in which these Group codes were issued and we believe an explanation has been uncovered from documents researched at Kew. These reveal that a new 'Wrexham Group' was separated from 8C, North Wales Group, in October 1950, just three weeks before it was transferred to the Western Division following the boundary revisions in November. It appears probable that this was intended to be 10C which did not materialise, leaving the code available for later re-issue.

The Manchester District saw much reorganisation from the outset. First, Group 72C (Rochdale) was merged into 70C and 73C (South Manchester) into 67C, in December 1950. A further reorganisation of the District in September 1951 brought about the closure of Groups 65C, 66C and 71C, while concentrating particular services on the remaining Groups; 65C and 71C were combined to enlarge 74C, while 66C is believed to have been absorbed by 64C. The larger Oldham Group, 70C, was wound up during 1952, apparently split between various neighbouring Groups, and 68C, the local railway cartage Group based on the activities of Joseph Nall of Bolton, is believed to have been merged into 69C.

Lancaster District lost Group 27C in 1952, merged into 24C. One final code introduced during 1952 was 12C, 'Liverpool Port Control

Organisation' which offered a fleet of radio-controlled vans to monitor activities at the docks. It is not known whether any vehicles were numbered in this series.

NORTH EASTERN DIVISION (HQ Leeds)

Divisional letter 'D', BTC crest colour 'Road Haulage Red' (aka 'Ayres Red'). In general most new vehicle registrations were raised at Group level in each District but from late 1953 onwards batches of new vehicles also began to be registered from the Divisional Office in Leeds. Under the original network all Districts, except West Riding, had their own Parcels Group.

Tyne/Tees District

1D	Central Newcastle	HQ Cambridge Hall, Northumberland Road, Newcastle	? Currie & Co
2D	Haymarket	8 Lovaine Crescent, Newcastle 2	D48. Wallsend Road Haulage
3D	Gateshead	Second Avenue, Team Valley Trading Estate, Gateshead	D35. Northumbrian Transport
4D	Stockton	Church Road, Stockton-on-Tees	D45. Fred Robinson
5D	Middlesbrough	32 Cleveland Street, Middlesbrough	D95. T O Harrison
6D	Sunderland	Low Row, Sunderland	D20. Hepplewhite & Shaw
7D	Quayside	Baltic Chambers, Quayside, N'cstle	? J Baxter (and others)
8D	Sandyford	Dinsdale Road, Sandyford, N'cstle 2	B19. Mutter Howey (Edin.)
9D	Exchange	15 Queen Street, Newcastle 1 – later Dinsdale Road, Sandyford	D94. F Short & Sons
10D	Tyne/Tees Parcels	Gallowgate, Newcastle	? Fleet mainly from United Automobile Servs, Darlington

Leeds, York & East Riding District

20D	York	Foss Island, Walmgate Bar, York	D59. NMU Ltd
21D	No record		
22D	North Leeds	12 Rampart Road, Woodhouse Street, Leeds 6	D36. OK Carrier Co D124. Hutton & Grimes
23D	South Leeds	107 Water Lane, Leeds 11	C22. NWTS (Salford)
24D	Central Leeds	Wortley Low Mills, Whitehall Road, Leeds 12	D28. Holdsworth & Hanson
25D	Central Hull	Hyperion Street, Hull	D53. Barrick & Fenton
26D	Selby	Holme Lane, Selby	D37. Onward Transport
27D	North Hull	Myton Street, Hull	D13. C A & F Cook Ltd
28D	East Hull	13 South Street, Hull	D23. R Hodgson (Hull) Ltd
29D	Leeds, York & East Riding Parcels	Brown Lane, Leeds 12	A34. Carter Paterson (London)

West Riding District

40D	Halifax	Horton Street, Halifax	D24. I W Holdsworth
41D	Ripponden	Chapel Field Works, Ripponden	D6. Beaumont Bros
42D	Huddersfield	Savile St, Milnsbridge, Huddersfield	D19. Joseph Hanson

1950-1953 Group Codes

43D	South Bradford	38 Legrams Lane, Bradford	D10. Bradford-Leicester Transport D25. Holdsworth & Burrill
44D	Central Bradford	16 Leeds Road, Bradford	D90. Blythe & Berwick
45D	Airedale	Albion Garage, Main Street, Bingley	D88. L Butterfield D154. W C Forder & Sons
46D	Dewsbury/Batley	Crown Garage, Bradford Rd, Batley	D99. Geo Oldroyd
47D	West Bradford	Prospect Wks, Wakefield Rd, Bradford	D17. City Express Motors + Ryburn Utd Tpt (division of Bouts Tillotson)

South Yorkshire District

60D	Central Sheffield	80 Eyre Lane, Sheffield 1	D49. Warringtons Tpt
61D	Chesterfield	Walton Road, Chesterfield	D57. Chesterfield Tpt
62D	Attercliffe	Shepcote Lane, Tinsley, Sheffield	D98. Geo Pickin
63D	Park	Worthing Road, Sheffield 9	? John Grocock Ltd
64D	Doncaster	North Bridge Road, Doncaster	? Currie & Co (Newcastle)
65D	Barnsley	Meadow Street, Barnsley	D134. Walter Fisher
66D	Hallam	Star Garage, Penistone Rd, Sheffield 6	D161. Glossops Transport
67D	South Yorkshire Parcels	Transport House, Penistone Road, Sheffield	A3. Bouts Tillotson (London)

In November 1950 one additional Group was added:

68D	Sherwood	Dock Road, Worksop	E32. Sergeants Transport

This was transferred in from the Midland Division following boundary revisions, when the northernmost portion of Nottinghamshire was added to N E Division control and had formerly been a part of Group 65E, Dukeries. The Newark depot 60E was added to 67D at the same time.

Amendments

No major alterations were made to the N E Division, apart from the addition of Group 68D, until 1952. In that year 5D was merged into 4D which was renamed 'Teeside Group' as a result; 7D was abolished, believed merged into 3D; 9D was merged into 8D, both having shared joint management for some time already; 24D and 29D were merged to form an enlarged Parcels Group; 25D was wound up and split between 27D and 28D; 66D was similarly split, between 60D and 63D. One other small alteration was to add the Dunham-on-Trent depot to the 68D Group network – this had formerly been part of 65E Group like others in the area but had initially been transferred to 42H, Gainsborough Group, at the time the other bases were combined as 68D.

The merger of 24D and 29D was unusual in that the 24D fleet, being the larger of the two, was simply recoded from 24D to 29D, following which the 29D fleet was renumbered and became 29D168-209.

MIDLAND DIVISION (HQ Birmingham)

Divisional letter 'E', BTC crest colour 'Nut Brown'. Initially new vehicle registrations were raised at Group level but, in 1952, the District Offices at Birmingham, Wolverhampton, Leicester and Nottingham became responsible for new registrations and from mid-1953 onwards the Divisional Office in Birmingham assumed responsibility for all new registrations.

The Division comprised five Districts when first set up but underwent much change over successive years, as explained below. First, the original network:

Birmingham & Coventry District

1E	Bullring	HQ Well Lane, Allison Street, B'ham 5	E9. A J Gupwell Transport
2E	Coventry	Quinton Road, Coventry	E15. John Morton & Son
3E	Witton	147 The Broadway Perry Barr B'ham 20	? Broadway Transport
4E	Cheapside	Cheapside, Birmingham 5	A32. Tillings Transport (London)
5E	Aston Cross	Dartmouth Street, Aston, B'ham 6	E61. Caudle Ltd
6E	Tyburn	229 Tyburn Rd, Erdington, B'ham 24	E8. S Green & Sons
7E	Birmingham Parcels	Walter Street, Nechells, B'ham 7	A34. Carter Paterson (London)
8E	Hockley	107 Whitmore St, Hockley, Birmingham	E79. Transport Economy
9E	Hay Mills	George Road, Hay Mills, B'ham 25	E65. Hurst & Payne
10E	Nuneaton	Tuttle Hill, Nuneaton	E24. W. Midland Roadways E152. Archers Ltd.

Staffordshire & Shropshire District

20E	Wellington	Watling Street, Wellington	E177. J T Stone
21E	Walsall	Wolverhampton Road, Bentley	E4. T S Charnell & Sons E7. J T Elwell & Co
22E	Wolverhampton	Ettingshall Road, Wolverhampton	E3. C & L Transport
23E	Shrewsbury	Minsterley, nr Shrewsbury	E67. Lewis Bros (Haulage) Ltd
24E	Kidderminster	34 Lower High Street, Stourbridge	E126. S T W Priest E23. Talbot Transport
25E	West Bromwich	121 Spon Lane, West Bromwich	E10. R Harrison
26E	Stafford	Wolseley Road, Rugeley	E184. R Gee & Sons Ltd
27E	Dudley	Tipton Road, Dudley (new site combining all Units)	E81. Dudley & Blowers Transport Co and others

Leicester & Northampton District

40E	North Leicester	Groby, Leicestershire	E13. S Lathom & Son
41E	South Leicester	Lutterworth Road, Blaby, Leics	E12. Kinders Transport
42E	Leicester Parcels	9 Belgrave Road, Leicester	A34. Carter Paterson (Lond.)
43E	Northants Parcels	High Street, Rushden	E49. P X Carriers E50. Bert Scroxton
44E	Leicester Tipping	Hinckley Road, Stoney Stanton	E68. Lane & Peters
45E	Northampton	Gladstone Road, Northampton	E196. A W Darby

Nottingham & Derby District

60E	Nottingham Parcels	Triumph Road, Lenton, Nottingham	E6. Donaldson, Wright
61E	South Nottingham	Iremonger Rd, London Rd, Nottingham	E64. Robin Hood Transport
62E	Derby	Meadow Lane, Alvaston, Derby	E104. Benjamin Keeling
63E	North Nottingham	64 The Wells Road, Nottingham	E37. R Keetch & Son
64E	South Derbyshire	Lichfield Road, Branston, nr Burton	E24. West Midland Roadways
65E	Dukeries	Nursery Street, Mansfield	E18. Scott (Mansfield) Ltd
66E	North Derbyshire	Unity Garage, Darley Dale	E30. Toft Bros & Tomlinson

Oxford & Worcester District

80E	Oxford	Long Lane, Littlemore, Oxford (jointly with Cowley Group)	E20. Chas. Scott Road Services
81E	Droitwich	Chapel Bridge, B'ham Rd, Droitwich	E147. H B Everton
82E	Worcester	Graham Garage, Bromyard Rd, St Johns	E100. P K Matthews
83E	Livestock	LMR Goods Station, Milverton, Warwick	E34. E G Oldham
84E	Cowley	Long Lane, Littlemore, Oxford	E103. J Harding

This was the network finally established and effective from early in 1950. However, it is interesting to ponder what might have been, for an earlier Group schedule dated July 1949 reveals several further proposed Groups that did not come into being, particularly in the Staffordshire & Shropshire District where codes up to 31E were originally considered.

We find, for example, that 20E was originally proposed as 'Shifnal Group' and 29E 'Wellington'; in the event the two were merged and the code 20E was taken by Wellington. Similarly, a Group 25E to be 'Darlaston' was proposed but this became part of 21E 'Walsall'. Two Groups were proposed at Wolverhampton, 22E 'North' and 28E 'South' but materialised as the single Group 22E. A Group 31E was proposed at 'Stourbridge' but this became part of 24E 'Kidderminster'. And finally 'West Bromwich', originally allocated the code 30E, became 25E instead after the voiding of 'Darlaston'.

In the Notts & Derby District the original proposal was for 62E to be 'Riddings Group' and 67E 'Derby'. Activities in both areas were instead combined under the 6wE banner as 'Derby Group'; and in the Oxford & Worcester District it was originally proposed that 81E should be 'Leamington Group' and 85E 'Droitwich' – again, both areas were combined as 81E 'Droitwich Group'. One final revision was the name 'Aston Cross' for 5E Group – this was originally to be named 'Erdington'.

Amendments

The first Group to be disbanded within the network set up from early 1950 was 1E 'Bullring' which was abolished around July 1950. Its fate is unclear, believed at least partly absorbed into 4E.

Next, from November 1950, came a major reorganisation especially affecting the Midland Division, after BRS regional boundaries were redrawn, which resulted in the loss of the Oxford, Worcester and Shropshire areas to the Western Division, and the northernmost portion of Nottinghamshire to the N. E. Division, whilst gaining the Potteries area from the N.W. Division and a portion of Bedfordshire, to the west of the A1, from the Eastern Division. As a consequence most of Groups 80E-84E, 20E and 23E and portions of 24E and 65E left Midland control, while the following new Groups were added:

28E	North Staffs	HQ Hamil Rd, Burslem (ex 41C) plus two depots in Crewe (ex ??) and one in Whitchurch Shropshire (ex 23E)	C23. North Staffs Haulage C185. Gordon Hill, Crewe & others E181. Denmans
29E	Tunstall	High Street, Tunstall (ex 42C)	C14. Beresford, Caddy & Pemberton
30E	Stoke	Whieldon Road, Stoke (ex ??)	C113. Beckett Bros
31E	Longton	Church Street, Longton (ex 45C)	C252. Longton Transport
46E	Livestock	Milverton, Leamington (ex 83E)	E34. E G Oldham
47E	Luton	Dunstable Road, Luton (ex ??)	H13. W T Parrott
48E	Leighton Buzzard	Grovebury Rd, L.Buzzard (ex 26H) plus one depot in Dunstable (ex ??)	H123. A C Biggs ?

There were also expansions at 2E (which gained the Leamington portion of 81E); 6E (gaining Redditch from 81E); 26E (gaining Newport, Shropshire, from 20E); 45E (gaining Bedford from Eastern Division, old Group code unknown) and 65E (gaining the Riddings portion of 62E).

With the loss of Shropshire the opportunity was taken to re-title as 'Staffordshire District' the area now covered by Groups 21E-31E, while Group 25E, West Bromwich, was transferred to the Birmingham & Coventry District and merged with 8E (Hockley) to form an enlarged new Group 11E, West Bromwich.

Once the dust had settled from this reorganisation further consolidation of Groups occurred. 31E was merged into 28E in December 1950; 24E was merged into 27E in March 1951 – despite 24E being the larger of the two the Dudley premises were more suitable for expansion; 3E was wound up and split between 5E and 6E in March 1952; and 29E was scheduled for absorption into 30E, also early in 1952. Further mergers in 1952 involved the loss of 48E, merged into 47E; 40E, merged into 41E and 10E, absorbed by 6E.

The claim by Ingram and Mustoe in their book 'The Early Years' that in North Notts there were two further Groups – 68E (Sherwood) and 69E (Gainsborough) – is as yet unsubstantiated. Apart from the fact that the single depot at Dunham-on-Trent would not have been large enough to justify a new Group 69E, there would not have been two Groups with the same name (Gainsborough already existed as 42H). Further it is on record at Kew that N.E. Division gained these areas direct from Dukeries, Group 65E, in November 1950 (Dunham-on-Trent in 1952, from 42H).

SOUTH WESTERN DIVISION (HQ Bournemouth)

Divisional letter 'F', BTC crest 'Road Haulage Green'. Yet again new vehicle registrations were initially raised at Group level but from late in 1951 all began to be raised by the Divisional head office at Bournemouth.

The original network comprised three Districts. Subsequent years saw amendments that added two further Districts to the Division and, for ease of reference, all five Districts are outlined below:

Bristol District

1F	Central Bristol	HQ Cheese Lane, Bristol 2	?? H W Hawker
2F	East Bristol	46 Days Road, St Phillips, Bristol 2	F23. Pioneer Transport
3F	South Bristol	116 Bath Road, Totterdown, Bristol 4	F24. Henry Russett
4F	Bath & Wells	Princes Road, Wells	F53. George Willmott
5F	Taunton & N. Devon	27 High Street, Taunton	F141. A G Bowerman
6F	S. Devon & Cornwall	24 Wolborough St, Newton Abbot	F10. Frank White (Tpt) Ltd
7F	Bristol Parcels	Albert Road, St Phillips, Bristol 2	A34. Carter Paterson (London)

In 1951 a new Group was added:

8F	South Gloucestershire	Westerleigh Road, Yate, nr Bristol	

This had originally begun life as Group 43G in the Western Division but was transferred to the S.W. Division during the boundary revisions of November 1950 and initially became part of 1F, Central Bristol Group. During 1951, however, the decision was taken to set up a separate Tipping Group in the area and, as this included most of the former 43G fleet, all were made over to the new Group 8F.

Southampton District

20F	Poole & Yeovil	West Quay Road, Poole	F7. Southern Roadways
21F	Parkstone	Cranbrook Road, Parkstone	?? Geo Maidment (Tpt) Ltd
22F	Southampton	121 Regents Park Road, Southampton	F12. Geo Baker & Son
23F	Portsmouth	8 Powerscourt Road, Portsmouth	F168. Parks of Portsmouth
24F	Exeter	1 Ferndale Road, St Thomas, Exeter	F55. Crews Bros
25F	Eastleigh Parcels	Dutton Lane, Eastleigh	A34. Carter Paterson (London)

26F	Isle of Wight	6 Quay Street, Newport IoW	A34. Carter Paterson (London)
27F	Railway Cartage	30 Christchurch Road, Bournemouth	A35. Chaplins (London)
28F	Exeter Parcels	Church Road, St Thomas, Exeter	A34. Carter Paterson (London)

Reading District

40F	Reading	Cardiff Road, Reading	F13. Talbot-Serpell Transport
41F	Swindon & Salisbury	9 High Street, Swindon	F8. Swindon Transport Co
42F	Melksham & Frome	Spa Road, Melksham	F17. W A & A G Spiers

Late in 1952 add:

43F	Guildford	Ex 65F (see below)	

The Division was expanded from January 1st 1952 by transferring the Kent & Surrey area from S.E. Division to form a new Home Counties District:

60F	East Kent	ex 1A
61F	Mid Kent	ex 2A
62F	Medway	ex 4A
63F	Rother Valley	ex 8A
64F	Brighton	ex 20A
65F	Guildford	ex 26A – later transferred to Reading District as 43F as shown above

At the end of 1952 a new Exeter District was set up by re-coding as follows:

80F	Exeter	ex 24F
81F	Taunton & N. Devon	ex 5F
82F	S. Devon & Cornwall	ex 6F
83F	Exeter Parcels	ex 28F

The Reading District had no specific Parcels Group, while Parcels work in the Home Counties area continued to be carried out by South Eastern Division through its 'South of Thames Area' grouping, 35A (with vehicles actually coded 34A).

WESTERN DIVISION (HQ Cardiff)

Divisional letter 'G', BTC crest colour 'Lead Grey'. New vehicle registrations were again initially raised at Group level, later adjusting to District level.

Although by far the smallest Division in terms of numbers of vehicles – and Groups – it had numerous internal reorganisations as well as expansion following the Divisional boundary alterations of November 1950. In South Wales individual large Groups were set up rather than a selection of smaller Groups as in other Divisions. The original network follows:

Newport/Cardiff District

| 1G | Newport | 57 Dock Street, Newport, Mon | G1. All British Carriers |
| 2G | Cardiff | Ferry Road, Grangetown, Cardiff (new site combining older Units) | G5. Lansdowne Motors and others |

Swansea District

| 20G | Swansea | 237 High Street, Swansea (Depot – new site at North Dock) | G3. Jacksons Haulage G4. S J Jeffrey |
| 21G | West Wales | Station Road, Carmarthen | G45. G J Bland & Co |

Gloucester District

40G	Forest of Dean	Hill Street, Lydney, Glos	G79. T S Thomas
41G	Gloucester	Wessex Bldgs, Clarence St, Gloucester	G6. Stephens Transport
42G	Hereford	38 Edgar Street, Hereford	?? Morgan & Friend
43G	South Gloucestershire	Westerleigh Road, Yate, nr Bristol (new site)	G113. W A Febry (Yate) G94. S Ball & Sons (Chipping Sodbury)

Amendments

Following the boundary changes of November 1950 in which portions of Oxfordshire, Worcestershire and Shropshire were transferred from the Midland Division, and Central Wales from the N.W. Division, the network was significantly altered. It now comprised:

South Wales District

Groups 1G, 2G, 20G and 21G as above plus 25G – an additional code introduced for vehicles held in the 'South Wales Pool', a selection of vehicles held in reserve at Barry Dock and numbered in the same series as Swansea's (20G).

Oxford/Gloucester District

Groups 40G and 41G, plus:

44G	Oxford	ex 80E
45G	Cowley	ex 84E
46G	Worcester	ex 82E
47G	Droitwich	ex 81E

Shrewsbury/Central Wales District

30G	Wrexham/Welshpool	ex N.W. Division, possibly 10C(?), previously 8C. HQ Berse, nr Wrexham
31G	Shrewsbury	ex 23E
32G	Wellington	ex 20E
42G	Hereford	ex former Gloucester District (no code change) and now also including Clee Hill (ex 24E)

Group 43G was transferred to the South Western Division during these boundary changes, initially being merged into Group 1F before being separated to set up the new Group 8F in 1951.

It is not known whether separate numbering sequences were ever introduced for Groups 30G-32G. From the outset all records for vehicles in this area show them to be numbered in a common 31G series but using district blocks of numbers to distinguish different depots. Thus 31G upwards was Wellington; 31G100+ was Shifnal; 31G200+ was Dawley; 31G250+ was Wrexham; 31G380+ was Welshpool; 31G420+ was Minsterley; 31G450+ was Oswestry, and so on. 31G itself was renamed 'Shrewsbury/Central Wales District' and by 1953 the Divisional network now read as follows:

1G	Newport District
2G	Cardiff District
20G	Swansea District plus sub Group 21G, West Wales
31G	Shrewsbury/Central Wales District plus sub Group 42G, Hereford
41G	Gloucester District plus sub Groups 46G, Worcester and 47G, Droitwich
46G	Oxford District

Groups 46G and 47G were merged into 41G early in 1953, leaving the Division with just two sub Groups. (Groups 40G and 45G had already been absorbed into 41G and 44G respectively in 1952). No Groups were specifically dedicated to parcels carriage in the Western Division; this activity was instead carried out by appropriate depots within each District.

EASTERN DIVISION (HQ Norwich)

Divisional letter 'H', BTC crest colour 'Turquoise Blue'. The final geographical Division of BRS set up by the BTC. Once again, new vehicle registrations were initially raised at Group level, a policy that continued in use in most Districts until at least 1953. An original Group network covering East Anglia and the adjoining Peterborough District was drawn up before the boundary revisions of November 1950 and as this affected subsequent amendments it is shown below:

1950-1953 Group Codes

	Original Proposal, Norwich Dist.		Original Proposal, Peterborough Dist.
1H	Norwich	20H	Huntingdon and Isle of Ely
2H	Ipswich	21H	Peterborough
3H	North Norfolk	22H	Wisbech
4H	Kings Lynn	23H	Cambridge
5H	Beccles	24H	? assumed to be Group in Luton/Bedford area
6H	Yarmouth	25H	? assumed to be Group in Luton/Bedford
7H	Bury St Edmunds	26H	Leighton Buzzard
8H	Stowmarket		
9H	Bishops Stortford		
10H	Fordham		

With the transfer of the western portion of Bedfordshire to the Midland Division in November 1950, Eastern Division chose to redraw the boundaries between the Norwich and Peterborough Districts, adding Kings Lynn, Fordham and Bishops Stortford to the Peterborough catchment area and the Group structure finally adopted became as follows:

Norwich District

1H	Norwich	91 Hall Road, Norwich	H22. Eastern Roadways
2H	Ipswich	London Road, Ipswich	H7. East Anglian Transport
3H	North Norfolk	Quay Garage, Wells-next-the-Sea	H23. T C Grange
4H	Stowmarket (ex 8H)	Station Road, Stowmarket	?? O G Barnard
5H	Beccles	London Road, Beccles	H17. Robinsons (Beccles) Ltd
6H	Yarmouth	Maincross Road, Gt Yarmouth	H62. Toby Transport
7H	Bury St Edmunds	Roudham East Harling, Norfolk	H26. R T Lawrence

Peterborough District

20H	Hunts & Isle of Ely	Bury Road, Ramsey, Hunts	H8. Greenwoods
21H	Peterborough	165 Cromwell Road, Peterborough	H56. Airlandwater, Fengate
22H	Wisbech	Cromwell Road, Wisbech	H10. H W Jones
23H	Cambridge	450 Cherry Hinton Road, Cambridge	H61. Moss (Cambridge) Ltd
24H	Kings Lynn (ex 4H)	North Everard Street, Kings Lynn	H34. Giles & Bullen
25H	Bishops Stortford (ex 9H)	Stansted Road, Bishops Stortford	H22. Eastern Roadways (Norwich)
26H	Fordham (ex 10H)	New Path, Fordham, Ely	H35. H A Newport

A further Group was added following the 1950 boundary revisions, after extending the District northwards:

27H	South Lincolnshire	Pode Hole, Spalding	H68. A E Dodson

Whether this held a previous Group code in the Lincoln District (48H?) or was part of an existing Group such as 44H is not known.

Lincoln District

40H	Grimsby	Regent Gge, Convamore Rd, Grimsby	H18. J J McVeigh
41H	Louth	22 Nichol Hill, Louth	H99. A W Jaines
42H	Gainsborough	Wembley Street, Gainsborough	H226. R H Wild/J Bradshaws (after separation from H8)
43H	Boston	1 Mill Hill, Boston	H110. Boston Haulage Co
44H	East Lincolnshire	Marsh Lane, Boston	H182. T E Dabbs
45H	Lincoln	Monks Road, Lincoln	H33. Thacker & Saltergate
46H	Scunthorpe	5 High Street East, Scunthorpe	H89. J Harvey (Haulage) Ltd
47H	Brigg	Bigby Road Garage, Brigg	H11. W H Martin H137. Fergus Proctor
??	South Lincs.	Transferred to 27H 1950/51 (see above)	

Colchester District

60H	Colchester	Victoria Chase, North Station Road, Colchester	H58. Days

All vehicles in this area were combined into one large Group rather than a number of smaller Groups as in the other Districts.

Parcels services in the Eastern Division continued to be carried out by the original BTC Units and were ungrouped at this time. These were as follows:

Unit A34	Carter Paterson	Bases at Cambridge, Chelmsford, Clacton and Ipswich
Unit H39	P X Eastern	Bases at Cambridge, Ipswich, Lowestoft and Norwich
Unit H59	Holdsworth & Hanson	Base at Chelmsford
Unit H60	E R Ives	Bases at Kings Lynn and Norwich

It was not until 1952 that these were combined to form a new Group 8H 'Norfolk and Suffolk Parcels'. Later the Group's coverage was extended into Lincolnshire by adding bases at Boston and Scunthorpe, effectively becoming 'Eastern Parcels'.

During 1951, 41H was merged into 40H which was renamed 'Grimsby & Louth' and 42H was absorbed by 47H.

1952 saw considerable reorganisation affecting especially the Groups in East Anglia. 7H was merged into 1H; 6H was merged into 5H, which was renamed 'Beccles & Yarmouth'; 24H (Kings Lynn) was merged into 3H, which was renamed 'West Norfolk Group' and then became that Group's headquarters; and the resultant network was reconstructed such that Norwich District now comprised Groups 1H, 3H, 5H and 8H, while a new 'Ipswich District' comprised Groups 2H, 4H and 60H. The 'Colchester District' was wound up.

Elsewhere, 20H was abolished, split between 22H and 23H, and 44H was merged into 43H.

2

1953-1956

With a change in government in October 1953 the new Conservative administration wasted no time in legislating for the majority of the BRS fleet to be returned to private ownership once again. The BTC was obliged to set up a Disposals Board to organise denationalisation of their vehicles. Of a fleet that had peaked at 41,265 vehicles in 1952 and stabilised at around 36,000 after various adjustments such as withdrawal of elderly and non-standard types and replacement of many smaller vehicles with fewer larger ones, the government proposal was that BRS should dispose of 32,500 and retain around 3,500 (rather less than 10%) which would then be set up to work alongside all other operators under equal trading conditions.

The Disposals Board selected vehicles from locations throughout the country from all nine Divisions, including Special Traffics, giving each vehicle (or batch of vehicles) a Unit number, each preceded with the reference '66', and published lists of Units available for disposal at intervals of around a month. Prospective buyers were invited to apply for these lists and then send their tenders for any particular Unit(s) for consideration. In total 28 lists of Units were published, the first on November 18th 1953 and the last on June 13th 1956, detailing Units numbered from 66/1 to 66/10173. A total of 31,703 vehicles were offered for disposal during this exercise, many more than once as larger Units that failed to sell were often then broken up into smaller Units and given new Unit numbers. Large numbers of Units were of one vehicle only to appeal to smaller operators but Units varied in size up to those containing significant quantities of vehicles complete with premises, many of which were duly re-occupied by their former operators. And of course, apart from denationalisation, other vehicles continued to be replaced by new ones and disposed of by auction in the normal course of business at the same time.

The 28 Disposal lists were numbered 1-15; R1-R6 (R = Reject, re-offering Units that had failed to sell previously); S1-S4 ('Special' lists containing larger, with-premises Units intended to appeal to the larger operator); and SC1-SC3 ('Special Scottish' lists offering similar large with-premises Units in Scotland). After a cautious start interest in the Units available gained momentum and apart from prospective operators themselves, a number of specialist dealers began to make repeated successful tenders for significant quantities of vehicles, then applying for the 'Special A' licences required by the new owners to operate them, and selling them on, complete with the requisite licences. This often resulted in former BRS vehicles ending up in completely different parts of the country after the new owners acquired them from those middle men rather than from BRS direct. It is surprising this was allowed to happen as, at first, licensing authorities had been refusing some grants on the grounds that vehicles would not be working in the same areas as before.

List S4 published in March 1955 was the one that caused a major rethink over the entire denationalisation process. It had offered 160 large Units with a total of 6115 vehicles at many major locations but the response to it was disastrous: only 19 Units with 436 vehicles were sold initially, with 14 more (406 vehicles) awaiting a decision, while no bids were received at all for 74 Units (2986 vehicles) and all tenders for another 53 (2287 vehicles) were rejected.

All tenders for the Parcels and Meat Haulage operations, which had been prepared for sale in the form of companies under the provisions of Section 5 of the Transport Act 1953, were also rejected and legislation had to be introduced enabling the BTC to retain far more vehicles than had originally been intended; in fact 7750 general haulage vehicles (to enable BRS to continue to operate trunk services effectively), plus 1425 on contract agreements, 4400 on parcels work, 500 on meat haulage and 925 on 'Special Traffics' (furniture removals, heavy haulage and tankers) were retained, making a total of 15,000. Decisions upon offers for Units from the final list published were made in July and August 1956 and the process of denationalisation was considered complete in August.

The vehicle fleet of necessity underwent much upheaval while the denationalisation process unfolded. Ian Allan were unable to produce their 'ABC' booklets on BRS during this period and instead published two versions of a new booklet – 'The ABC of British Lorries' – each of which contained a page at the back acknowledging to their army of BRS enthusiasts that constant changes in the fleet rendered it impossible to publish details on BRS for the time being. These ABCs are now particularly hard to come by.

The following summary outlines, in the first section, the various alterations that occurred to BRS Group codes during denationalisation, i.e. the period not covered by Ian Allan between their booklets of 1953 and

1957, which is largely previously unrecorded. There follows a second section that identified the major companies that benefited from denationalisation by acquiring 'Special A' or 'S' licences as they came to be termed, within the catchment area of each BRS Division.

Following acceptance of tenders for vehicles offered in the first Disposals list, ex-BRS vehicles began to appear on the road, in the service of their new owners, from January 1954 onwards.

AMENDMENTS TO BRS GROUP CODES

SOUTH EASTERN DIVISION

Among Groups to be wound up as denationalisation proceeded 45A was closed and merged into 53A, 25A was absorbed into 46A and 62A into 64A. These were some of the earliest to finish. Contracts Services were also concentrated, by winding up 42A (split between 9A and 49A), while both 52A and 63A were closed and merged into 70A.

Early in 1955 the Parcels Groups 33A-37A were transferred to the control of the newly formed company BRS (Parcels) Ltd and the fleet numbers were prefixed 'P'. See further on. Also early in 1955 the S E Division acquired control of the following Groups from the South Western and Eastern Divisions following their closure: 20F, 22F, 23F, 26F, 27F, 43F, 60F-62F, 64F, 1H and 60H. As vehicles from these Groups passed through paint shops they began to receive BTC crests with the Royal Blue roundel of their new Division but no change to the old codes was made at this stage.

With the setting up of further limited companies, BRS Ltd and BRS (Contracts) Ltd at the beginning of 1956, all Contracts fleet numbers were prefixed 'C'. Also in 1956 a new armorial design was granted to the BTC, now with the lion standing and the wheel held aloft, and the S E Divisional roundel colour was revised from Royal Blue to Road Haulage Green from this time; it was applied to cab doors as they attended paint shops.

Further fleet contraction occurred in which 7A was wound up, merged into 64A, and 64A itself was finally attached to the Covent Garden Organisation, providing that service with a vehicle fleet and the fleet was recoded to 99A. The Railway Cartage Group, 27F, was transferred to the control of British Railways in 1956.

By the end of denationalisation, S E Division was controlling Groups 5A, 6A, 43A, 53A and 66A; 46A, 61A and 99A; C9A, C49A and C70A; 20F, 22F, 23F, 26F, 43F, 60F-62F, 64F, 1H and 60H.

SCOTTISH DIVISION

Denationalisation, between 1954 and 1956, saw a huge reduction in the BRS fleet in Scotland; percentage-wise this Division experienced the highest proportion of vehicles sold of the eight Divisions. Several Groups, notably 3B, 5B and 68B, were entirely wiped out and others were severely pruned, especially 62B, 67B and 69B. As fleet contraction continued numerous fleet renumbering exercises were introduced.

At the end of 1954 a new Group, 7B 'Aberdeen', was introduced combining what remained of Groups 1B and 2B before this, too, was almost entirely sold. Group 20B was renamed simply 'Dundee' and 40B, Edinburgh, at the same time. A new Group, 26B 'Fife', was introduced probably around the same time, merging the survivors from 23B and 24B. Also in the Dundee District, 22B was absorbed by 21B. In the Edinburgh District, 42B was merged into 40B and part of 43B into 44B, before this too was merged into 40B.

The Glasgow District saw many changes. 63B was renamed 'Glasgow' at the end of 1954 and duly absorbed 64B, followed by what remained of 67B at Falkirk and 69B at Ayr and, finally, Grangemouth which appears to have gone from 67B to 43B first, before also ending up at 63B. The survivors from 62B were merged into 60B. What became of 65B is unknown but as it is believed to have included much contracts work and all contracts work was eventually centred on 60B, this may have been another merger. 66B remained virtually unaffected by all this turmoil.

The four Parcels Groups were transferred to BRS (Parcels) Ltd at the beginning of 1955, after which the company letter 'P' was prefixed to all their fleet numbers. 61B appears to have been retitled 'Glasgow Parcels' from this time. In 1956 the Scottish Division was reorganised into just two Districts: 'North of Scotland' controlling Groups 7B, 20B and 21B north of the Tay, and 'South of Scotland', controlling 60B, 63B, 66B, 40B and 26B, the final surviving Groups. The new BTC armorial crest retained the same roundel colour of 'Road Traffic Blue'.

NORTH WEST DIVISION

As denationalisation proceeded Group mergers began to occur in the N W Division. Among the first Groups to be abolished 21C was merged into 24C, 25C into 22C and 61C into 64C. There then followed a much larger reorganisation, at the end of 1954, which saw the four main Liverpool Groups, 1C-4C, merged to form a new Group 13C 'City of Liverpool'. Some months afterwards Group 10C was also broken up, the haulage work also joining 13C while contracts work (mainly for Co-ordinated Traffic Services) was transferred to 62C. The specialist ICI Dyestuffs contract work at 60C was also transferred to 62C which effectively became 'North Western Contracts'.

It is likely that 12C also became part of 13C during this but no records are available. The three Parcels Groups 9C, 20C and 63C were moved to BRS (Parcels) Ltd in early 1955 and the codes prefixed 'P'.

Still further consolidation occurred in 1956 but, as wholesale fleet renumbering was now on the cards, no further interim fleet number adjustments were made; for example, after all depots of Rossendale Group 26C had been disposed of, a handful of surviving vehicles transferred to Blackburn but retained their 26C fleet numbers. Likewise, in South Lancashire and North Cheshire, the six remaining depots from 5C, 6C, 7C and 11C were combined as the new 'Warrington Branch' but no renumbering was introduced; rather, the vehicles were regarded as interchangeable between the six sites and deployed as required regardless of their fleet numbers.

One final amendment during 1956 was for 74C to absorb 69C and became renamed 'Bolton Branch' – in this case the 74C code was substituted for 69C on former Bolton vehicles. At the end of denationalisation N W Division was administering vehicles only in the series 5C, 6C, 7C, 8C, 11C, 13C, 22C, 23C, 24C (including 26C), 62C, 64C, 67C and 74C. The Divisional crest colour remained 'Sea Green' after introduction of the new-style crest in 1956.

NORTH EASTERN DIVISION

As in other areas the N E Division underwent much revision at the end of 1954, when a series of new Groups was introduced, following Group mergers as follows:

30D	York	A merger of 20D and 26D
31D	Hull	Merging 27D and 28D
32D	Leeds	Merging 22D and 23D
49D	West Riding General	Merging 41D, 43D, 44D and 45D
50D	West Riding Parcels	Merging 40D, 42D, 46D, 47D and so establishing a fourth Parcels Group in the Division. Code 48D was not used

The Parcels Groups 10D, 29D, 67D and the newly-formed 50D, passed to BRS (Parcels) Ltd early in 1955 with appropriate 'P' prefix. Just six months later, in mid-1955, 49D being now the sole member of the old 'West Riding District' was merged into 32D, which duly took the title 'West Riding General', and Groups 30D-32D now comprised a new 'Yorkshire District'.

Elsewhere, in the North East, 3D was merged into 2D, 6D into 1D and 8D was also abolished, its fate unresolved (any survivors remain untraced), while in South Yorkshire 61D was absorbed by 60D and 65D and 68D were both merged into 64D.

Early in 1955 N E Division acquired control of the Lincoln District after the Eastern Division was wound up and the remaining Groups of this District – 40H, 45H and 46H – were added to an enlarged 'South Yorks & Lincs District'. The BTC crest colour would change from turquoise to red following this transfer as they underwent repainting.

At the end of de-nationalisation, N E Division was administering Groups in the series 1D, 2D, 4D, 30D, 31D, 32D, 60D, 62D, 63D and 64D plus 40H, 45H and 46H. The BTC crest roundel colour continued to be 'Road Haulage Red' after the new design was introduced in 1956.

MIDLAND DIVISION

The resultant reduction arising during de-nationalisation brought about much Group consolidation from 1954 onwards, including the closure of Group 9E, merged into 4E; the merger of 21E into 22E which was retitled 'South Staffs Group'; the absorption of 45E by 47E and the closure of 61E which was merged into 63E and retitled simply 'Nottingham'. Group 66E was also wound up (no survivors are known; all were apparently sold), while 44E and 46E were dispersed as the BTC pulled out of specialist tipping and livestock transport.

During 1955 the Division was re-organised into just two Districts – 'West Midland', which combined the remaining Groups of the former 'Birmingham & Coventry' and 'Staffordshire' Districts with the exception of Coventry itself, and 'East Midland', a merger of the old 'Leics/Northants' and 'Notts/Derby' Districts plus Coventry. A third District was then added, the Peterborough District, transferred in after Eastern Division was dissolved and comprising its remaining Groups of 21H, 22H and 23H, which involved alteration of their BTC crest colour from turquoise to nut brown upon repainting.

Meanwhile the four Parcels Groups, 7E, 42E, 43E and 60E, passed to BRS (Parcels) Ltd control and were prefixed 'P', also early in 1955. The Staffordshire District had never included a Parcels Group, the two depots devoted to such work in this area being attached to other Districts (Willenhall with 7E and Stoke 60E).

Following these events still further concentration occurred: 6E was disbanded, the Tyburn and Tamworth portions merging with 22E and Redditch with 27E; the Wolverhampton portion of 22E was transferred to the control of 4E; 28E was merged into 30E and 64E into 62E. The Wolverhampton portion of 4E was transferred again, to 11E which was renamed 'Wolverhampton' and absorbed what remained of 26E; and the Tyburn portion of 22E was transferred to 4E.

The new BTC armorial crest was introduced in 1956 and the opportunity was taken to revise the roundel colour to the turquoise formerly used by the Eastern Division, which began to be applied to all Midland Group vehicles as repainting occurred. The Division now controlled only 2E, 4E, 5E, 11E, 22E, 27E, 30E, 41E, 47E, 62E, 63E, 65E, 21H, 22H and 23H.

SOUTH WESTERN DIVISION

Parcels Groups 7F, 25F and 83F passed to BRS (Parcels) Ltd at the beginning of 1955 and were prefixed 'P'. Then, owing to the reduction in the fleet resulting from denationalisation, the decision was taken early in 1955 to disband the South Western Division completely. The Bristol District (Groups 1F-4F) and the Exeter District (80F-82F) were transferred as existing Districts to the Western Division, while the Southampton District (20F, 22F, 23F, 26F and 27F) and Home Counties District (60F-64F) went to the South Eastern Division, except 63F which was closed in 1954 and merged into 61F. The Reading District was dismantled. Reading (40F) and the Swindon portion of 41F went to Western Division, joining Oxford District, while the Melksham portion of 42F was added to the Bristol District, also joining the Western Division. The Salisbury portion of 41F and the Gillingham portion of 42F were attached to the Poole/Yeovil Group of the Southampton District and Guildford (43F) to the Home Counties District, all going to S E Division.

No fleet renumbering was introduced for any of these transfers and the only indication, to observers of the time, that any change had occurred would have been the gradual alteration of the BTC crest roundel colours to Lead Grey (Western Division) or Royal Blue (S E Division) from 1955 onwards – and, in due course, the subsequent further crest colour variation after the new crest was introduced in 1956, now to Deep Cream (Western Division) or Road Haulage Green (S E Division).

WESTERN DIVISION

The already streamlined Western Division network of just six District codes and two sub-Groups remained in place as fleet reduction occurred and no codes were eliminated. In the continued absence of Specific Parcels Groups, when BRS (Parcels) Ltd was set up as a separate company at the beginning of 1955, selected depots from 2G, 20G, 31G, 42G and 44G were made over to this new company and their vehicle numbers prefixed 'P', in fleet number sequences that then became separated from those used by the existing haulage series.

Also early in 1955 the Western Division gained control of a large portion of the former S W Division after that was dissolved. The areas involved consisted of the Bristol District (Groups 1F-4F and 42F), the Exeter District (Groups 80F-82F) and Groups 40F (Reading) and 41F (Swindon portion), both of which became sub-Groups within Oxford District. The BTC crest roundel colour of these vehicles would gradually have changed to 'Lead Grey' in the event of a repaint and, from mid-1956, to 'Deep Cream' for all Western Division vehicles after the new armorial design was adopted.

No further contraction of District or Group codes occurred. Indeed in

Bristol, where only two depots remained at the conclusion of the sales programme, vehicles from 1F, 2F and 3F had long been regarded as interchangeable and deployed as required; so examples from all three series were still in use at the end of 1956 even though no depot from the original 3F network remained. At the end of de-nationalisation Western Division was still administering codes 1G, 2G, 20G, 21G, 31G, 41G, 42G and 44G plus 1F-4F, 40F, 41F, 42F and 80F-82F.

EASTERN DIVISION

As the already much-reduced Group network faced de-nationalisation the resultant fleet reduction brought about further Group mergers during 1954. 3H and 5H were both merged into 1H which effectively became 'Norwich District', while 2H, 4H and 25H were all merged into 60H which, similarly, became 'Ipswich District'. In the Peterborough District 26H was merged into 22H and, later, 27H into 21H while, in the Lincoln District, what remained of 47H is believed to have been absorbed by 46H and, finally, 43H was merged into 45H. One further loss at the beginning of 1955 was the Parcels Group 8H which passed to the control of BRS (Parcels) Ltd and was prefixed 'P'.

Shortly after this the Eastern Division itself was dissolved and split three ways: the East Anglian Districts, 1H and 60H, passed to the S E Division; the Peterborough District (Groups 21H, 22H and 23H) to the Midland Division; and Lincoln District (Groups 40H, 45H and 46H) to the N E Division where they were combined with the south Yorkshire District. No fleet renumbering was involved and the only difference noted by the observer would have been the gradual change in BTC crest colour as vehicles passed through paint shops.

DISPERSAL OF EX-BRS VEHICLES

Having accounted for the alterations to Group codes for the vehicles retained as de-nationalisation proceeded, let us now account for some of those that left the BRS fleet.

It is on record that 19,303 vehicles were sold during de-nationalisation. In order to operate an ex-BRS vehicle the new owner was required to obtain a 'Special A' licence and details of all 'S' licences were published in each Traffic area's edition of 'Applications and Decisions'. From summaries of these announcements made in the transport press and now held on archive, a good idea of the distribution of all such vehicles can be made.

A comprehensive analysis of all these reports has given a fascinating insight into the vehicle movements that took place. In fact, just over 19,500 vehicles are credited to final owners – rather more than the total number said to have been sold (this discrepancy could partly be due to imprecise reporting of details from certain Traffic Areas, particularly

Yorkshire, Western and South Wales, by the press reporters involved) and they were involved in some 31,000 transactions which is an indication of the number of assignments and re-assignments of vehicles that took place between individuals, dealers and operators and, in due course, limited liability companies set up by their founders.

The reports also indicate that these vehicles were split between nearly 6,100 operators, thus confirming that one aim of the Transport Act of 1953 had been achieved, this being to spread the former state-owned vehicle fleet among a larger number of operators than had existed prior to nationalisation. The road haulage industry had become significantly fragmented.

The following observations identify the businesses that benefited most from the acquisition of 'S' licences, related to the comparable BRS regional Divisions to give an idea of the main operators BRS was now competing with in each area. It should be remembered the quantities of 'S' licences held by many of these businesses in no way reflected their overall fleet size, for the vehicles often joined existing fleet of lorries already operating within the required 25-mile radius on 'B' and 'C' licences as directed during the days of nationalisation. To quote just two examples: when H Gilbraith of Accrington acquired three ex-BRS vehicles in February 1954 they joined an existing fleet of 50 vehicles (mainly tippers and tankers) and when Mortons (Coventry) Ltd obtained five ex-BRS vehicles in June 1954 they were said to be joining a fleet of 75 vehicles that had been operating within the 25-mile radius.

SOUTH EASTERN DIVISION

'S' licence grants were made to approximately 835 owners, operators and dealers in the area corresponding to BRS S E Division. A huge proportion of these were persons obtaining grants for just one vehicle (351 instances or 42%), many of which may have been newcomers to the industry 'testing the water', while others were further re-assigned to other operators later.

Detailed study of the records indicates the largest operators to benefit from 'S' licence grants were Davis Bros (Haulage) Ltd (66 vehicles) and C Bristow (84), two related haulage companies operating nationwide services, though some 18 of those acquired by C Bristow were further assigned on to others. Other major users were J & H Transport Services of Peckham (56, less 8 assigned), G L Baker (47, less 8), Home Counties Plant Hire, Ilford (47), Hays Wharf Ltd, Tooley St (46), Rand & Brunt, Welwyn Garden City (43, less 21) and L T Redburn, Enfield (41, less 9).

There were several significant dealers in ex-BRS vehicles in this area, chief among which was Percy D Sleeman Ltd of Ealing (nearly 80 vehicles acquired and assigned on) along with its related company Valliant Direct Coaches Ltd of Uxbridge (about 55). Five separate members of the

Regan family (T, J, Miss P, M and V Regan) whose registered addresses were variously quoted as either 118 Solebay St, E3, or 43a Settles St, E1 (itself a former BRS depot) between them also acquired over 150 vehicles for onward assignment. For dealers it is not possible to give precise figures as the origins of re-assigned vehicles are frequently not given in the records.

Several other dealers became involved on a smaller scale, notable among these being Whalebone Motors, Chadwell Heath (nearly 30), W J Taylor, Leytonstone (also about 30), T W Hodge, SE14 (at least 27) and Boardmans of Stratford Ltd (about 20). Finance companies also supported some purchases and one, Transport Unit Finance, London EC4, were involved in 32 deals, acquiring licences for operators mainly based in South Wales and the North East.

The largest single former BRS depot to be sold to new operators in this area was that at New Malden, whose 40 vehicles passed to Dallas (Kingston) Ltd. Other significant depots to pass on were at 123 Solebay St, Mile End (35 vehicles to Davis Bros (Haulage) Ltd; Christchurch Way, Greenwich; (26 vehicles to P A Carter), and Chiswick Common Road (23 vehicles to J Coales & Son).

Three depots in the area were sold to the Salford dealers, Hacketts Haulage Ltd; these were at Purfleet (38 vehicles), Greenwich (54) and Bethnal Green (30). Hacketts later assigned a portion of those at Purfleet to another dealer, Comberhill Motors Ltd of Wakefield and the vehicles from all their sites were dispersed throughout the country accordingly.

SCOTTISH DIVISION

A clear difference was apparent in Scotland where there was a higher preponderance of larger fleet sizes than in any part of the country and a correspondingly lower number of single vehicle 'S' licence grants than anywhere else. In all just over 525 operators obtained 'S' licences in the Scottish Traffic Area, including just 176 (33%) of one vehicle each.

Two important businesses were set up in accordance with Section5 of the 1953 Transport Act for Disposal Units to be set up in the form of companies as going concerns to be taken over by acquiring their shares. The first of these was Road Services (Caledonian) Ltd which eventually acquired 133 'S' licences including 110 at depots in Dumfries, Lockerbie, Stranraer, Abington and Glasgow; and the second was D McKinnon (Transport) Ltd which obtained the 46-vehicle depot at Kilmarnock, duly building up a fleet of 57 'S' licensed vehicles.

The largest number of 'S' licence grants made to one operator was the 227 vehicles acquired by Charles Alexander & Partners (Transport) Ltd of Aberdeen, though 76 of these were later reassigned to another company, Sutherlands of Peterhead (Road Hauliers) Ltd, which eventually obtained 128 'S' licences but, again, 54 of these were further reassigned to Highland Haulage Ltd of Inverness. Another large beneficiary was Inter City Road

Services (Forth) Ltd. Yet another prominent operator was London Transport & Trading Co Ltd which obtained 'S' licences for 150 vehicles though, again, 93 of these were only reassigned to get another company, Scottish Transport Ltd whose founder, W S Dick, obtained 'S' licences for 156 vehicles, duly assigning all to this company – sadly, following his death, this company failed in 1956.

Further major Scottish operators were Sam Anderson of Newhouse (88 'S' licences but at least 42 of these were assigned on so they were also dealing in ex-BRS vehicles); Allisons Transport (Contracts) Ltd of Dundee (68 vehicles); Highland Haulage (61, 54 of which came via W R Wisely through his connection with Sutherlands of Peterhead); Russell of Bathgate (49 less 9 assigned on); and Alexander Scott (Contractors) Ltd of Glasgow (40 less 3).

Three names became prominent as dealers in ex-BRS vehicles, chief of which was Central Garage (Bathgate) Ltd which handled well over 120 vehicles. E Sanderson of Bearsden, Glasgow processed about 70 vehicles and Pentland Garage (Loanhead) Ltd nearly 50, assigning at least 33 of these to new owners but also keeping a nucleus to operate its own services. The statistics suggest Sam Anderson was also involved in such dealings.

The largest depot to change hands was that at Old Ford Road, Aberdeen, where 84 vehicles were acquired by Charles Alexanders. The 49 vehicles at Peterhead depot also went to Charles Alexander but were assigned to Sutherlands of Peterhead; as described above, the Dumfries depot (39 vehicles) and the Kilmarnock depot (46 vehicles) changed hands under Section 5, while the depots at Falkirk (36 vehicles) and Denny (32 vehicles) went to Inter City Transport, duly passing to Road Services (Forth) Ltd. The Inverness depot (30 vehicles) was acquired by W R Wisely and, through his connection with Sutherlands of Peterhead, passed on to become the headquarters of Highland Haulage. Depots at Dunfermline (29 vehicles), Leven (33 vehicles), Alloa (18 vehicles) and Alva (11 vehicles) passed to London Scottish Transport.

NORTH WESTERN DIVISION

Back in England the S E Division pattern was repeated and of some 1000 owners, operators and dealers that obtained 'S' licences in the North Western catchment area, nearly 40% (393 individuals) were single-vehicle grants. Consequently the number of operators to obtain significant quantities of vehicles was quite low. The largest single contractor was Smiths of Eccles Ltd which acquired 61 'S' licences but assigned 15 of these vehicles to others.

Other prominent fleets of 'S' licence vehicles to emerge at this time were Robsons Border Transport of Carlisle (49 vehicles less 14 assigned; Runcorn Transport Services, the trading name of Arthur Wood (also 49 vehicles); Harris Road Services Ltd (48 vehicles, less 9); Fred Rose Ltd of

Blackrod (44 less 5) and Liverpool Warehousing Co Ltd (40). After these came Sutton & Son (St Helens) Ltd (36 less 16); O B Transport, the trading name of Offley Bros of Ellesmere Port (32); and Topham Bros (Manchester) Ltd with 30 vehicles less 17 assigned.

Among others to obtain between 20 and 30 vehicles was W H Bowker of Blackburn, Jack Bradley & Co of Accrington, John Buckley & Co Ltd of Warrington, David Hall & Sons of Bury Robertson Buckley & Co of Liverpool, Fearings Transport of Burnley, M A Keenan of Liverpool and Athersmith Bros of Barrow-in-Furness.

The largest vehicle fleet, complete with former BRS depot, to pass to new operators was that at Lostock Gralam, nr Northwich, whose 39 vehicles passed to Harris Road Services Ld. The Cecil Street depot in Manchester went to Topham Bros with 29 vehicles, 14 of which were assigned to Smiths of Eccles. The 28-vehicle fleet at Stanley Street, Runcorn, passed to Runcorn Transport Services; the 26-vehicle fleet at Blackrod nr Chorley to Fred Rose Ltd; the 26-vehicle fleet at Knott Street, Weaste, Oldham to Cusick (Oldham) Ltd; and the 22-vehicle depot at Tarporley to O B Transport.

Numerous dealers specialising in the acquisition of ex-BRS vehicles grew in the area. By far the biggest of these was Hacketts Haulage Ltd of Salford which, along with its associated companies, J W Fieldsend (originally a coaching company) and Woodcocks (Chorley) Ltd of Heskin (a subsidiary haulage company in its own right) processed several hundred vehicles. Records suggest that Hacketts handled at least 280 vehicles, Fieldsend nearly 45 and Woodcocks about 150, less some 110 also assigned on, leaving them a basic operational fleet of around 40 vehicles. During 1955 Hacketts acquired several complete depots (three in London, three in the Midlands and one each in the South Western and Western Divisions) as well as a 32-vehicle batch in Cardiff, all for assignment.

Another very significant trader was A Cusick of Oldham which processed well over 200 vehicles, many of which passed to his company Cusick (Oldham) Ltd, itself involved in such dealing and attributed with at least 215 vehicles, over 170 of which were also assigned. Other such dealers were Wilde & Bennett Ltd of Hadfield (over 50 vehicles), J W Ratcliffe & Sons Ltd, Ashton-in-Makerfield (nearly 30), Northern (Allied) Transport & Trading Co Ltd, Penrith (also about 30) and, particularly, two businesses in Warrington – T H Prince which handled some 90 vehicles, 30 of which went to his company Prince Transport (Warrington) Ltd, and the Warrington Warehousing Co Ltd (Prop. J Mees) which processed over 100 vehicles.

Most former BRS depots in this area went to local operators. The largest to go elsewhere was that at Vickers Street, Collyhurst, Manchester whose 25-vehicle fleet passed to Alexander Scott (Contractors) Ltd of Glasgow in 1955.

NORTH EASTERN DIVISION

Unsurprisingly the largest number of 'S' licence grants was in this area as it covered a whole swathe of the country from Berwick-on-Tweed in the north down to Chesterfield and Worksop in the north midlands. Over 1050 individual businesses obtained 'S' licences in the area and, again, a high proportion of these were grants in respect of one vehicle only (nearly 400, or 37%).

The largest outfit to appear during this time was undoubtedly NMU (1954) Ltd of York, set up as a company under the terms of Section 5 of the 1953 Transport Act, which acquired 272 vehicles most of which were operated on six contracts but included 74 operating under 'S' licences. Of businesses purely engaged in haulage the largest to benefit from 'S' licensing was Ackworth Transport Co Ltd which is credited with around 120 vehicles, though some 75 of these were assigned on to others as the company also became involved in dealing in ex-BRS vehicles under the guidance of its founder Willie Storey. Other prominent users were J W Capstaff, Newcastle (49 vehicles less about 17); McPhees (Newcastle) Ltd (46 less 2); and Parkers Luxury Tours of Selby (39 less 10) – this company was actually owned by R Britton who duly revived his pre-nationalisation name of Onward Road Transport Ltd for his haulage interests.

Next in size came Tees-side Carriers Ltd (31 vehicles less 4 assigned on), then numerous operators obtained between 20 and 30 vehicles, including S A Bell, Bridlington; J G Fielder (Haulage) Ltd, Bradford; Gardner Bros (Langley Moor) Ltd, Co Durham; G K Levitt, North Newbald nr York; Henry Long (Manningham) Ltd, Bradford; T A Metcalfe, Darlington; Mason Bros (Haulage & Storage) Ltd, Rotherham; Pickering Road Haulage Ltd, Hull; F & F Robinson (Stockton-on-Tees) Ltd; Trowbridge (Sheffield) Ltd; and Woodseats Transport Co, Sheffield which traded as The Wheeler Road Transport Co.

A large number of dealers in ex-BRS vehicles grew in this area. A particularly significant one was E Waters of Monkseaton, nr Sunderland which processed over 220 such vehicles. Central Yorkshire must have been flooded with ex-BRS vehicles as no fewer than four such dealers became involved, the main one being the above-mentioned Willie Storey of Ackworth; the records show he processed nearly 220 vehicles, including those assigned to his own companies – Ackworth Transport Co (86 vehicles) and Woodseats Transport Co (21 vehicles). Also at Ackworth, S Sykes handled nearly 20 vehicles, while nearby at South Elmsall B T Weaver dealt with some 65 vehicles, and C Grace over 50.

Still in this area, at Wakefield, R Heath dealt with around 40 vehicles while Comberhill Motors Ltd processed around 90, including 42 at Rotherham; S Hughes (Commercial) Ltd of Mirfield, nearly 60 vehicles; T J Hughes of Bradford, about 40; Ernest Crabtree of Queensbury, Bradford, 35; and his company Wescol Motors Ltd, later Wescol (Bradford) Ltd, working from two bases at Queensbury and Ripon, well over 70.

The largest BRS depot to pass to an operator was that at St Pauls Road, Bradford, where 26 vehicles passed to Henry Long (Manningham) Ltd. The 20-vehicle fleet in Pickering Road, Hill, passed to Pickering Road Haulage. W Storey acquired two depots, duly assigning the one at Ackworth with 27 vehicles to his own company; the second, with 20 vehicles at Bentley, nr Doncaster, was split up. The largest depot to be sold in this area, with 42 vehicles at Rotherham, was acquired by Comberhill Motors of Wakefield, also for assignment, in 1955. Most depots successfully sold in this area were of less than 20 vehicles.

MIDLAND DIVISION

Once again, a huge number of the approximately 930 operators and dealers to obtain 'S' licences in this area acquired just one vehicle (356 or 38%), repeating the pattern elsewhere throughout England. There were some larger operators, however. The largest to arise and benefit from 'S' licensing was Sunley Transport (Stafford) Ltd, which acquired 82 vehicles together with the former BRS depots at Rugeley and Stafford − that of Rugeley with 46 vehicles being the largest to be sold as an operational unit in the Midlands. This company failed only a short time later, however, possibly around 1957 (from memory?).

Other significant fleets of 'S' licensed vehicles were built up by Beresford Transport Ltd, Tunstall (75 vehicles less over 30 assigned on); Murphy Bros (Transport division) Ltd, Loughborough (60 vehicles less 4); R G Bassett, Tittensor (50 vehicles less 30) and his company Bassetts Roadways Ltd (57 less 9, many assigned to them by R G Bassett); E & J Davis of Birmingham (54 less 6); Gleaves Transport (Audlem) Ltd (47 less 20); Mansfield Haulage Ltd (38 less 13), Longton Transport Ltd, Stoke (39 less 23); Wild, Condon Ltd, also of Stoke (31 less 12); and Shenstone Transport Co Ltd, Birmingham (30).

Others to acquire between 20 and 30 vehicles were Caudle Ltd, Birmingham; A & H Davey (Roadways) Ltd, Stoke; James Gamble (Transport) Ltd, Nottingham; Oldbury Transport Ltd; Fredk Ray Ltd, Bedford; Shepherd & Hough Ltd, Earlswood; E A Smith (Transport) Ltd, Wolverhampton; Red House Garage Ltd, Coventry; A M Walker Ltd, Cosby; and J Watts & Sons (Contractors) Ltd, Nottingham.

Numerous dealers in ex-BRS vehicles came into prominence in the midlands. Largest by far was Murphy Bros Ltd with bases at Leicester, Thurmaston and Syston, which processed over 300 vehicles including those at Loughborough where the depot, plus 37 vehicles, were assigned to its operating subsidiary, Murphy Bros (Transport Division) Ltd. Also in Leicestershire, John Brindley of Sharnford, Hinckley, handled over 140 vehicles. Still in the east Midlands, John Ball Ltd, Mansfield, dealt with about 90, A Rhodes of Nottingham some 110, and Hamblins Suppliers Ltd, Leics, over 55. E E Bamford of Alfreton was another early dealer, duly forming a company E E Bamford (Contractors) Ltd to continue the work until it collapsed in 1956 following fraud convictions on the founder. Bamford himself processed around 15 of 35 vehicles acquired and the limited company a further 25 of the 35 it acquired, then A G B Burney was appointed as receiver and manager, duly processing another 55 vehicles.

In the West Midlands names to the forefront were L Gleave of Audlem which processed around 150 vehicles, assigning many to its subsidiary Gleave Transport (Audlem) Ltd, as did K Beresford of Bignall End which handled some 35 vehicles, passing many of these to Beresford Transport Ltd. N Beech of Hanley similarly dealt with around 90 vehicles. Further to the south, the Richardson Brothers of Oldbury were heavily involved in this work. T J Richardson dealt with over 70 vehicles, R N Richardson nearly 40, G Richardson about 35 and D B Richardson nearly 30. Some of these were assigned to their own business, Oldbury Transport Ltd.

Apart from the depots sold to Sunley Transport, other important depots sold as operating bases were at Loughborough (the 37 vehicles going to Murphy Bros); at Tyseley, Birmingham, 30 vehicles to Shenstone Transport Co Ltd; at Darley Dale, 25 vehicles to North Derbyshire Engineering Ltd, trading as Toft Bros & Tomlinson; and at Leighton Buzzard, 22 vehicles to Fredk Ray Ltd. Other depots were sold to dealers, the fleets being split and assigned to other operators. These included the largest to be sold, with 53 vehicles, at Moxley, nr Wednesbury, to T J Richardson of Oldbury; one at Mansfield, with 42 vehicles, to John Ball Ltd; and Fazeley, nr Tamworth, with 24 vehicles, to R E G Mason of Littleover. Three depots, at Swadlincote (30 vehicles), Wirksworth (29) and Hartington (23) went to the Salford dealers, Hacketts Haulage Ltd.

SOUTH WESTERN DIVISION

Despite BRS boundary changes in 1952 that had added the Home Counties to this area, it remained a relatively small catchment area for transport operation. Only about 600 operators obtained 'S' licences in the area and, again, a large number of the grants were to operators of single vehicles (236 or 39%).

The largest single purchase by one operator was that of the Thatcham depot in Berkshire, with 85 vehicles, acquired by Cropper & Coldthrop Transport Ltd, which eventually built up to 89 'S' licensed vehicles. Another prominent operator was Western Transport Ltd of Bristol which obtained 90 vehicles, less 10 assigned on, based at locations throughout the country for nationwide services. A third large beneficiary was S Ball & Son (Transport) Ltd of Old Sodbury which obtained 84 vehicles, though about 60 of these were assigned to others, indicating involvement in dealing in ex-BRS vehicles as well as operating them.

Other useful fleets of 'S' licensed vehicles were amassed by Reed Transport Ltd, Larkfield (35 vehicles, including the depot); Parkstone Transport Ltd (33 vehicles), a new company formed by Cusick (Oldham) Ltd after A Cusick had purchased the Parkstone depot and assigned it on; Amey Transport (Oxford) Ltd of Abingdon, with 27 vehicles; R & W Febry of Chipping Sodbury (23 vehicles); John Jempson & Son, Rye (25 vehicles); HHV Guest Road Services Ltd, Bath (29 vehicles); Brown Bros (Sittingbourne) Ltd (27 vehicles); A D Forsey (Transport) Ltd, Worle, nr Weston-super-Mare (22 vehicles); Hill & Sons (Botley & Denmead) Ltd (23 vehicles); and H Rackliffe which acquired 27 vehicles less some assigned on, leaving 19 to form his new company Rackliffe (Guildford) Ltd.

Largest depot to be sold was that at Thatcham, reported above. Next in size was that at Parkstone where Allan Cusick of Oldham acquired 46 vehicles, retaining 32 for operation of his new subsidiary company Parkstone Transport Ltd and assigning the others. The 35-vehicle fleet at Larkfield was acquired by Albert E Reed & Co Ltd, the newsprint processors, and set up as a transport subsidiary. The 32-vehicle fleet at Bath was acquired by Pierrepoint Garages Ltd, a company in which HHV Guest had an interest, and duly made over to the new company bearing his name. At Yatton, the 28-vehicle fleet was acquired by Western Transport Ltd and at Rye, Sussex John Jempson & Son acquired the 23-vehicle fleet.

Other depots in the area again went to dealers for assignment. Largest of these, the 35-vehicle depot at Cheese Lane, Bristol, was acquired by the conglomerate 'Febry, Ball & Baylis', three operators whose managers combined forces to make a joint tender and then assigned the vehicles. Similarly, 'Febry & Ball' had separately acquired the 20-vehicle depot at Yate nr Bristol some months earlier.

There were some specialist dealers in ex-BRS vehicles in the area though none anything like as committed as those further north. Principal among these was E E Tucker of Taunton which appears to have processed around 80 vehicles; the 27-vehicle fleet at Wellington, some (including 23 milk floats) were among these. Another such dealer was F A Wiltshire of Reading who are credited with over 30 such assignments. The Regan family already mentioned in London had a third registered base at Chun Farm, Horsmonden, Kent, and many of their acquisitions and assignments specified this address, crediting them with a further 75 deals on top of the 140 or so administered from London. On a smaller scale, others involved in such dealings were Hardwick & Parsons of Bristol (15 vehicles), E A A Foot of Ringwood (14) and Rogercraft Ltd, Old Sodbury (13).

Depots acquired by dealers further afield included the 32-vehicle fleet at Mapledurwell, Basingstoke which was acquired by T Regan of 118 Solebay St, London; the Folkestone depot (25 vehicles) by Gleave Transport (Audlem) Ltd; and the Wells depot (20) by Hacketts Haulage Ltd, Salford.

WESTERN DIVISION

This was another small catchment area regarding transport operation even though the area covered had been expanded into Warwickshire, Worcestershire and Shropshire during the boundary revisions in 1950. Some 550 operators and dealers obtained 'S' licences in the area and, again, a large proportion of these involved operation of only one vehicle (233 or 43%).

Among the largest 'S' licence users to emerge in the area was George Read of Mitcheldean and its limited liability company G Read (Transport) Ltd, which between them obtained licences for over 60 vehicles, less at least 11 assigned on. Another was The Storage Co (Penarth) Ltd, granted 'S' licences for 55 vehicles but most of these were assigned on – at least 13, possibly more – to its associated company Welsh Transport Services Ltd, Cardiff (the records from South Wales Traffic Area were not consistently reported in full). A third important operator was Valley Carriers of Penarth, the trading name adopted by E W S & L S Hayman, accredited with 26 vehicles, and its associate Grove Garages (Penarth) Ltd, with at least 9, until the limited liability company Valley Carriers Ltd was formed; this duly obtained around 60 'S' licensed vehicles but many were assigned on and the full picture is unclear.

Others building up significant 'S' licensed fleets were Hills Transport (Dinas Powis) Ltd with 43 vehicles, less 2 assigned on; Andys Transport Ltd, Banbury (30 vehicles); R Mann of Worcester with at least 23 vehicles; H B Everton (Roadways) Ltd, Droitwich (28); S Harfoot & Sons Ltd, Barry Dock (25 less 7); and Newport Haulage Services Ltd (20). Largest in Shropshire was J H Ferringtron of Wellington with 16 vehicles and, in Herefordshire, H S Williams (Haulage) Ltd of Whitchurch with 11. The growth of R Mann was largely the result of acquiring two small depots in the north west, with 11 vehicles at Bury and 5 at Sale.

In addition to The Storage Co (Penarth) Ltd, others to spring up as dealers in ex-BRS vehicles were Putson Motor Engineering Co Ltd of Abergavenny which handled some 25 vehicles; Prails (Hereford) Ltd with nearly 25; J Costelloe of Cheltenham which acquired and assigned some 40 vehicles, and Cleeve Hill Transport Ltd, also of Cheltenham, which processed over 30.

Few BRS depots of any size found new operators in this area and none in industrial South Wales – one of the largest batches to be sold here, of 32 vehicles in Cardiff, did not include premises. Those went to Hacketts Haulage Ltd of Salford. Largest depots to find new operators were at Droitwich where 28 vehicles passed to H B Everton (Roadways) Ltd; at Banbury where the 25-vehicle fleet went to Andys Transport Ltd; at Mitcheldean where George Read acquired the 19-vehicle fleet; and at Llanelly where the 20-vehicle fleet passed to Edwin J Phillips. The Lydney depot, with 23 vehicles, was sold to The Storage Co (Penarth) Ltd which duly assigned them on to Hacketts Haulage Ltd.

EASTERN DIVISION

Around 580 operators, owners and dealers obtained 'S' licences in this area and yet again a high proportion were of single vehicle grants (261 or 45%), though some significant larger operators also came into being. Far and away the most important of these was Tower Hill Transport, the trading name of Boston Stevedores Ld set up by E A Moffatt, which is accredited with 124 'S' licensed vehicles distributed at bases throughout the country, indicating considerable success when tendering for Disposal Units.

Other important operators included Welch Bros (Foxton) Ltd, granted 60 'S' licences, and its successor Welchs Transport Ltd, centred on Stapleford, Cambs, to which most of these presumably passed but which also gained a further 10 licences. Another big player was Turner Bros (Soham) Ltd which acquired several small depots and built up a fleet of nearly 80 'S' licensed vehicles, less 8 assigned on. A third was McVeigh Transport Ltd of Grimsby, granted 53 'S' licences, while F W Williams (Transport) Lt, Wisbech, acquired 35, all assigned to them by Dawbarns Ltd of Wisbech, presumably its parent company.

Several operators acquired between 20 and 30 vehicles, including Roudham Transport, East Harling (27 vehicles, mostly assigned to them by R T Lawrence); J Bradshaw & Son, Sturton-by-Stow (accredited with 32, though other reports suggest many more); Greenwoods (Contractors) Ltd, Ramsey (25); B & B (Lowestoft) Ltd (21 less 15 assigned on); and Yoxford Transport Ltd (also 21); while another operator Vickers Transport (Peterborough) Ltd obtained 34 but assigned at least 12 on to others, indicating involvement also as a dealer.

At Scunthorpe, D N Holloway acquired 14 vehicles and his company, North Lincs Haulage of Grimsby, at least 28, possibly including these 14. G E Johnson of North Kelsey, with 24 vehicles, and the partnership between G E Johnson and J E Staniland, which acquired another 11 vehicles, assigned many of these to their company, G&C Johnson (Clixby) Ltd, also of North Kelsey, which amassed over 35 vehicles as a result. One other interesting company to emerge at this time was D M T Transport Ltd of Lincoln, accredited with 19 'S' licences. The initials were said to be those of 'Denationalised Motor Transport'.

A major dealer in BRS vehicles in this area was V J Grange of Peterborough which processed over 150 vehicles. Another big name in this field was O G Barnard & Son of Stowmarket, a former haulier now more committed to trailer manufacture, which acquired and duly assigned some 75 vehicles. Other smaller outfits involved in such deals were Peterborough Engineering Co Ltd (over 30 vehicles); Reads of Peterborough Ld (at least 19); M J Dwane of Leadenham, Lincoln (at least 17); and F A Houchell of Ipswich (also about 17) trading alongside his haulage business of

Orwell Roadways (Ipswich) Ltd which itself acquired 16 vehicles.

Largest BRS depots to pass on as operating bases were that at Grimsby (40 vehicles) acquired by Two Counties Transport and assigned to McVeigh Transport; Fordham (30 vehicles) acquired by Turners (Soham) Ltd; Newark Road, Lincoln (27 vehicles) passing to E R Wright & Sons (Bracebridge) Ltd; and Bury St Edmunds (22 vehicles) acquired by R T Lawrence and assigned on to Roudham Transport. Tower Hill Transport acquired just one depot during its growth, at Marsh Lane, Boston with 20 vehicles. Depots acquired for assignment on to others included Tiptree, Essex (34 vehicles) acquired by Kilby & Davison Ltd, Bedford on behalf of a number of independent hauliers in Bedfordshire, each of which took one or more vehicles. The depot at Ely (20 vehicles) went to Peterborough Engineering Co Ltd and that a Louth (18 vehicles) to T Regan, Horsmonden Kent, both for assignment.

General Observations

To summarise, the names mentioned give just a few of the many hundreds of 'Hire or Reward' operators that BRS enthusiasts were obliged to begin following in pursuit of former BRS vehicles. Study of their early entry (or, in many cases, re-entry) to the haulage business from 1954 onwards provided a basis from which many transport fans began to observe their vehicles keenly in subsequent years as well, especially if they gave their vehicles fleet numbers to assist in building up records. While most of the companies recalled here have long since ceased to exist, like BRS itself, they have left lasting memories for enthusiasts of the varied haulage scene of their day.

Meanwhile, the hugely reduced BRS fleet remained large enough to continue its appeal to its fans. We learnt that the fleet was being prepared for a complete renumbering exercise more appropriate to its new size, so we remained happy to continue following it closely, as explained in the next section.

3

1956-1964

The vehicles remaining in service with BRS Ltd and its close associate BRS (Contracts) Ltd after de-nationalisation ceased in October 1956 were termed the 'Retained Fleet'. The fleet numbers in use within the six surviving Divisions of BRS had become inappropriate to the much-reduced depot network and a new numbering system was urgently required. Whereas before, each Division comprised several Districts, each controlling a number of individual Groups having their own codes, it was now the Districts that adopted their own codes and individual depots - or 'Branches' as the old Groups were now termed - no longer had their own identity. In the following summary identifying the various locations holding each new code, Branch names are all upper case, with their constituent depots in lower case; there were also several depots that were controlled directly from District level and were not members of Branches. Also included are details identifying the previous Group codes held by each location, as this information was not given in the Ian Allan ABCs that appeared at this time.

SOUTH EASTERN DIVISION

Continued to use Divisional letter 'A'. BTC crest colour had become Road Haulage Green since the new armorial design was granted in 1956. New vehicle registrations continued to be raised at Divisional level from the HQ in London the new District network was as follows:

1A London District

BRENTFORD	Commerce Road	ex 53A
COVENT GARDEN	Offices at Covent Garden, Spitalfields and Rotherhithe and depots at Mile End	All ex 99A
HAMPSTEAD	Depots at Cressey Road NW3 and Holmes Rd, Kentish Town	Both ex 43A

HAYES & SLOUGH	Depots at Hayes and Chesham	Both ex 46A
PURFLEET	Stanford-le-Hope plus sub-depot at Rochford	Both ex 61A
STRATFORD	High Meads, Temple Mills Lane	Ex 66A
TOWER BRIDGE	Depots at Royal Mint Street and Edgware	Both ex 5A
TUFNELL PARK	Junction Road N19	Ex 6A

2A Southampton District

SOUTHAMPTON	Depots at Regents Park Road and Portswood Road plus Docks office	All ex 22F
PORTSMOUTH	Depots at Fratton and Camber Quay	Both ex 23F
POOLE	Depots at West Quay Road, Poole and Yeovil	Both ex 20F
	also at West Harnham, Salisbury	Ex 41F
	and at Shaftesbury Road, Gillingham	Ex 42F
ISLE OF WIGHT	Depots at Newport and Cowes, plus transfer depots at Southampton and Portsmouth	All ex 26F

3A East Anglia District

NORWICH	91 Hall Road	Ex 1H
KINGS LYNN	Estuary Road	Ex 1H
IPSWICH	London Road	Ex 60H
COLCHESTER	North Station Road	Ex 60H
CHELMSFORD	Navigation Road	Ex 60H
	Depots at Beccles, reporting directly to District Office	Ex 1H
	And at Stowmarket and Bishops Stortford, likewise	Both ex 60H

4A Home Counties District

BRIGHTON	Warwick Street	Ex 64F
CANTERBURY	1a Wincheap plus offices at Faversham, Minster and Folkestone	All ex 60F
GUILDFORD	Shalford Goods Yard	Ex 43F
MAIDSTONE	Sutton Road, Maidstone & Priory Road, Tonbridge	Both ex 61F
ROCHESTER	Priory Road, Strood & Queenborough Road, Sheerness	Ex 62F
SITTINGBOURNE	Crescent Street	Ex 62F

C5A London Contracts District

NEWINGTON BUTTS	Searles Road SE1. Cubitt Street WC1. Drummond Road SE16. Lansdowne Road, Croydon. Centaur Street SE1	All ex C9A
VICTORIA PARK	Cambridge Heath Road E2. Batemans Row EC2 and Walmgate Road, Perivale	All ex C70A
CHISWICK	612 Western Avenue W3	Ex C51A

Some comments on the fleet numbering systems adopted are relevant at this stage. All four of the General Haulage Districts introduced new fleet numbers around November 1956 and employed four-figure serials, e.g. 1A1001, 3A1101, etc. However, a directive from BRS Head Office early in 1957 that these numbers were too unwieldy required a further revision in fleet numbering to be introduced from February 1957. In the London and Southampton Districts the new systems incorporated 'secret' series that enabled the individual operating Branches to be identified; the Home Counties District had originally used a four-figure series that did likewise, but the revised 1957 system failed to do so. We will return to this topic in greater detail later. Retained fleet sizes were for 1A, 822 vehicles; 2A, 336 general plus 19 contracts; 3A, 300 general plus 30 contracts; 4A, 258 general and 18 contracts. Also 14 staff cars received fleet numbers in this District. With a fleet of just over 1000 vehicles there was no option but to use four-figure numbers in the London Contracts District so the Head Office directive did not apply to this fleet.

SCOTTISH DIVISION

Continued to use Divisional letter 'B'. BTC crest colour 'Traffic Blue', and to licence all new vehicles through the Divisional Workshops at Linlithgow, using West Lothian CC for vehicle registrations, the original revised network was as follows:

1B Southern Scotland District

DOUGLAS	West Street; North Wallace Street; Kessock Street and Midland Street (office) all in Glasgow, plus Orchard Street, Paisley	All ex 60B
GLASGOW	Lister Street, Mount Vernon and Ingram Street (office) plus Falkirk, Grangemouth and Ayr	All ex 63B
ARGYLL	Warroch Street, Glasgow; Campbeltown; Lochgilphead; Inveraray, Strone; Tarbert and Oban	All ex 66B
EDINBURGH	Newington and Leith, both in Edinburgh; Bathgate; Haddington; Galashiels, Kelso and Dunbar	All ex 40B
FIFE	Dunfermline, Kirkcaldy, Strathkinness and Alva	All ex 26B

2B Northern Scotland District

DUNDEE	54 East Dock Street	Ex 20B
ANGUS	Forfar, Arbroath, Montrose, Perth and Coupar Angus	All ex 21B
ABERDEEN	56 Virginia Street plus Inverness and Elgin	All ex 7B

Retained fleet sizes were, for 1B, 698 general (including service vehicles) plus about 28 on contracts; 2B, 291 general and service and 7 on contracts. The new fleet numbers were not introduced until February 1957 and no four-figure series were adopted; all went straight to series from 1B1 and 2B1 upwards.

In June 1958 the Southern Scotland District was reduced in size by separating a new 'Edinburgh District', coded 3B, covering all the depots of the former Edinburgh Branch. 1B was retitled 'Glasgow District' from this time.

NORTH WESTERN DIVISION

Divisional letter 'C'. BTC crest colour 'Sea Green'. New vehicle registrations continued to be raised at Branch level for general haulage vehicles but at Trafford Park Office for all contracts vehicles, exactly as before.

1C Liverpool District

LIVERPOOL	Studholme Street depot plus Fruit Office at Victoria Street and Shipping Office at North John street	All ex 13C
WARRINGTON	Battersby Lane, Warrington; Sherdley Road, St Helens; also Runcorn, Widnes, Hindley and Sandbach	Ex 5C, 6C, 7C and 11C
N. WALES	Bretton, nr Chester	Ex 8C

2C Manchester District

GREENHEYS	Wentworth Street, Ardwick, Manchester 12	Ex 64C
TRAFFORD PARK	Richmond Road, plus Rochdale	Both ex 67C
BOLTON	Kay Street, plus North Street, Manchester and Salford	All ex 74C
CONTRACTS	Ashburton Road, Trafford Park; Stalybridge; Stockport; Kearsley nr Farnworth; Ford Street, Liverpool	All ex 62C
	'Manchester Storage' office at Deansgate, Manchester, reporting to District	Ex 62C

3C Preston District

PRESTON	Water Lane	Ex 22C
IRISH FERRY	Albert Edward Dock, Preston and Larne Harbour, N Ireland	Both ex 22C
BLACKBURN	Bennington Street	Ex 24C & 26C
	Depots at Carlisle and Howgate, nr Whitehaven, reporting to District	Both ex 23C

Retained fleets were for 1C, 388 (including service vehicles); for 2C, 324 general plus about 245 on contracts and, for 3C, 218. The Liverpool District did not become effective until 1957 so no four-figure numbers were raised – numbering was simply from 1C1 upwards. At 2C and 3C new series were introduced from November 1956 onwards using four-figure serials; at 2C the 'thousand' was eliminated as directed by Head Office early in 1957, 2C1001 becoming 2C1, etc, but 3C never took this action and retained the four-figure series throughout its existence.

NORTH EASTERN DIVISION

Divisional letter 'D' and BTC crest colour 'Road Haulage Red' continued as before and new vehicle registrations continued to be raised mainly by the Divisional Office from Leeds. The original network was as follows:

1D Tyne/Tees District

NEWCASTLE CENTRAL	The Close and Stepney Bank, both in Newcastle plus Silksworth Row, Sunderland	All ex 1D
NEWCASTLE HAYMARKET	High Street East, Wallsend and Second Avenue, Team Valley, Gateshead	Both ex 2D
TEES-SIDE	Stockton, Thornaby, Darlington, Bishop Auckland and Yarm-on-Tees	All ex 4D

2D Yorkshire District

YORK	60 Lawrence Street, York plus Malton and Harrogate	All ex 30D
HULL	53 Walton Street	Ex 31D
	Plus Bridge Street, Goole	Ex 30D
LEEDS	11 Marshall Street, Leeds and Bell Hill, Rothwell	Both ex 32D
	Plus Maltkiln Lane, Castleford	Ex 30D
BRADFORD	181 Thornton Road, Bradford, plus Ovenden, Bingley and Batley	All ex 32D

3D South Yorks & Lincs District

SHEFFIELD	Eyre St and Penistone Rd, both in Sheffield & Walton Rd, Chesterfield	All ex 60D
	Plus Staniforth Road, Sheffield	Ex 63D
	and Shepcote Lane, Sheffield	Ex 62D
DONCASTER	10 North Bridge Road, plus sub-depot at Barnby Dun and depots at Barnsley and Worksop	All ex 64D
SCUNTHORPE	Station Road	Ex 46H
LINCOLN	Monks Road, Lincoln, plus Boston and Newark	All ex 45H
GRIMSBY	22 Julian Street	Ex 40H

Retained fleet sizes were, for 1D, 476 general plus 22 contracts; for 2D, 427 general and 23 contracts; and for 3D, 494 general and 32 contracts. Few vehicles of 1D and 2D received four-figure numbers as the new schedules were not drawn up until December 1956 and most went straight to series from 1 upwards from 1957. 3D, however, was functional from October 1956 and the majority of vehicles received their numbers in the series 3D1001 upwards, altering to 3D1 upwards in 1957 after the four-figure numbers were cancelled. In the case of 1D, care had to be taken when recording vehicles in deciding whether the number being carried represented the old Central Newcastle Group series or the new Tyne/Tees District series.

From January 1st 1959 a new 'West Yorkshire District' was set up, coded 4D, by combining the last two General Haulage depots of 2D, in the Bradford Branch, with the four Parcels depots of BRS (Parcels) Ltd West Riding Parcels Branch, P50D, which became P4D. There had always been a close relationship between all these sites owing to their commitment to transport for the woollen trade, so perhaps this was not such a surprising move as it also confirmed the continuing close links between the two companies. 96 General and 398 Parcels vehicles were simply recoded from 2D and P50D to 4D/P4D and a new joint series, from fleet no 901 upwards, was introduced from 1959, used by both companies. Contracts vehicles were first introduced from mid-1959. 2D was retitled 'East Yorkshire District', also from 1959.

MIDLAND DIVISION

Divisional letter 'E'. BTC crest colour had become 'Turquoise Blue' from mid-1956 after the new armorial design was introduced but some vehicles still carried the old crest with nut brown roundel. Unusually the three Districts in existence prior to renumbering of the Retained Fleet were re-organised into six new Districts, coded 1E-6E, from October 1956. New vehicle registrations were raised at District level for 1E-4E but at Branch level for 5E and 6E. The Districts were as follows:

1E Birmingham District

BIRMINGHAM	Cheapside and Bromford Lane, both in Birmingham, plus Arthur Street, Redditch	All ex 4E
BIRMINGHAM CONTRACTS	Dartmouth Street, Aston, Birmingham	Ex 5E
WOLVERHAMPTON	Steelhouse Lane, plus Black Lake, West Bromwich	Both ex 11E
WALSALL	Wolverhampton Road, Bentley, plus Amington Road, Tamworth	Both ex 22E
DUDLEY	Tipton Road, plus Wordsley, nr Stourbridge	Both ex 27E
	Also Stone depot, nr Kidderminster, reporting to District	Ex 27E

2E Stoke District

| | Depots at Whieldon Road, Stoke; High Street, Tunstall; Mill Street, Crewe; Common Lane Goods Station, Stafford, all reporting to District | All ex 30E |

3E Leicester District

LEICESTER	Lutterworth Road, Blaby, plus Rugby and Loughborough	All ex 41E
COVENTRY	Quinton Road and London Road, both in Coventry, plus Milverton, Leamington Spa	All ex 2E
BURTON	Lichfield Street	Ex 62E
	Also Corby depot (Gretton Road, Weldon) reporting to District	Ex 41E

4E Luton District

NORTHAMPTON	Lincoln Road, Northampton, plus Bedford	Ex 47E
	Depots at Luton, Dunstable, Aylesbury and Stevenage, reporting to District	All ex 47E

5E Notts & Derby District

DERBY	Meadow Lane, Alvaston	Ex 62E
NOTTINGHAM	104 The Wells Road	Ex 63E
MANSFIELD	Carfax Garage, Chesterfield Road, plus Riddings	Both ex 65E

6E Peterborough District

PETERBOROUGH	Fengate, Peterborough, plus Whittlesey	Both ex 21H
WISBECH	Cromwell Road	Ex 22H
CAMBRIDGE	450 Cherry Hinton Road	Ex 23H
	plus Bourne depot, Lincs, reporting to District	Ex 21H

For the record, the retained fleet sizes were as follows: 1E, 429 plus 79 contracts; 2E, 194 but no contracts; 3E, 266 plus 15 contracts; 4E, 146 plus around 20 contracts; 5E, 222 plus 4 contracts; and 6E, 213 plus 23 contracts.

It is known that all six Districts produced four-figure series of fleet numbers late in 1956 identifying which Branch their vehicles operated from, but only three of these – 1E, 2E and 6E – were ready from October, enabling them to be physically applied. The others were raised so late that before more than a handful had been altered, the 1957 instruction to abandon four-figure numbers was issued and each District was then obliged to introduce a further renumbering exercise. In the Stoke District the 'thousand' figure was simply abolished, resulting in a series 2E1 upwards that no longer identified the individual Branches. In all the others blocks of three-figure numbers were instead introduced that still identified individual Branches within each series, as was the case in the London and Southampton Districts of the SE Division.

The Birmingham Contracts Branch was separated from Birmingham District in July 1958 and set up as a new 'Birmingham Contracts District' with code C11E (the codes 7E-10E) being unavailable, having been taken up by BRS (Parcels) Ltd.

A new Branch was opened at Melton Mowbray in 1959 in the Leicester District (3E) following acquisition of the company Hills Transport (Melton Mowbray) Ltd which was allowed to trade as an independent business within the BRS organisation until the end of 1961, alongside a small fleet of BRS vehicles, and then merged into the BRS fleet.

The Luton District was wound up in January 1961. Northampton, Bedford and Stevenage were transferred to 6E. Luton was closed and merged with Dunstable. Dunstable and Aylesbury then passed to 3E. To accommodate this expansion the Burton Branch was transferred from 3E to 5E, also from January 1961. The Northampton Branch did not sit readily in Peterborough district's activities and was duly transferred from 6E to 3E in April 1961, while the Bedford Branch also transferred from 6E to 3E early in 1964.

Shortly before the 1964 fleet renumbering exercise was introduced, three Branches of the South Yorks & Lincs District (3D) in the N E Division were transferred to Midland Division control. Chesterfield and Newark joined 5E and Boston joined 6E. The former 3D fleet numbers were not altered at this late stage and were retained, simply altering their prefix from 3D to E5G, E5H or E6J, these being the internal depot codes by which the individual sites were identified in Directories.

WESTERN DIVISION

Divisional letter 'G'. BTC crest colour had been 'Deep Cream' from mid-1956 with the introduction of the new armorial crest but some former Western and South western vehicles may still have carried the earlier lead grey or 'Road Haulage Green' roundels, respectively, of the previous crest. The Division was organised into six Districts, each responsible for their own new vehicle registrations from their respective District Offices.

1G Cardiff District

CARDIFF	Ferry Road, Grangetown and Norbury Road, Fairwater, both in Cardiff	Ex 2G
NEWPORT	Malpas Road and Dock Street, both in Newport, Mon	Ex 1G
	Depots at Ebbw Vale and Pontypool and at Merthyr Tydfil, all reporting to District Office	Both ex 1G Ex 2G

2G Swansea District

SWANSEA	North Dock	Ex 20G
WEST WALES	Station Yard, Carmarthen	Ex 21G
	Depots at Bridgend and Llanelly reporting to District	Both ex 20G

3G Gloucester District

GLOUCESTER	Great Western Road	Ex 41G
WORCESTER	Bromyard Road, St Johns	Ex 41G
WELLINGON	Watling Street	Ex 31G
WREXHAM	Berse, New Broughton, nr Wrexham	Ex 31G
HEREFORD	38 Edgar Street	Ex 42G

	Depot at Ross-on-Wye reporting to District	Ex 42G
	Offices at Lydney and Stroud and changeover point at North Leach, Gloucs, all reporting to District	All ex 41G
	Depots at Shifnal (ex 31G) and Evesham (ex 41G) closed shortly before renumbering was introduced	

4G Oxford District

OXFORD	Long Lane, Littlemore	Ex 44G
READING	Cardiff Road	Ex 40F
	Depots at Kidlington, High Wycombe and Marlow and at Swindon, all reporting to District	All ex 44G Ex 41F

5G Bristol District

BRISTOL	Spring Street, Bristol 3 and Days Road, Bristol 2	Ex 1F, 2F and 3F
	Depots at Melksham and Bradford-on-Avon and at Clutton, Somerset, all reporting to District	Both ex 42F Ex 4F
	Office at Avonmouth, reporting to District	–

6G Exeter District

EXETER	Marsh Barton Trading Estate	Ex 80F
PLYMOUTH	Sutton Road, off Commercial Road	Ex 82F
TAUNTON AND BRIDGWATER	High Street, Taunton and Bristol Road, Bridgwater	Both ex 81F
	Depots at Cullompton and Barnstaple reporting to District	Both ex 81F
	Depots at Newton Abbot & St Austell reporting to District	Both ex 82F

Retained fleet sizes were at 1G, 279 general plus about 70 contracts; 2G, approx 190 general and 33 contracts; 3G, 203 general plus 12 contracts; 4G, 342 general, 73 contracts, also 15 staff cars received numbers; 5G, 282 general and 24 contracts; and 6G, 138 general, 12 contracts and 7 staff cars.

The Exeter District, 6G, was wound up and merged into the Bristol District, 5G, in June 1961. 5G was renamed 'West of England District' following this merger.

A number of other amendments to the District network occurred shortly before the new renumbering exercise of 1964. Two Branches from the Gloucester District, Hereford and Ross-on-Wye, were transferred to control of the Cardiff District in January but complete renumbering was not involved. Instead the internal depot codes G1G and G1H were substituted for the 3G prefix of their existing fleet numbers. Similarly, the Oxford District gained Aylesbury from the Leicester District, also in January 1964. Again, the existing 3E fleet numbers were simply recoded to G4H, the new internal depot code.

1956-1964 District Codes

'HIDDEN' FLEET NUMBER SEQUENCES

Brief mention has already been made of the fact that the London and Southampton Districts, and all Midlands Districts, adopted 'secret' series of fleet numbers that enabled the operating Branch to be identified, in contravention of the Head Office directive that the new numbering sequences should be simple joint series. To enable those of you who may wish to identify the bases of vehicles shown in their photograph collections, the following details should be of interest. For many of the sequences involved they enable much more to be learnt from the numbers than might at first have been realised. This helped to keep enthusiasts interested!

London District

1956 series	1957-1959	Branch identification
1A1001-1108	1A1-113	Brentford
1A2001-2054	1A500-570	Covent Garden
1A3001-3135	1A200-364	Hampstead
1A4001-4082	1A400-495	Hayes
1A5001-5060	1A600-679	Purfleet
1A6001-6097	1A700-799	Stratford
1A7001-7137	1A800-961	Tower Bridge
1A8001-8132	1A1000-1173	Tufnell Park

The apparent duplication of Brentford's 1956 series with Tufnell Park's 1957 series did not affect observations at the time but could give rise to difficulty in identifying photographs many years later.

At Stratford, upon reaching 1A799 and completing the allocation, the next vehicles to arrive were given seven re-issued vacant numbers within the sequence, which contravened a long-established understanding that fleet numbers should be cancelled and not re-issued once they became vacant. Head Office, upon learning of this misdemeanour, immediately decreed that London District should discontinue its 'secret identification' numbering and, from autumn 1959, all further additions were raised in a common series, regardless of base, issued in the order 1A496-499, 680-699, 114-199, 365-399, 571-599, 962-999 and 1174 onwards, to reach 1A1241 by January 1965 when the next renumbering exercise took place. All existing numbers were 'frozen' and no longer subject to alteration in the event of transfer from one Branch to another as they had done previously

Other changes to affect this District were: In 1957 the Edgware depot of Tower Bridge Branch was closed. In 1958 the Kentish Town depot of Hampstead Branch was closed but the premises were retained for use as a stores depot by Tufnell Park Branch. In 1959 Covent Garden Branch was renamed 'Mile End' – a logical move as this was, after all, the location of the vehicle fleet. Also in 1959 Purfleet Branch was renamed 'Grays' and a new continental ferry service was introduced from the site.

49

In 1960 Hayes Branch was wound up; the Hayes depot was closed and the fleet transferred to Brentford, which was renamed 'Brentford/Hayes Branch', and the Chesham depot became directly controlled from District Office. In 1961 the Tower Bridge Branch was relocated to the old Kentish Town depot latterly in use as stores, and renamed 'Kentish Town Branch'. Also in 1961 Stratford Branch was closed, the vehicle fleet being split between Mile End and Kentish Town.

Southampton District

This District drew up a four-figure series of new fleet numbers in 1956 using distinct blocks of numbers to differentiate between each Branch but, unlike the London District, all were in the same series of 1001 upwards, so it became a simple matter to eliminate the 'thousand' yet still maintain separate Branch identification from 1957, thus:

1956 series	1957-1965	Branch identification
2A1001-1141	2A1-238	Southampton
2A1301-1350	2A301-387	Portsmouth
2A1401-1470	2A401-500 then 701-730	Poole
2A1501-1574	2A501-647	Isle of Wight

Each number remained unique: In the event that a vehicle transferred from one Branch to another it retained the same number and was not given one in the new Branch series. Numbers not attained in each block by 1965, such as 2A239-300 at Southampton, were unused. The Gillingham depot of Poole Branch was closed in 1957.

Home Counties District

It was observed earlier that the Home Counties District did not use fleet numbering to differentiate between Branches from 1957 onwards but, as the 1956 allocation did, it is appropriate to consider this District also at this stage. In fact, the 1957 joint series placed the vehicles in depot-by-depot order so, until inter-depot transfers began to occur, the bases of each could still be determined, as below:

1956 series	1957 series	Depot identification
4A1001-1029	4A1-31	Brighton
4A1200-1259	4A32-90	Canterbury
4A1400-1423	4A91-115	Guildford
4A1600-1637	4A116-158	Maidstone
4A1800-1853	4A159-213	Rochester
4A2000-2009	4A214-221	Sheerness
4A2200-2239	4A222-261	Sittingbourne
4A2400-2430	4A262-296	Tonbridge
4A2600-2602 (unconfirmed)	4A297-299	Canterbury Repair Centre

The new joint series continued from 4A300 onwards regardless of base and still including staff cars as well as general and contracts vehicles, to reach 4A709 by 1965.

MIDLANDS DIVISION
General Remarks

The 1956 numbering sequences all comprised a joint series from 1 upwards that combined all Branches, with a fourth 'thousand' figure ingeniously identifying the operating Branch or depot. For example, in Birmingham District 1E5030 was the 30th vehicle in the overall series, the '5' indicating Dudley Branch; in Stoke District 2E3006 was 6th in the series, the '3' indicating Crewe depot. Thus, should inter-Branch transfers occur later within Districts only the 'thousand' figure would require alteration.

In the three Districts for which full schedules were implemented, 1E, 2E and 6E, the vehicles were placed in year-by-year order at each Branch and, in the overall series, the oldest carrying the lowest numbers – though in the Stoke District this order was somewhat arbitrary. The new three-figure numbers introduced in 1957, after Head Office cancelled the four-figure series, were raised in the same order at each Branch and indicate that 3E, 4E and 5E also placed their vehicles in year order, the oldest first, but full records for their four-figure series did not survive.

Birmingham District

1956 series	1957 issue	Series extent (1964)	Identification
1E1xxx	1E101-241	1E300 then 322-423	Birmingham Branch
1E2xxx	1E301-318	1E321 (by 1958)	Birmingham (Aston)
1E3xxx	1E501-590	1E663	Wolverhampton Branch, including Walsall from 1960
1E4xxx	1E701-788	1E848	Walsall Branch. Tamworth only from 1960
1E5xxx	1E901-982	1E1100 then 1101-1118 duplicating earlier Stone series	Dudley Branch, Oldbury from 1962. Including Stone from 1958 onwards
1E6xxx	1E1101-1115	1E1118 (by 1958)	Stone depot, nr Kidderminster
C1E7001-7079 (separate series)	C1E1301-1379	C1E1398 (by 1958)	Contracts series

The Birmingham (Aston) general haulage vehicles were a small nucleus offering back-up to the main Contract Hire fleet based at this site. After the Contracts fleet was formed into the new Birmingham Contracts District in 1958 and recoded C11E, using the same fleet numbers, the general vehicles were absorbed into Birmingham Branch and renumbered 1E268-277. 1958 also saw the Stone depot added to Dudley Branch and the vehicles renumbered 1E1007-1022.

In 1960 Walsall Branch was wound up. Walsall depot was transferred to Wolverhampton Branch control and all further new vehicles were numbered in the Wolverhampton series, leaving the old Walsall series to be used by Tamworth depot only, which now reported direct to District.

In 1962 the Dudley, Wordsley and West Bromwich depots were all closed and the fleets combined at a new depot at Oldbury. The new Oldbury Branch, still with Stone as a sub-depot, continued to use the former Dudley Branch series of numbers for new vehicles.

Stoke District

Only the 1956 numbering system identified each vehicle's base, thus:

1956 series	Identification	Vehicles
2E1xxx	Stoke (general service)	62
2E2xxx	Tunstall	78
2E3xxx	Crewe	13
2E4xxx	Stafford	10
2E5xxx	Stoke (shipping services)	31

From 1957 the first figure (the 'thousand') was eliminated from the fleet numbers, leaving a joint sequence 2E( )001 upwards that no longer identified individual Branches. The four-figure series had reached 2E1195, a Stoke vehicle that duly became 2E195, and continued from 2E196 to reach 2E371 by 1964, including the batch 2E342-370 transferred from the North Western Division at Sandbach late in 1963. In due course the computer-style numbers such as 2E001 were further revised as repainting occurred, to read simply 2E1 upwards.

Contract Hire vehicles were not introduced until mid-1958 by which time general vehicles were numbered at around 2E230, so contract vehicles received numbers C2E301 upwards in a series that eventually reached C2E329. Meanwhile, general vehicles duly received numbers in the 300's, so duplicating the contracts numbers.

Leicester District

Vehicles were identified as follows:

1956 series	1957 issue	Series extent (1964)	Identification
3E1xxx	3E701-787	3E866, also C3E701-742	Leicester Branch
3E2xxx	3E302-343	3E388, also C3E301-304	Corby depot
3E3xxx	3E501-584	3E691, also C3E501-509	Coventry Branch
3E4xxx	3E101-156	3E193, also C3E101-118 (by 1961)	Burton Branch

The District was late in preparing its four-figure numbering series in 1956 so few examples were seen. Highest number found was 3E1285, a new Leicester Branch vehicle based at Loughborough. The Burton series is deduced, none were noted physically. Burton Branch was transferred to Notts/Derby District in January 1961 and renumbered into a new series 5E801 upwards.

Leicester District was prolific in introducing new sequences of numbers identifying separate Branches after 1957 and the following additional series came into use:

Add	Series extent (1964)	Identification
3E901+	3E972, no contracts	Melton Mowbray: new branch 1959, including former Hills Transport vehicles at 3E930-958
3E1101+	3E1185, C3E1101-1114	Dunstable – ex Luton District Jan 1961
3E1301+	3E1317, C3E1301-1316	Aylesbury – ex Luton District Jan 1961
T3E1501+	Trailers only	Overspill for Coventry Branch after trailer series reached T3E700
3E1701+	No record	Not known if raised
3E1901+	3E1935, C3E1901-1932	Northampton – ex Peterborough District April 1961
3E2101+	3E2112, no contracts	Rugby – separated from Leicester Branch Jan 1962
3E2301	3E2317, no contracts	Loughborough – separated from Leicester Branch Jan 1962
3E2501+	3E2528, C3E2501-2504	Leamington – separated from Coventry Branch Jan 1962
3E2701+	Series cancelled	Bedford – ex Peterborough District 1964. Proposed but not activated

Luton District

Identifications were as follows:

1956 series	1957 issue	Series extent (1961)	Identification
*4E1xxx	4E101-136	4E175, also C4E101-115	Luton
4E2xxx	4E301-313	4E330, also C4E301-314	Aylesbury
*4E3xxx	4E501-533	4E545, also C4E501-506	Dunstable
*4E4xxx	4E701-715	4E723, no contracts	Stevenage
4E5xxx	4E901-949	4E994, also C4E901-917	Northampton Branch (including Bedford)

Again, the District was late in producing its 1956 schedule and few examples were physically recorded. No examples from the series asterisked above were seen and these are assumed.

In 1959 Bedford was separated from Northampton Branch and set up at new premises as a Branch in its own right with a new fleet number series 4E801 upwards, which reached 4E834 (no contracts). The District was abolished in January 1961, as observed previously.

Notts/Derby District

Vehicles were identified as follows:

1956 series	1957 issue	Series extent (1964)	Identification
*5E1xxx	5E101-151	5E193	Derby

1956 series	1957 issue	Series extent (1964)	Identification
*5E2xxx	5E301-403	5E483	Nottingham (Wells Road)
5E3xxx	5E501-540	5E589	Riddings
*5E4xxx	5E701-728	5E753	Carfax depot, Mansfield
C5E9001-9004 (separate series)	Same	C5E9152	Nottingham Contracts (Comery Avenue)

This District was very late in producing 1956 schedules and only one example of a four-figure number was seen. The other sequences, asterisked above, are assumed.

Burton Branch was added to the District, transferred from Leicester District from January 1961, in a further series 5E801 upwards, which reached 5E849. Contracts vehicles at this Branch were renumbered C5E9070-9081 in the contracts series, which now covered the whole District.

No new series were introduced at Chesterfield and Newark on their addition in 1964 s further renumbering was imminent.

Peterborough District

Identities were as follows:

1956 series	1957 issue	Series extent (1964)	Identification
6E1xxx	6E101-168 and	6E210, no contracts	Peterborough (including Whittlesey 1956)
	6E301-331	6E347, no contracts	Whittlesey (1957 onwards)
6E2xxx	6E701-746	6E773, C6E701-761 (by 1962)	Cambridge
6E3xxx	6E501-554	6E620, C6E501-537	Wisbech
6E4xxx	6E901-915	6E927, C6E901-908	Bourne

After Luton District was closed in January 1961, three further series were introduced:

6E1001 upwards, reached 6E1062, plus C6E1000	Bedford
6E1201 upwards, reached 6E1223 by Apr '61, plus C6E1201-1216 by Apr '61	Northampton
6E1401 upwards, reached 6E1415, plus C6E1400-1404	Stevenage

Following on from these a further series T6E1500 upwards for trailers only was introduced at Wisbech as an 'overspill' after their original trailer series reached T6E700.

Yet another series, 6E1700 upwards, was proposed for Boston Branch after this site joined the District in 1964 but, in the event, this series was cancelled and the former S Yorks & Lincs District numbers were retained as further renumbering was imminent.

The Northampton Branch spent only four months under Peterborough District control before passing to Leicester District in April 1961. The Cambridge Branch was transferred to East Anglia District in April 1962.

OTHER DISTRICTS' NUMBERING SYSTEMS

The remaining Districts did not adopt 'secret identities' within their numbering series but, as many chose to renumber their 'Retained Fleets' in Branch-by-Branch order, the initial locations were identifiable until transfers began to occur. For completeness, comments to help identify the home bases of vehicles in some of these Districts follow:

East Anglia District (3A)

The district was unique in providing each item of equipment with its own serial number under the 1956 four-figure system. Contract vehicles were allocated the block C3A1001-1100; general vehicles 3A1101-2000, and trailers T3A2001 upwards. In 1957 it became a simple matter of eliminating the 'thousand' from contracts vehicles and from trailers to produce series from 1 upwards, but 1100 had be taken from the general vehicles – thus 3A1101-1400 became 3A1-300.

The haulage vehicles were renumbered, apart from the first three, in year-by-year order, oldest first, in two distinct blocks: 3A1104-1217 (later 3A4-117) and 3A1218-1400 (later 3A118-300), so their locations were randomly distributed. There was no obvious pattern to the vehicles in either block – they were not in make order or depot-by-depot – nor was there any apparent reason for the two separate blocks of numbers.

The series eventually reached 3A595 in 1964, which included the batch 3A491-528 transferred in from Cambridge, ex-6E, in April 1962. The Contracts series reached C3A119.

London Contracts District (C5A)

Pre-1955 vehicles were renumbered into a new series, C5A1001-1385, which included trailers, in alphabetical order of customers' names, with further larger batches of vehicles for particular customers taking the series to C5A1452. A handful of further pre-1955 vehicles added from 1957 onwards eventually brought this series to C5A1468.

Post-1955 all new London Contracts vehicles were already numbered in a joint series for 3001 upwards, again including trailers, only the Group codes (C9A, C49A, C70A, etc) varying, and it was a simple matter to recode all these to C5A from the end of 1956 onwards, by which time the series had reached around C5A3500. It eventually attained a high of C5A5482 by early 1965, after which further fleet renumbering occurred.

Operating bases were not indicated in either of these series, the numbers forming joint sequences covering all Branches. However, the Branch name was frequently lettered above the fleet number on the inside of the cab doors, a favourite location for the numbers to be placed on contracts vehicles.

Southern Scotland District (1B)

Effective 1957 so no four-figure series. The vehicles were renumbered in Branch-by-Branch order and also in depot-by-depot order within each Branch, so the initial distribution can be established as follows:

1B1-122 Douglas Branch (ex 60B)	1-72, Douglas (West Street): 73-97, Townhead (North Wallace Street): 98-104, Paisley: 105-119, Port Dundas (Kessock Street): 120-122, 7.5% reserve
1B123-295 Glasgow Branch (ex 63B)	123-214, Lister Street: 215-237, Mount Vernon: 239-255, Falkirk: 256-282, Grangemouth: 283-290, Ayr: 291-295, Reserve
1B296-375 Argyll Branch (ex 66B)	296-335, Warroch Street: 336-343, Campbeltown: 344-348, Lochgilphead: 349-355, Strone: 356-358, Oban: 359-375, Reserve
1B376-598 Edinburgh Branch (ex 40B)	376-419, Newington: 420-506, Leith: 507-529, Haddington: 530-555, Bathgate: 556-565, Galashiels: 566-577, Kelso: 579-585, Dunbar: 586-598, Reserve
1B599-681 Fife Branch (ex 26B)	599-630, Dunfermline: 631-654, Kirkcaldy: 655-666, Strathkinness: 667-678, Alva: 679-681, Reserve
1B682-683	New vehicles
1B684-699	Service vehicles and mobile cranes

The '7.5% Reserve' was a hangover from the days of the Suez crisis and fuel rationing, whereby BRS had been required to impose a 7.5% fleet reduction to conserve fuel. Some Districts chose to include these vehicles in their assets when renumbering their 'Retained Fleets' even though they were usually the most elderly, were standing out of use and were unlikely ever to turn a wheel in BRS service again; indeed, most were disposed of during 1957.

The series continued with new vehicles from 1B699 onwards, reaching 1B787 by June 1958 when Edinburgh was separated as a new District and then continued as 'Glasgow District' from 1B788 to reach a high of 1B1029 by October 1964, when further renumbering occurred. Contracts, in a separate series C1B1 upwards, reached C1B99.

Northern Scotland District (2B)

Also a 1957 series, so no four-figure numbers. In this case vehicles were renumbered in order of their old fleet numbers, Branch by Branch, so individual depot allocations could not be determined. The allocation was as follows:

2B1-92	Dundee Branch (ex 20B)
2B93-197	Angus Branch (ex 21B)
2B199-265	Aberdeen Branch (ex 7B)
2B266-282	7.5% Reserve, all branches: 266-273, Dundee: 274-276, Angus: 277-282, Aberdeen
2B283-291	Service vehicles and cranes

The series continued to reach 2B515 by October 1964 and the separate contracts series, C2B16.

Edinburgh District (3B)

This new District, formed in June 1958, simply renumbered from 3B1 upwards all vehicles from the former Edinburgh Branch of Southern Scotland District in order of their old 1B numbers (between 1B376 and 1B776) reaching 3B207. As some inter-depot transfers had already occurred and many new vehicles had joined the fleet since 1957, it was no longer in depot-by-depot order. The series duly reached 3B368, with contracts in a series C3B1-17, by October 1964.

Liverpool District (1C)

Another 1957 schedule so no four-figure numbers. The vehicles were renumbered in Branch-by-Branch order but within each batch there was no discernible pattern to the allocation nor were the six depots of Warrington Branch differentiated. The following was apparent:

1C1-132	Liverpool Branch (ex 13C)
1C133-319	Warrington Branch (six depots, former series 5C, 6C, 7C and 11C intermixed)
1C320-379	North Wales Branch (ex 8C)
1C380-388	Recovery vehicles and Port Control radio vans

The series duly reached 1C681 by June 1964, including two batches: 1C461-486 at Wrexham (ex 3G) in 1958 and 1C607-617 at Crewe (ex 2E) in 1963. The Sandbach depot was later transferred to Stoke District at the end of 1963 after Crewe was closed. All Contracts vehicles in this District were administered by Manchester Contracts.

Manchester District (2C)

The original series, 2C1001-1324, was drawn up in October 1956 and revised to 2C1-324 in 1957. The vehicles were numbered in Branch-by-Branch order, in order of their old fleet numbers so individual depot allocations were not apparent. The series revealed the following:

2C1-101	Greenheys Branch including 77-101 ex Contracts (ex 64C)
2C102-200	Trafford Park Branch (2 depots) including 192-200 ex Contracts (ex 67C)
2C201-324	Bolton Branch (3 depots) including 311-324 ex Contracts (ex 74C). In this case it is known that the vehicles between 2C201 and 267 originated from Cornbrook Group (depots at Cheetham and Salford) always 74C, while those between 2C268 and 310 were original vehicles from Bolton Group itself, formerly 69C

The series eventually reached 2C492 by July 1964. Contract Hire vehicles were also renumbered in order of their old fleet numbers but in a separate series from C2C5001 upwards, which reached C2C5781 by July 1964 – again not identifying their home bases.

Preston District (3C)

The original series 3C1001-1218 was drawn up in October 1956 and the four-figure numbers remained in use after 1957, the series eventually reaching 3C1460 during 1963 and then mysteriously continuing from 3C1556 to 1566 during 1964.

The original fleet was again put in Branch-by-Branch and/or depot-by-depot order but in no particular order within each batch, as follows:

3C1001-1050	Preston Branch (ex 22C)
3C1051-1127	Blackburn Branch (ex 24C and 26C)
3C1128-1155	Whitehaven depot (ex 23C)
3C1156-1173	Carlisle depot (ex 23C)
3C1174-1218	Irish Ferry Branch (ex 22C) – these were immediately replaced by a fleet of new vehicles, 3C1219-1262, at the end of 1956

After the Whitehaven and Carlisle depots were made over to the new Northern District and the Irish Ferry Branch to British Road Ferry Services, early in 1964, what remained of the Preston District was wound up and transferred to control of Manchester District where the fleet numbers had their 3C prefixes adjusted to C2S at Preston and C2T at Blackburn, their new internal depot codes, pending further renumbering. As at Liverpool, all contracts work in this District was administered by Manchester Contracts.

Tyne/Tees District (1D)

The schedule was drawn up late in 1956 and only a few vehicles had received their four-figure numbers in the series 1D1001-1476 before the numbers were revised to 1D1-476 early in 1957. They were numbered in Branch-by-Branch order and also depot-by-depot within that, enabling their initial allocation to be established before transfers occurred,.

1D1-170	Newcastle Central Branch (ex 1D)	1-78, Stepney Bank: 79-138, Mansion House Wharf (The Close): 139-170, Sunderland
1D171-303	Newcastle Haymarket Branch (ex 2D)	171-239, Team Valley: 240-303, Wallsend
1D304-446	Tees-side Branch (ex 4D)	304-367, Stockton: 368-413, Thornaby: 414-428, Darlington: 429-444, Bishop Auckland: 445-446, Yarm-on-Tees
1D447-476	All Branches	New vehicles Oct-Dec 1956, part of 1956 replacement programme

In 1959 the Central and Haymarket Branches were combined as one 'Newcastle Branch' at new premises in Eastern Avenue, Team Valley and the vehicles at Stepney Bank, Wallsend and Second Avenue were relocated to this site. The Mansion House Wharf depot closed in 1962, these also going to Eastern Avenue.

Meanwhile, also in 1959, the Tees-side Branch was concentrated on two sites – Thornaby which absorbed the Stockton vehicles and Darlington which took over the Bishop Auckland and Yarm fleets.

The fleet series reached 1D727 by the end of 1963. Contracts, in a separate series C1D1 upwards, reached C1D94.

Yorkshire District (2D)

This District was unusual in that it chose to number all its equipment – general and contracts vehicles and trailers – in one continuous series, whereas all other Districts had at least separated their trailers into different series. The original series was drawn up around October 1956 and the 'thousand' figures were initially applicable, an overall series 2D1001-1690 (including trailers) being revised to 2D1-690 from 1957, comprising 387 general vehicles, 10 service vehicles, 30 new vehicles, 23 contracts vehicles plus two additional and 214 trailers plus 19 additional, accounting for 685 numbers, plus 5 unidentified.

All equipment was numbered in former Group order, depot by depot, before – for example – Castleford and Goole left control of York Branch and joined Leeds and Hull Branches respectively – and the initial batches can be identified as follows:

2D1-111	Ex 30D, former York Group	1-38, York: 39-74, Castleford: 75-96, Goole: 97-103, Harrogate: 104-111, Malton
2D112-194	Hull Branch (ex 31D)	All at Walton Street
2D195-261	Leeds Branch (ex 32D)	195-232, Leeds: 233-261, Rothwell
2D262-357	Bradford Branch (ex 32D – previously 49D)	262-279, Batley: 280-323, Bradford: 324-339, Ovenden: 340-357, Bingley
2D358-387	7.5% Reserve	358-364, Hull: 365-367, Leeds: 368-376, Bradford: 377-387, York
C2D388-410	Contracts vehicles	
T2D411-624	Trailers	411-454, ex 30D: 455-522, ex 31D: 523-566, ex 32D: 567-624, ex 32D/49D
2D626-635	Service vehicles	
2D625 and 636-690		New vehicles (30), trailers (19) and contracts vehicles (2) added Oct-Dec 1956 plus 5 unknowns

Having reached fleet no 2D748 in July 1957, trailers and contracts vehicles were at last separated into their own series from T2D1 and C2D1 upwards. The three series then progressed to 2D806, T2D53 and C2D12 by December 1958. The Bradford Branch was then separated to form a new 'West Yorkshire District', along with the neighbouring Parcels Branches, and recoded 4D. The remaining 2D fleet, now retitled 'East Yorkshire District', continued from 2D807 to reach 2D888 by February 1964, the separate Contract series reaching C2D110, plus one trailer CT2D1 and general trailers T2D154.

There were several administrative changes over the years. In 1957 the

Rothwell depot of Leeds Branch ceased to operate road services and was instead retained as a Divisional Stores; the fleet was split between Leeds and Castleford depots. In 1959 the depots at Harrogate, Castleford and Goole were removed from their respective Branches and instead controlled directly from District Office. The Malton depot of York Branch closed around 1962/63.

South Yorks & Lincs District (3D)

One of the first new series to be introduced from October 1956, the sequence 3D1001-1494, was adjusted to become 3D1-494 from 1957. As in the rest of North Eastern Division, vehicles were placed in depot-by-depot order, in former Group order, enabling their initial bases to be identified as follows:

3D1-218	Sheffield Branch	1-13, Eyre Street: 14-75, Penistone Road: 76-109, Chesterfield (all ex 60D): 110-167, Staniforth Road (ex 63D): 168-218, Shepcote Lane (ex 62D)
3D219-323	Doncaster Branch (ex 64D)	219-268, Doncaster: 269-288, Barnby Dun sub-depot: 289-300, Worksop: 301-323, Barnsley
3D324-347	Grimsby (ex 40H)	All at Julian Street
3D348-406	Lincoln Branch (ex 45H)	348-381, Lincoln: 382-392, Newark: 393-406, Boston
3D407-450	Scunthorpe (ex 46H)	All at Station Road
3D451-462	All Branches	New vehicles Oct-Dec 1956
3D463-472	Scunthorpe (ex 46H)	New vehicles 1955
3D473-481		Recovery and yard vehicles
3D482-494	All Branches	Further new vehicles Oct-Dec 1956

During 1957 the Eyre Street and Penistone Road depots in Sheffield were closed, the vehicles relocating to Staniforth Road; and the Barnby Dun depot closed, the vehicles moving to Doncaster.

The series reached 3D884 by February 1964 and the separate Contracts series, C3D99. The Chesterfield, Newark and Boston depots were transferred to Midland Division control early in 1964.

West Yorkshire District (4D)

This new District was set up from January 1st 1959 using the existing fleet of Bradford Branch vehicles simply recoded from 2D to 4D but not without considerable reorganisation. Only two of the former depots were retained – those at Bradford and Bingley – though the Bradford site relocated from Thornton Road to the former Parcels depot in Legrams Lane. The depots at Batley and Ovenden were closed but a third depot was instead introduced at Dewsbury, another former Parcels depot that had earlier been mothballed. Consequently the fleet was completely redistributed and the numbering sequence gave no indication of the vehicles' bases.

It functioned jointly with West Riding Parcels Branches (P4D) and a new series of fleet numbers from 901 upwards was introduced and used by both companies. Upon reaching 999 it continued from 100, reaching 118 by February 1964. Contracts, in a separate series, reached C4D26.

Birmingham Contracts District (C11E)
This was the former Contracts Branch of Birmingham District, separated and set up as an entirely new District in 1958, by which time fleet numbering had reached C1E1398. The code simply altered to C11E and continued from 1399 to reach C11E1669 by February 1964.

The majority of vehicles were indeed based at Birmingham, though such bases as Tamworth and Wolverhampton also operated vehicles numbered in the series. The new District had a remit to expand within the West Midlands and two large important contract customers were in fact engaged in subsequent years – Scribbans Kemp Bakeries late in 1958 and C Kunzle, cake makers, in 1961 – both of which operated extensive fleets of vans located throughout the country.

Cardiff District (1G)
As with all Districts of the Western Division, schedules were not finalised until 1957 and no four-figure series were introduced. The Cardiff District prepared a careful numbering schedule that divided the fleet first into petrol- and diesel-engined vehicles and then Branch by Branch within each category, such that the original bases were identifiable until inter-depot transfers began to occur. Thus:

Petrol	Diesel	Identification
1G1-20	1G61-145	Cardiff (ex 2G series)
1G21-29	1G146-152	Merthyr Tydfil (ex 2G series)
1G30-52	1G153-221	Newport (ex 1G series)
	1G222-247	Ebbw Vale (ex 1G series)
	1G248-274	Pontypool (ex 1G series)
1G53-60	1G275-279	Service vehicles

Great care needed to be exercised by enthusiasts at the time in deciding whether the 1G numbers of vehicles seen represented the new Cardiff District series or the old Newport Group series as renumbering proceeded, as many were very similar.

The series duly attained a high of 1G543 by 1964 and contracts, in a separate series, reached C1G239. Two further depots added to the District's control in 1964 – Hereford and Ross-on-Wye – simply had their former Gloucester District 3G fleet numbers amended to carry the prefixes G1G and G1H (the new depot codes) pending the 1964 renumbering that was imminent.

Swansea District (2G)

The 1957 renumbering system did not enable individual bases to be identified. The vehicles were divided into vehicle types, the largest quantity being their famous fleet of Leyland Octopus 8-wheelers, of which 120 survived de-nationalisation. These became 2G1-120 in order of the numerals of their registration numbers (from JCY38 to HCY998). There followed smaller blocks of numbers for other types of vehicles in reducing quantities, e.g. next came 17 AECs, then 15 Fodens, etc. Some 190 vehicles were renumbered and, while the schedule did not identify home bases, it did result in most former 20G vehicles – the mainstream 8-wheelers – holding all numbers up to about 2G160, while Carmarthen's (ex 21G) featured among the miscellany of smaller vehicles towards the end of the series, even including three wartime Internationals still in service.

New deliveries in later years took the series to 2G371 by 1964. Contracts, in a separate series, reached C2G163.

Gloucester District (3G)

This District also produced a 1957 renumbering schedule that failed to assist in identifying individual bases. In this case they merged all vehicles from the three previous series, 31G, 41G and 42G, and renumbered them jointly from 3G1 upwards in order of year of registration, the oldest first. Within each year they were further placed in order of first letter of the registration numbers regardless of vehicle make or base, e.g. for 1950 vehicles, from 3G98 (DFK841 at Worcester) to 3G114 (TRE806 at Wellington). The original allocation took the series to 3G203 but it had reached 3G210 by the time it was implemented late in January 1957.

The series continued to reach 3G485 by 1964. Branches at Wrexham (transferred to N W Division in 1958) and Hereford and Ross-on-Wye (to Cardiff district early in 1964), left the District's control. Contracts, in a separate series, reached C3G112.

Oxford District (4G)

A fourth District and a fourth method of renumbering their vehicles. This time, most of the fleet was renumbered in order of the previous fleet numbers and, as a result, individual bases were not apparent – only a general idea from their origin. The following was apparent:

4G1-229	Ex 44G. At Oxford Branch. Also depots at Kidlington, High Wycombe and Marlow. All vehicles up to 1955, in old fleet no order
4G230-288	Ex 40F and 41F, mixed, at Reading and Swindon, added to the District in 1955. These were renumbered n order of the numerals of their registration numbers, from CDP26 to GHR948, regardless of previous Grouping
4G289-337	Ex 44G. New vehicles delivered 1955/56, now to all six locations – again in old fleet no order

| 4G338-342 | Service vehicles |
| 4G343-357 | Staff cars |

The series continued from 4G358 to reach a high of 4G787 in February 1964. A series of numbers 4G787-800 allocated to vehicles at Aylesbury, transferred in from Leicester District (3E) in January 1964, was cancelled, the vehicles instead retaining their old numbers now prefixed G4H.

Contracts, in a separate series, reached C4G238. A proposed sequence C4G238-245 for contracts vehicles at Aylesbury was similarly cancelled, the old numbers being prefixed CG4H.

Bristol District (5G)

Again, the numbering system adopted failed to identify individual bases. Broadly similar to the system adopted by Gloucester District, Bristol put all vehicles from the five former Group series 1F, 2F, 3F, 4F and 42F in order of year of registration, renumbering them 5G1 upwards, the oldest first. Unlike Gloucester, however, there was no pattern shown by the vehicles within each year, although in some cases they appeared to be in depot-by-depot order this was not always the case. The old fleet numbers also failed to indicate the current base as vehicles had been regarded as communal and transferred between depots with no change in their numbers for some months prior to the renumbering.

In 1961 the District was renamed 'West of England District' after absorbing the Exeter District. The former 6G general haulage vehicles were renumbered 5G400-528 and in this case they were numbered in depot-by-depot order, thus:

5G400-432	Bridgewater
5G433-438	Barnstaple
5G439-455	Plymouth
5G456	St Austell
5G457-509	Exeter
5G510-528	Newton Abbot

The series finally reached 5G603 by February 1964. Contracts, in a separate series, reached C5G293. These included the batch C5G103-146 ex C6G in 1961 and also the batch C5G221-268 raised when all Western Division vans working on the Bowyers contract in other Districts were placed under West of England district control.

Exeter District (6G)

This District adopted a very precise renumbering system, very similar to that of Cardiff District, by dividing the fleet first into petrol- and diesel-engined vehicles and then raising new numbers in depot-by-depot order. Their original distribution was as follows:

Petrol	Diesel	Identification
6G1-3	6G57-70	Newton Abbot, ex 82F Grouping
	6G71	St Austell, ex 82F Grouping
6G4-11	6G72-83	Plymouth, ex 82F Grouping
6G12-28	6G84-105	Exeter, ex 80F Grouping
6G29-36	6G106-119	Taunton, ex 81F Grouping
	6G120-122	Bridgwater, ex 81F Grouping
6G37-43	6G123-135	Cullompton, ex 81F Grouping
		Barnstaple, ex 81F Grouping
6G44-49	6G136	Service vehicles
6G50-56		Staff cars

Barnstaple had a permanent allocation of only one container at this time but was retained as an 'outstation' and, in fact, certain contracts work was later based there after Cullompton depot closed.

This was only the third District to allocate fleet numbers to staff cars after 1956, the others being Home Counties (4A) and Oxford (4G).

The series continued from 6G137 to reach around 6G212 by June 1961 when the District was wound up and merged with 5G, Bristol District, which was then renamed 'West of England District'. The Contracts series reached C6G70.

4

1964-1972

The BTC was wound up in 1963 and control of BRS and its associated companies passed to a new body, the Transport Holding Company. The first indication of this action was the gradual elimination of the BTC crest from the cab doors of BRS vehicles.

Under THC control the old divisional structure of BRS was disbanded and the divisional tier of management was discontinued. The 26 Districts in existence at the beginning of 1964 were reorganised into 14 new Districts, each trading autonomously. New fleet numbers were raised comprising two-letter codes – the first letter signifying the district and the second the Branch within the District – rather than the number-and-letter codes used previously

The sixth and final edition of Ian Allan's 'ABC of BRS' had only been published in 1963, just before this fleet numbering revision occurred and, to our knowledge, no guide has ever been published since that explains vehicle numbering from 1964 onwards to the enthusiast. It is hoped the following pages will resolve many queries and aid photograph collectors in identifying their vehicles.

To follow up on the observation above, that the BRS crest fell out of use as part of the vehicle livery, other aspects may help to date photographs of vehicles bearing two-letter coded fleet numbers. Apart from vehicle registrations (year letter 'B' corresponded to the 1964 renumbering and all licensing authorities were obliged to introduce 'C' registrations from 1965), if the view is of an older vehicle with new-style number but still carrying the BTC crest it is relatively early, taken before the crest had been eliminated. If the livery is entirely plain with only the fleet number providing relief on the cab sides it dates from before 1969. If the livery includes the new triple arrowhead motif it dates from 1969, after the new logo was introduced.

The first letter of the new codes, identifying the Districts, was as follows. Letters A-E and G corresponded to the outgoing Divisional letters in use since 1956.

A	South Eastern District	HQ London	H	Northern	HQ Newcastle
B	Scottish	Glasgow	J	South Yorks & Lincs	Sheffield
C	North Western	Manchester	K	North Midland	Derby
D	Yorkshire	York	L	East Anglia	Norwich
E	West Midland	Birmingham	M	South Midland	Oxford
F	East Midland	Leicester	R	South Western	Bristol
G	South Wales	Cardiff	X	London Contracts	London

Unlike the 'Retained Fleet' renumbering exercise which was achieved within a period of 4-5 months (Oct 1956-Feb 1957) the THC exercise took much longer. The first revised numbers were observed in February 1964 but it was July 1965 before the final new districts were operational. As changes in registration patterns and other events also occurred during this period of time, the new Districts are dealt with in chronological sequence rather than alphabetical order.

Northern District (H)

First to become functional, from February 1964. It comprised the former Tyne/Tees District plus Carlisle and West Cumberland Branches from the old Preston District, with the following codes for general haulage vehicles:

HA	Newcastle	Old internal code D1A	HD	Darlington	Old code D1H
HB	Sunderland	Old internal code D1C	HE	Carlisle	Old code C3E
HC	Tees-side	Old internal code D1G	HF	West Cumberland	Old code C3F

Contracts vehicles were numbered in a joint series for all Branches using just the District letter 'H' plus the BRS (Contracts) Ltd company letter 'C' as a suffix, e.g. H1C, H2C, etc.

New vehicle registrations began to be raised by District HQ (the old Tyne/Tees District Office) at Newcastle and later, after its relocation to Gosforth in 1968, from Northumberland CC.

West Midland District (E)

Examples first seen late in March 1964. This was a merger of the whole of the Birmingham and Birmingham Contracts Districts, along with Coventry and Leamington from the Leicester District and Wellington and Worcester from the Gloucester District, coded as follows:

EA	Cheapside	Old code E1A	EH	Tamworth	Old code E1H
EB	Birmingham (Bromford Ln)	Old code E1B	EJ	Oldbury	Old code E1J
EC	Redditch	Old Code E1C	EK	Kidderminster	Old code E1L

ED	Wolverhampton	Old code E1E	EL	Wellington	Old code G3D
EE	Walsall	Old code E1G	EM	Worcester	Old code G3B
EF	Leamington	Old code E3F	ER	Birmingham Contracts (Tyburn Road)	CE11A
EG	Coventry	Old code E3E			

All Contracts vehicles within the original Birmingham District were initially numbered within the series ER1C upwards, including those at Wolverhampton and Tamworth, but those at Leamington, Coventry, Wellington and Worcester were numbered in the same series as their general vehicles, with the 'C' suffix.

The District Office was the former Midland Divisional Office at Harborne Road, Birmingham which raised all new registrations from Birmingham CBC. Codes EN, EP and EQ were not used.

East Midland District (F)

Also functional from late March 1964, this comprised the remainder of the old Leicester District including most of the former Luton District, disbanded in 1961, plus Bedford from the Peterborough District. Codes were as follows:

FA	Leicester	Old code E3A	FE	Melton Mowbray	Old code E3J
FB	Rugby	Old code E3B	FF	Dunstable	Old code E3K
FC	Loughborough	Old code E3C	FG	Northampton	Old code E3N
FD	Corby	E3D	FH	Bedford	Old code E6F

Contracts vehicles were numbered in separate series from general haulage at each Branch with company letter 'C' as a prefix, e.g. CFA1, CFG1, etc.

The former Leicester District Office at London Road continued as HQ and to raise new vehicle registrations from Leicester CBC as before.

South Western District (R)

The next District to become operational, examples first seen during April 1964. It comprised the whole of the former West of England district (a merger of the Bristol and Exeter Districts in 1961) plus Yeovil from the old Southampton District and Gloucester from the old Gloucester District, as follows:

RA	Bristol (Spring Street)	Old code G5A	RH	Bridgwater	Old code G5L
RB	Days Road (Bristol sub-depot)	Old code G5B	RJ	Taunton (Office)	Old code G5K
RC	Avonmouth (Office)	Old code G5E	RK	Newton Abbot	Old code G5M
RD	Melksham	Old code G5C	RL	St Austell	Old code G5N
RE	Wells	Old code G5G	RM	Barnstaple	Old code G5P
RF	Exeter	Old code G5H	RN	Yeovil	Old code A2E
RG	Plymouth	Old code G5J	RP	Gloucester	Old code G3A

The District Office remained at Canynge Road in Bristol and raised new registrations from Bristol CBC as before. The old Gloucester District Office was closed and no further registrations were raised here.

The codes RB, RC and RJ were not physically held by any vehicles at this time. All Days Road vehicles were numbered in the RA series used at Spring Street and codes for Traffic Offices were later discontinued. Contracts vehicles were numbered in the same series as general with company letter 'C' as a suffix.

North Midland District (K)

Early in May 1964, first examples from this District appeared. It was a merger of the old Notts/Derby and Stoke Districts, with control continuing from the old Notts/Derby Office in Derby.

The Stoke District Office was closed and Stoke registrations ceased:

KA	Derby	Old code E5A	KG	Chesterfield	Old code E5G
KB	Nottingham (Wells Road)	Old code E5B	KH	Newark	Old code E5H
KC	Riddings	Old code E5C	KJ	Stoke	Old code E2A
KD	Carfax (Mansfield)	Old code E5D	KK	Tunstall	Old code E2B
KE	Nottingham Contracts (Comery Ave)	Old code E5E	KL	Stafford	Old code E2D
KF	Burton	Old code E5F	KM	Sandbach	E2? (ex C1K)

All new registrations were raised from Derby CBC by the District Office in Ashbourne Road, Derby. All this District's contracts vehicles were numbered jointly in the 'Nottingham Contracts' series with 'C' prefix from CKE1 upwards, regardless of base at this time.

South Midland District (M)

Also early in May 1964 this District began functioning, completing the reorganisation in the Midlands. It comprised the whole of the former Oxford District, plus Chesham added from the old London District:

MA	Oxford	Old code G4A	ME	Swindon	Old code G4F
MB	Banbury	Old code G4G	MF	Aylesbury	Old code G4H
MC	Reading	Old code G4B	MG	Chesham	Old code A1M
MD	High Wycombe	Old code G4D			

The old Oxford District Office in George Street continued in use and to raise new registrations from Oxford CBC as before. Contracts vehicles were numbered in the same series as general at each Branch, with suffix 'C'.

Yorkshire District (D)

Mid-May 1964 saw the first examples from this new District which was a merger of the former East Yorkshire and West Yorkshire (general) Branches once again, with the following network:

DA	York	Old code D2A	DF	Castleford	Old code D2H
DB	Harrogate	Old code D2C	DG	Bradford	Old code D4E
DC	Hull	Old code D2D	DH	Bingley	Old code D4F
DD	Goole	Old code D2E	DJ	Dewsbury	Old code D4G
DE	Leeds	Old code D2F			

The split of the old North Eastern Division into three separate trading Districts brought about the closure of the old Divisional Office in Leeds and, at first, the old East Yorkshire district Office at Walmgate Bar, York, was used by the new Yorkshire district and the first new registrations were raised from York CBC. However, a new, more centrally located, office was opened later in June 1964 in Lady Lane, Leeds after which all further new registrations were from Leeds CBC.

Contracts vehicles were initially numbered in the same series as general at each Branch with suffix 'C'. Early in 1965, however, a new series DK1C upwards, 'Yorkshire Contracts Branch', was established into which all their contracts vehicles were renumbered.

South Yorks & Lincs District (J)

Completing the reorganisation in the North East, this new District also first materialised during mid-May 1964. It was simply a continuation of the same District as before, excluding three Branches transferred out at the beginning of the year, controlled from the same office at Eyre Street, Sheffield, with the following network:

JA	Sheffield	Old code D3A	JE	Worksop	Old code D3H
JB	Attercliffe	Old code D3D	JF	Scunthorpe	Old code D3J
JC	Doncaster	Old code D3F	JG	Lincoln	Old code D3K
JD	Barnsley	Old code D3G	JH	Grimsby	Old code D3N

New vehicles began to be registered from Sheffield CBC for the first time, administered by the District Office. Contracts vehicles were numbered in the same series as general, with suffix 'C'.

North Western District (C)

June 1964 saw the first examples of the new North Western District's reorganised general haulage fleet but inspection of registration dates suggests it was July before adjustment of the Contracts fleet was completed. This large District covered almost all the former N W Division territory with the exception of the Carlisle and Whitehaven bases, already part of the new Northern District, and the Irish Ferry service which had passed to the new company, British Road Ferry Services, earlier in the year. The network was as follows:

The BRS Reference Book

CA	Liverpool City (Studholme Street)	Old code C1A	CN	Salford (Dock Office)	Old code C2D
CB	Dock Office (Liverpool)	Old code C1B	CP	Cheetham	Old code C2F
CC	Fruit Office (Liverpool)	Old code C1C	CQ	Bolton	Old code C2G
CD	Warrington	Old code C1E	CS	Preston	Old code C2S
CE	St Helens	Old code C1F	CT	Blackburn	Old code C2T
CF	Runcorn	Old code C1G	CU	Trafford Park Contracts (Ashburton Road)	Old code C2H
CG	Kitt Green	Old code C1H	CV	Stalybridge Contracts	Old code C2J
CH	North Wales	Old code C1J	CW	Stockport Contracts	Old code C2K
CJ	Widnes	Old code C1L	CX	Liverpool Contracts (Great Howard Street)	Old code C2M
CK	Wrexham	Old code C1M	CY	Salford Contracts (Vere Street Warehouse)	Old code C2Q
CL	Greenheys	Old code C2A	CZ	Contracts Services (Head Office)	-
CM	Trafford Park (Richmond Road)	Old code C2B			

The policy of the old N W Division continued regarding new vehicle registrations. For general haulage each Branch raised its own locally but, for contracts, all new vehicles were licensed via the Contracts Office at Trafford Park – formerly from Lancashire CC but adjusting to Manchester CBC from mid-1964. General haulage continued to be controlled from the old Divisional Office in Corporation Street, Manchester.

General vehicles were numbered in series from 1 upwards at each operational Branch – there were no vehicle fleets at office locations CB, CC or CN at this time. Contracts vehicles, however, were numbered in a joint series from 1 upwards, only the codes CU, CV, CW or CX varying as appropriate, while 'out-stationed' vehicles based, for example, at Preston or certain customer's premises such as Llandudno, were all coded CU.

There was no vehicle fleet at CY (warehouse only) or CZ (internal office code) the code CR was not used at this time. In due course office codes were phased out and became vacant.

East Anglia District (L)

Another two months were to pass before this new District's examples first appeared in August 1964 but registrations suggested the Norwich office in Thorpe Road and now responsible for raising new vehicle licensing from Norwich CBC was operative from April onwards. The District was a merger of the old East Anglia and Peterborough Districts and the Peterborough office was closed, so ending vehicle registrations from this area. The network was as follows:

LA	Norwich	Old code A3A	LJ	Cambridge	Old code A3L
LB	Kings Lynn	Old code A3B	LK	Peterborough	Old code E6A
LC	Beccles	Old code A3C	LL	Whittlesey	Old code E6B
LD	Ipswich	Old code A3D	LM	Wisbech	Old code E6C

LE	Colchester	Old code A3E	LN	Bourne	Old code E6E
LF	Chelmsford	Old code A3F	LP	Stevenage	Old code E6H
LG	Stowmarket	Old code A3G	LQ	Boston	Old code E6J
LH	Bury St Edmunds	Old code A3K			

Contracts vehicles were numbered in separate series at each Branch with prefix C, e.g. CLA1, CLH1 and, in this context, Bury St Edmunds was a contacts-only Branch providing a fleet of eight-wheeled tippers for the British Sugar Corporation. Chelmsford operated no vehicle fleet and was effectively a traffic office only at this time.

South Wales District (G)

Examples first noted in September 1964. This was a merger of the former Cardiff and Swansea Districts, including two Branches only recently transferred in from the Gloucester District (Hereford and Ross-on-Wye). Both former District offices were closed, the former Divisional office at Queen Street, Cardiff, being retained to administer the fleet with responsibility for new vehicle registrations from Cardiff CBC, so no more Swansea registrations. Branch codes were as follows:

GA	Cardiff	Old code G1A	GG	Ross-on-Wye	Old code G1H
GB	Newport	Old code G1B	GH	Swansea	Old code G2A
GC	Ebbw Vale	Old code G1D	GJ	West Wales	Old code G2B
GD	Pontypool	Old code G1E	GK	Bridgend	Old code G2C
GE	Dowlais	Old code G1F	GL	Contracts Services	-
GF	Hereford	Old code G1G			

All contracts in this District were numbered in the joint series GL1C upwards, with no indication of Branch ownership.

Scottish District (B)

Registration patterns suggested the new network was functional from October 1964, though first examples were not seen until January 1965. Codes were as follows:

BA	Glasgow (Lister Street)	Old code B1F	BN	Arbroath	Old code B2C
BB	Douglas (West St, Glasgow)	Old code B1A	BP	Perth	Old code B2E
BC	Townhead (Nth Wallace St)	Old code B1B	BQ	Coupar Angus	Old code B2F
BD	Paisley	Old code B1C	BR	Aberdeen	Old code B2G
BE	Ayr	Old code B1L	BS	Inverness	Old code B2H
BF	Grangemouth	Old code B1K	BT	Elgin	Old code B2J
BG	Argyll (Warroch St, Glasgow) Plus sub-depots: Campbeltown – Old code B1N Lochgilphead – Old code B1P Dunoon – Old code B1R Tarbert – Old code B1S Oban – Old code B1T	Old code B1M	BU	Newington (Edinburgh)	Old code B3A

BH	Dunfermline		Old code B1XB	BV	Leith, Edinburgh	Old code B3B
BJ	Kirkcaldy		Old code B1MC	BW	Bathgate	Old code B3D
BK	Alva		Old code B1 XE	BX	Haddington	Old code B3C
BL	Dundee		Old code B2A	BY	Galashiels	Old code B3E
BM	Forfar		Old code B2B	BZ	Kelso	Old code B3F

The new District was simply a reorganisation of the previous Scottish Division, with control continuing from the former Divisional Office at Bothwell Street, Glasgow; all three earlier District Offices were closed. New vehicle registrations continued to be raised by the District Workshops at Linlithgow using West Lothian CC, apart from a few Contracts Vehicles that were registered locally.

Contracts vehicles were numbered in separate series at each Branch that offered the service with company letter 'C' as a prefix, e.g. CBB1, CBL1, etc. There was in addition a small fleet of 'District Spares' numbered simply CB1 upwards, administered by the Head Office, for use at any Branch requiring them.

London Contracts District (X)

Some months were to pass before reorganisation was completed in the South East. Registration patterns suggest the new Contracts format was operational from May 1965. There is some doubt over the precise Branch code allocation but most sources suggest the following:

XA	Newington Butts Branch	Old code A5A	XE	Victoria Park Branch	Old code A5F
XB	Sub-depot Cubitt Street	Old code A5B	XF	Sub-depot Batemans Row	Old code A5G
XC	Sub-depot Croydon	Old code A5D	XG	Brentford Branch	?
XD	Sub-depot Centaur St	Old code A5E	XJ ?	Perivale	Old code A5H

Other sources, however, suggest that XC may have been Drummond Road sub-depot (formerly coded A5C in Newington Butts Branch, a site later becoming AZ in the S E District) while Croydon had been uncoded; and that XF may have been Western Avenue, Acton (formerly the site of Chiswick Branch, coded A5J, which closed about the time of the reorganisation) while Batemans Row was uncoded. Also, it is not clear where the new Contracts Branch at Brentford originated from; why the code XH was not listed at this time, as it is known to have been used later; or when Perivale closed.

The only vehicles to be renumbered in this District were those delivered new from January 1965 onwards, a total of 52 vehicles duly being numbered in a new series from 1 upwards with Branch codes XA, XE or XG – the sub-depot codes were not used. All remaining vehicles retained their existing fleet numbers which had reached C5A5482.

Around August 1965 the bulk of Brentford's general haulage fleet was attached to London Contracts District and given the code XL, with fleet numbers XL109-153 (vehicles) and TXL155-235 (trailers, in the same series). From this point onwards all vehicles, regardless of base, carried the prefix XL to their fleet numbers for several years and individual operating Branches were not identifiable. It was about 1968 before separate Branch codes began to be used again.

South Eastern District (A)

The final new District to be set up was functional from May 1965, as with the London Contracts District, and examples first appeared in June. It was a complex merger of the former Southampton (excluding Yeovil) and Home Counties Districts with the 'general services' only of the former London District (excluding Chesham), with the following network:

AA	Mile End	Old code A1C	AM	Rochester	Old code A4E
AB	Covent Garden (Fruit office)	Old code A1B	AN	Sheerness	Old code A4L
AC	Grays	Old code A1G	AP	Aylesford (new site under onstruction)	
AD	Rochford	Old code A1R	AQ	Sittingbourne	Old code A4F
AE	Brighton	Old code A4A	AR	Tonbridge	Old code A4G
AF	Canterbury	Old code A4B	AS	Southampton	Old code A2B
AG	Faversham (Traffic Office)	Old code A4H	AT	Portsmouth	Old code A2C
AH	Minster (Traffic Office)	Old code A4J	AU	Camber Quay (transfer depot)	-
AJ	Folkestone (Traffic Office)	Old code A4K	AV	Poole	Old code A2D
AK	Guildford	Old code A4C	AW	IoW (Newport)	Old code A2F
AL	Maidstone (pending)	Old code A4D	AX	Cowes (sub-depot)	Old code A2G

The 'long distance' services of the London District were dealt with separately, as will be seen below, and it was protracted negotiations with Unions and other involved parties that had caused the delay in finalising this new District.

A further delay was encountered in mid-Kent, where renumbering did not take place until August 1965, when the new depot at Aylesford became operational. Until then Maidstone and Tonbridge vehicles continued to be numbered in the old 4A series and when Aylesford opened it merged both fleets but took the code AL (not AP as originally proposed), leaving AP and AR unused, later voided.

How long the two office codes AB and AJ remained in use is not clear for they showed in later schedules as being Tilbury Dock Office and Dover Traffic Office respectively. The use of office codes was in fact discontinued in later years and, during their existence, no vehicles physically carried fleet numbers in the series AB, AG, AH or AJ, nor AU (a transfer depot) or AX (all vehicles on the Isle of Wight were coded AW).

London Contracts and South Eastern District continued to be jointly controlled from offices in Carlow Street, London with new vehicle registrations raised in the same blocks of numbers from the GLC, which included index marks formerly used by Middlesex, Croydon, East Ham and West Ham, from January 1966 onwards.

London Trunk Services

Changes within the former London District were what caused the delay in setting up the new network and arose because of resistance to the BRS Head Office determination to attach the London Trunking depots to the Districts to which they operated. Effective from around May 1965, however, the Branches were dispersed as follows:

- **Hampstead** (former code A1D): services to the N West
  Attached to N W District, coded CJ, the code being vacant since Widnes closure
- **Kentish Town** (former code A1S): services to the Midlands
  3-way split: part to West Midlands District, coded EZ
  part to East Midlands District, coded FZ
  part to North Midlands District, coded KZ
- **Tufnell Park** (former code A1K): services to the North East, Scotland & S. Wales
  5-way split:
  part to S Yorks & Lincs district, coded JZ
  part to Yorkshire District, coded DZ
  part to Northern District, coded HZ
  part to Scottish District, coded BZ, vacant since closure of Kelso
  part to South Wales District, coded GZ
- **Brentford** (former code A1A): services to the S West
  Small portion attached to S W District, coded RZ

The remainder were made over to London Contracts, providing feeder services, and coded XL from August 1965

British Road Ferry Services

Mention should also be made of this company which accounted for three further BRS sites when it was set up in March 1964 – those of Irish Ferry Branch (depots at Preston Docks, formerly coded C3A and Larne Harbour C3B) and the Continental Ferry Service at Grays (formerly coded A1T) working through Tilbury Docks.

As far back as 1958 the BTC had an interest in the carriage of freight containers by sea when the company ACCS Ltd (Anglo Continental

Container Services), established in 1949, became a subsidiary. ACCS duly set up two associated companies, Ferry Trailers Ltd and Irish Ferryway, specifically operating services to Ireland which, along with ACCS itself, passed to the THC as successor to the BTC in 1963. The new company British Road Ferry Services was set up in 1964 to develop the services already operated by BRS, absorbing both FTL and Irish Ferryway.

Initially trading as a member of the BRS Group of companies, BRFS retained the red livery of the former BRS vehicles and renumbered them into single series of 1-35 for 10-ton, 17 gtw auto-hitch tractors; 100-111 for 16-ton, 24 gtw tractors and 200-206 for 10-ton, 18 gtw fifth wheel tractors, the numbers not indicating the vehicles' bases.

From April 1965 the separate ACCS business began to trade under the name 'Containerway' and from this time the two fleets began to be jointly operated under the name 'Containerway & Roadferry Ltd', adopting a new livery of two-tone blue with white waist in which new vehicles, now of 19/20-ton capacity (28-32 gtw) began entering service, numbered 300 upwards. The merger between the two concerns was completed by April 1967. Owing to its specialist function the company was then attached to the 'Special Traffics' Group of companies within the THC and its links with the BRS Grouping were severed.

Amendments

The huge number of different codes introduced during 1964/65 and now in use, compared with the relatively stable allocation of District codes in use during the previous seven years, inevitably meant that code alterations now began to take place far more frequently. Enthusiasts – and indeed the BRS Districts themselves, at times – were hard-pressed to keep up with the numerous changes that occurred in successive years.

The addition of the London Trunk Branches to various regional Districts had already caused several additional codes to be added to the original allocations. A considerable number of further adjustments was made, particularly around 1970/71 following boundary alterations and mergers of Districts, and the mid-1960s were also the period of so-called 'back-door nationalisation' when several other haulage businesses were taken over by the THC, many joining the BRS network.

In the following notes covering the period up to 1972, when the next major reorganisation occurred, we need to account for the following revisions:

South Eastern	Reissue codes AB, AJ, AP. Add codes AY, AZ. Reissue codes AG, AH, AJ (again). Reinstate AA, AC, AD after earlier deletion; and several other deletions
Scottish	Reissue BZ as reported. Several deletions
North Western	Activate CN. Reissue CJ as reported. Add CR. Reissue CB. Some deletions

Yorkshire	Add DK and DZ as reported. Following boundary revision add DL-DS, also DA (reissued), DT, DU as 'Northern & Yorkshire District'. Following further boundary revision add DA (again), DQ, DV, DY, also DH and DK (reissued) as 'North Eastern District'.
West Midland	Add ES, EZ (as reported), ET, EQ, E/DS. Following boundary revision add EU, EV, EW, EY. Some deletions
East Midland	Add FZ as reported, also FJ. District closed
South Wales	Add GZ as reported, also GM, GN, GP, GQ, GR, GS, GT, also GKW
Northern	Add HZ as reported. District closed
S Yorks & Lincs	Add JZ as reported. Some deletions. District closed
North Midland	Add KZ as reported, also KP and K. Following boundary revision add KN, KQ, KR, KS, KT, KU and rename 'East Midlands District'
East Anglia	Reissue LF. Add LR, LS. Much reorganisation. Some deletions
South Midland	Add MM, MP, also MTS, MKX, MAX
South Western	Add RZ as reported. Reissue RB, also RC, RJ, RM and add RR following boundary revision
London Contracts	Add XL, XM following boundary revision. Also XH, XP, XS, XX. Some deletions
Miscellaneous	Add NA, ZA
New London District	Introduced by incorporating NA with further codes NB-NH but wound up 12 months later

South Eastern District (A)

1965?	Delete AB (Covent Garden and AJ (Folkestone). Substitute AB = Tilbury, AJ = Dover, both as Traffic Offices
10/65	Add AP, mid-Kent Contracts. All former Home Counties Contracts vehicles merged into new series. Add AY, Southampton Contracts. All former Southampton Contracts vehicles merged into new series
By 1967	Add AZ, Drummond Road. A former Contracts depot in Bermondsey, re-opened offering warehousing and distribution services
1/68	Delete AQ. Sittingbourne reclassified as a sub-depot of Aylesford and all vehicles renumbered in AL series. Depot later closed
1/70	Delete AA Mile End; AC Grays; AD Rochford; AZ Drummond Road. All transferred to new London District and recoded ND, NE, NG, NF respectively. No further reference to AB (Tilbury Dock office) at this time
Late 1970?	Delete AN. Sheerness Branch closed

During 1970 S E District Office was relocated from London to Sevenoaks and vehicle registrations began to be raised from Kent CC.

In January 1971 the London District was wound up after only 12 months' existence and merged into the South Eastern District. To accommodate this expansion the Southampton portion was transferred to control of the South Western District and the two new Contracts Branches, AP and AY, to London Contracts District. Thus:

	Add	AA	Mile End, ex ND (former code reinstated
	Add	AC	Grays, ex NE former code reinstated)
	Add	AD	Rochford, ex NG (former code reinstated)

	Add	AG	Tufnell Park, ex NA (code reissued following voiding of former Office codes)
	Add	AH	Kentish Town, ex NB & NH (code reissued following voiding of former Office codes)
	Add	AJ	Drummond Road, ex NF (code reissued following voiding of former Office codes)
	Delete	AS AT AV AW	Southampton Portsmouth Poole Isle of Wight (all recoded in S W District)
	Delete	AP AY	Mid Kent Contracts Southampton Contracts (both renumbered in London Contracts District)
Feb 71	Delete	AH	Kentish Town Branch closed
Late 71	Delete	AA	Mile End closed
Late 71	Delete	AJ	Drummond Road closed

The District Office relocated yet again in 1972, from Sevenoaks to Potters Bar, following which new registrations reverted to GLC issue.

Scottish District (B)

Early 1965	Delete	BZ	Kelso. Branch closed. Fleet to Galashiels and renumbered in BY series
5/65	Reissue	BZ	Tufnell Park, Scottish services
12/65	Add		12 former Gavin Wilkie vehicles to Douglas Branch. This Glasgow company's fleet had been acquired by the THC in July 65 and its 26 vehicles added to the Pickfords fleet, becoming M4359-M4384, but some of the work was deemed more appropriate to BRS General Haulage. At Douglas they became BB65-76.
3/66			Acquisition of associated companies, West Coast Transports and James McPhee Ltd in Argyll-shire. No separate existence, the fleets were merged into Argyll Branch becoming BG75-97
1966	Delete	BD	Paisley. Branch closed, fleet to BB
1/67	Delete	BZ	Tufnell Park reconstituted as a new Branch and coded NA
Mid 67	Delete	BC	Townhead. Branch closed, fleet to BB
8/67	Delete	BQ	Coupar Angus demoted to sub-depot of Forfar, fleet renumbered in BM series
8/68	Delete	BU	Newington Branch closed, vehicles renumbered in BV series and BV renamed 'Edinburgh'
1970			Acquisition of H & G S Bell Ltd, Granton, Edinburgh, a contract-hire and vehicle leasing company that continued to trade separately as a wholly owned subsidiary. The fleet was not numbered
6/71		BB	Douglas Branch reclassified as Contracts only. General haulage fleet wound up. Some transferred to BA, the rest mothballed

In August 1965 the THC acquired a 75% holding in the Tayforth group of companies – the remaining 25% was acquired in April 1970. This large grouping was allowed to trade as a separate entity within the THC, alongside the BRS activities.

North Western District (C)

10/64	Delete	CJ	Widnes Branch closed, vehicles dispersed
5/65	Reissue	CJ	Hampstead Branch, North Western services
1965	Activate	CN	A small fleet of vehicles numbered CN1-11 was introduced at Salford, previously a Dock Office code. The venture was short-lived and within 12 months the vehicles were back at Greenheys and Trafford Park. (Office codes CB, CC, CN and CZ duly fell out of use)
8/66	Add	CR	Preston Contracts. New premises at Bamber Bridge to house a vehicle fleet in the area, formerly coded CU and termed 'out-stationed', controlled by Trafford Park
4/68			All out-stationed Contracts vehicles at other sites were passed to control of their local Haulage Branches and recoded accordingly, e.g. CG at Kitt Green, CK at Wrexham, etc. though all continued to be numbered in the same overall Contracts series
6/69	Reissue	CB	Dockside Express; a new service introduced at Liverpool using vehicles in a new yellow ochre livery
1/70	Delete	CJ	Hampstead Branch transferred to the new London District, recoded NC
5/71	Delete	CM	Trafford Park Branch closed; some vehicles to CP and CL, the rest 'mothballed'

Yorkshire District (D)

4/65	Add	DK	Yorkshire Contracts. All Contracts vehicles throughout District renumbered into one series
5/65	Add	DZ	Tufnell Park, Yorkshire services
1/66			Acquisition of associated companies, Castle Bros (Hauliers) Ltd and E G Smith Ltd, with 80 vehicles based at Lowfields Road, Leeds. The business continued to trade separately as a fully owned subsidiary. The fleet was not numbered
1966	Delete	DA DH	York & Bingley. General Haulage at both was terminated, the Branches becoming 'Contracts only' and, as all Contracts were now at DK, these codes fell out of use
9/66			Acquisition of associated companies, F Crowther & Son (Wakefield) Ltd, F Crowther & Son (Sandal) Ltd, Pashleys (Newmillerdam) Ltd and Arthur Cooper Haulage (Wakefield) Ltd, operating 46 vehicles from Sandal, Wakefield. The business continued to trade separately under the F Crowther name as a wholly owned subsidiary. The fleet was numbered in a series that had reached no 148 by this time, with the exception of Cooper's vehicles which were later given the numbers 153-161 to conform
1/67	Delete	DZ	Tufnell Park reconstituted as new Branch, coded NA
2/67		DF	Castleford, relocated to, and renamed, Knottingley
5/67			Acquisition of associated companies, Castle Bros Transport (Leeds) Ltd and Dalby & Neild Ltd, with 23 vehicles – unusually all tippers – based at Elland Road, Leeds. The fleet, which was not numbered, continued to function as a wholly owned subsidiary
6/68			Acquisition of E Maeer & Son Ltd, Knottingley. No separate existence. The 15 vehicles were absorbed into Knottingley Branch, becoming DF98-112
Mid 1968			The Castle Bros (Hauliers) Ltd fleet began receiving fleet numbers in a series from 100 upwards; only 13 were physically held and no list was ever located to identify the others, currently numbering around 70 vehicles. There was no knowledge of this numbering at BRS District Office
7/69	Delete	DJ	Dewsbury demoted to sub-depot of Bradford; fleet renumbered to DG series
8/69			Castle Bros Transport (Leeds) Ltd fleet relocated to Lowfield Road premises of Castle Bros (Hauliers). A new series of fleet numbers allocated to both fleets; nos 1-21 for the tippers, nos 100-153 for the reducing haulage fleet

| 1/70 | Delete | DD | Goole demoted to sub-depot of Hull Branch. Fleet renumbered and/or recoded into DC series |
| 1/70 | | DA | Began to be prefixed to certain of the fleet numbers held by Castle Bros vehicles in Leeds as if adopting a Branch code. The action appeared to be unofficial as, again, there was no knowledge of the code at BRS District Office |

From June 1st 1970 the District was retitled 'Northern and Yorkshire District' after merging the former Northern District into its activities, this being the first phase of a major restructuring in the North East. The former Northern District Office at Gosforth was closed and, while more appropriately located offices were sought, several new vehicles began to be registered locally at Branch level, particularly at Newcastle (using Gateshead CBC) and Tees-side (Middlesbrough CBC). New offices were duly found in Harrogate at the end of 1970, after which all registrations were raised from West Riding CC.

The Branch network was now as follows:

DB	Harrogate	DM	Sunderland ((ex HB)
DC	Hull, including Goole	DN	Tees-side (ex HC)
DE	Leeds	DP	Darlington (ex HD)
DF	Knottingley	DR	Carlisle (ex HE)
DG	Bradford, including Dewsbury	DS	West Cumberland (ex HF)
DK	Northern & Yorkshire Contracts	Uncoded	Castle Bros (unofficially DA)
DL	Newcastle (ex HA)	Uncoded	F Crowther

Former Northern Contracts vehicles were renumbered into the existing DK series. All general haulage vehicles were simply recoded.

7/70	Add	DT	For the fleet of F Crowther, though their green and cream livery continued unaltered until the end of the year
11/70	Add	DU	For the fleet of J Rostron & Sons Ltd, papermakers of Selby, taken over to operate under Contract Hire terms on a national basis
12/70	Delete		No fewer than three Branches, all closed down: DM (Sunderland), DR (Carlisle), and DA (Castle Bros). Some vehicles found service elsewhere within the District, the rest were 'mothballed'

From January 1st 1971 the District was retitled yet again, now 'North Eastern District', after the second phase of the reorganisation became effective and the former South Yorks & Lincs District was absorbed into its activities. The resultant Branch network was now as follows:

DA	Sheffield (ex JA & JB)	DN	Tees-side
DB	Harrogate	DP	Darlington
DC	Hull, including Goole	DQ	Barnsley (ex JD)
DE	Leeds	DS	West Cumberland
DF	Knottingley	DT	Wakefield (ex Crowthers)
DG	Bradford, including Dewsbury	DU	Selby (J Rostron contract)
DJ	Doncaster, including Worksop (ex JC & JE)	DV	Scunthorpe (ex JF)
DK	Northern & Yorkshire Contracts	DY	Grimsby (ex JH)
DL	Newcastle		

Contracts vehicles at the five former South Yorks & Lincs Branches had been numbered in the same series as general vehicles and this continued to be the case. They were not renumbered into the 'DK' series as those of the Northern District had been six months earlier. All vehicles were simply recoded.

In October 1971, however, fleet numbering for all contracts vehicles was standardised by introducing new fleet numbers, from 1000 upwards, at each Branch and the former overall 'DK' series was discontinued. This necessitated the introduction of new codes for two Branches offering contracts only, thus DH – Bingley Contracts and DK – York Contracts.

Early in 1972 the Bingley Branch (DH) was closed, all operations passing to the nearby Bradford Branch. Grimsby (DY) was made over to 'Contracts only' work late in 1971, the surviving haulage vehicles being reclassified as 'Contracts spares'.

West Midland District (E)

Reference should first be made to two important acquisitions that took place within this District's catchment area although both, in fact, retained their independence and did not join the West Midland District.

In June 1964 the car transporting business of Furness & Parker Ltd, Coventry, was acquired by the THC and operated as a subsidiary within the BRS grouping. The work of this company was expanded in November 1964 when all car transporter vehicles operated by BRS throughout the UK were transferred to the control of Furness & Parker and the resulting combined fleet was then given a series of fleet numbers from S1 upwards, numbered on a national basis. The company was reconstituted as Cartransport (BRS) Ltd from March 1968.

In October 1966 the THC acquired the Morton group of companies – Mortons (Coventry) Ltd and four subsidiaries – with over 200 vehicles devoted to the carriage of motor parts, accessories and car bodies. This business was later reconstituted as Mortons (BRS) Ltd in 1968 and its existing fleet numbers were given the prefix 'W' as a company letter. Late in 1969 the BRS fleets at Coventry and Leamington were transferred to Mortons' control and renumbered into the W series of numbers. About 1971 all Mortons' car transporter work was transferred to Cartransport (BRS) Ltd, leaving Mortons to function as a specialist express motor parts and spares carrier within the BRS grouping.

West Midland District itself underwent the following amendments:

| 1/65 | Add | ES | Wolverhampton contracts. This new service was introduced partly to accommodate a large increase in contract activity in the area (previously the few vehicles operated were controlled by Birmingham Contracts ER) and also to administer existing vehicles that had, until now, operated as a 'General Haulage Contract' for GKN in the ED series of numbers |

5/65	Add	EZ	Kentish Town. West Midland services
10/65			Acquisition of the associated business of J E Cartwright Ltd, Roy Transport Ltd, Anslows (Midland Transport) Ltd and Alvagreen Transport Ltd, with a combined fleet of 50 vehicles based at Selly Oak, Birmingham, largely dedicated to motor spares transport. The fleet was numbered and was initially allowed to trade independently. However, in due course, surviving vehicles were absorbed into the BRS fleets at Bromford Lane and Redditch
10/66			West Midland District assumed responsibility for all Midlands trunk services at Kentish Town and the fleets formerly operated by East Midlands (FZ) and North Midlands (KZ) were merged into the EZ series
By 1968	Add	ET	Mortons Contracts. Why such a service should have been introduced is unclear as other contracts vehicles were numbered in Mortons own series of numbers at the same time – unless these were out-stations rather than home-based at Coventry. In this connection it may be significant that most ET vehicles later transferred to Rugby
1/69	Add	EQ	Overnight Express. This was a new service introduced by Birmingham Contracts offering next-day specialist deliveries in small vans
Late 1969	Delete	EF EG	Leamington and Coventry – both fleets transferred to control of Mortons (BRS) Ltd
11/69	Add	E/DS	A small fleet of vehicles used for the Driver Training School at Bromford Lane, Birmingham
1/70	Delete	EZ	Kentish Town Branch transferred to the new London District and recoded NB
Late 1970	Delete	EC	Redditch Branch closed
1/71			Four Branches from the former East Midland District, would up at the end of 1970, transferred to West Midland control:
	Add	EU	Rugby ex FB
	Add	EV	Dunstable ex FF
	Add	EW	Northampton ex FG
	Add	EY	Bedford ex FH
2/71	Delete	EY	Bedford Branch closed. Services and some vehicles to Dunstable
5/71	Delete	ED	Wolverhampton Branch converted to contracts only using second code ES. General Haulage fleet wound up
Late 1971	Delete	EK	Kidderminster Branch closed, fleet laid up
6/72	Delete	EQ	Overnight Express redefined as a Contracts Branch and vehicles absorbed into Birmingham Contracts series, ER
1972	Delete	EV	Dunstable Branch ceased operations. Fleet laid up, premises only retained. Also Tamworth Branch (EH) converted to Contracts only, surviving general haulage vehicles made over to 'Contracts Spares' with the same fleet numbers, now with C suffix

East Midland District (F)

5/65	Add	FZ	Kentish Town, East Midlands services
8/65	Add	FJ	Bourne Branch, transferred in from East Anglia District, formerly LN
9/65			Acquisition of Corringdon Ltd of Weldon, nr Corby, with a 70-vehicle fleet. This business continued to trade separately as a wholly owned subsidiary. The fleet was not numbered
10/66	Delete	FZ	All Midlands trunk services at Kentish Town passed to control of West Midlands District and vehicles renumbered into EZ series

The East Midland District was dissolved in December 1970 and the Leicester office closed. Control of most of their Branches passed to the

Derby office of North Midland District which was retitled 'East Midland District' to reflect the alteration in area covered. Four other Branches passed to the West Midland District, as shown above.

South Wales District (G)

5/65	Add	GZ	Tufnell Park, South Wales services
7/65			Acquisition of George Read (Transport) Ltd, Mitcheldean, Glos, with a 50-vehicle fleet. The business was allowed to trade independently as a wholly owned subsidiary. The fleet was not numbered
8/65	Delete	GZ	South Wales District uniquely took the decision to attach their 16 Tufnell Park vehicles to the Branches to which they nominally operated – 7 to Cardiff (GA), 3 to Newport (GB) and 6 to Bridgend (GK)
1965	Add	GM	Margam. A small fleet of internal and service vehicles serviced Port Talbot steelworks but by 1970 an operational revenue-earning fleet was in use
1/66	Add	GP	Forest of Dean the period of independent operation of George Read (Transport) Ltd was curtailed prematurely and the services set up as a normal BRS Branch; the vehicles now numbered GP1-58
3/66	Add	GQ	Gloucester Branch transferred in from South Western District, formerly RP, along with 4 'trunk' vehicles from Brentford (RZ). The Contracts vehicles were renumbered into South Wales' GL series
3/66			Acquisition of James Smith (Bicknor) Ltd, English Bicknor, Glos, with a 34-vehicle fleet. No independent operation, the vehicles were immediately absorbed into the Forest of Dean Branch, becoming GP59-95
1/67			Appropriate quantities of vehicles from Cardiff, Newport, Bridgend and Gloucester plus one from Swansea were made over to the new independent Tufnell Park Branch, coded NA
1/67	Delete	GE	Dowlais Branch closed
1968			Acquisition of Black Rock Haulage, Abergavenny. No separate existence; the fleet was absorbed into Pontypool Branch and numbered GD47-83
1/68		GKW	Introduced for a small fleet used on the Driver Training Sch. at Bridgend
Early 1970	Add	GR	Newport Timber Terminal. New fleet set up to serve important new business; certainly operational by May 1970
Late 1970	Add	GS	Cardiff Docks. Further new fleet established to serve new business obtained; certainly operational by February 1971
1971?	Add	GT	Sharpness. Directories of 1971 included this code and numbered trailers are known but there's no data to establish how long the service existed
11/71	Add	GN	British Tissues, Bridgend. The fleet of this company was acquired by BRS in May 1971 and the Bridgend based vehicles were set up as a separate costing exercise in November, though those at other sites were absorbed into existing BRS Branches

Northern District (H)

5/65	Add	HZ	Tufnell Park, Northern District services
1/67	Delete	HZ	Tufnell Park separated as new Branch, coded NA
1968			District Office relocated from Newcastle to Gosforth, resulting in change of vehicle registrations from Newcastle CBC to Northumberland CC

The District was wound up in June 1970 and merged into the Yorkshire District (D) which was then retitled 'Northern & Yorkshire District', and the Gosforth office was closed.

South Yorks & Lincs District (J)

5/65	Add	JZ	Tufnell Park, South Yorks & Lincs services
1965			Attercliffe Branch (JB) closed, vehicles transferred to Sheffield (JA) but not renumbered; they continued to work alongside Sheffield's vehicles while still carrying their JB fleet numbers
1/67	Delete	JG	Lincoln Branch transferred to control of North Midland District and fleet renumbered with new Branch code KP
1/67	Delete	JZ	Tufnell Park separated as independent Branch, coded NA
4/70			Worksop Branch (JE) demoted to become a sub-depot of Doncaster (JC). Existing vehicles not renumbered and continued to carry their JE fleet numbers but any additions were now numbered in Doncaster's JC series

The District was merged into the Northern & Yorkshire District (D) from January 1971 which was then retitled 'North Eastern District' and the Sheffield office was closed.

North Midland District (K)

5/65	Add	KZ	Kentish Town, North Midland services
10/66	Delete	KZ	All Midlands trunk services at Kentish Town transferred to control of West Midland District; fleet renumbered into EZ series
1/67	Add	KP	Lincoln Branch transferred in from South Yorks & Lincs District, ex JG. Contracts vehicles renumbered into Nottingham Contracts' joint CKE series
1970			Variation to Contracts fleet. All North Midlands contract vehicles recoded from the former overall code KE to the code of each individual operating Branch, e.g. KA at Derby, KJ at Stoke, etc. KE now became unique to the Nottingham depot only, at Comery Avenue. All vehicles continued to be numbered in the same joint series, only the codes varying
8/70			Lincoln Branch converted to Contracts only. KP general haulage discontinued
1/71			The District was renamed 'East Midland District' following closure of the former District holding this name and its Leicester office, and absorption of six additional Branches from this source, as follows: Add KN Leicester, ex FA Add KQ Bourne, ex FJ Add KR Loughborough, ex FC Add KS Corby, ex FD Add KT Melton Mowbray, ex FE Add KU Weldon, ex Corringdon Ltd which lost its identity **Note:** A series of fleet numbers from K1 upwards had been used in North Midland District since being set up in 1964, for service vans, recovery vehicles and slave tractors. It had reached K97 by January 1971, resumed from K1 again on acquiring the former Leicester-controlled vehicles until reaching K37 and then continued from K98, reaching K107 by September 1972
4/71	Delete	KQ	Bourne Branch closed but premises retained for storage purposes
Mid 1971	Delete	KD	Carfax Branch closed. Some vehicles to Nottingham, the rest laid up
	Delete	KW	Weldon Branch closed. Some vehicles to Corby, the rest laid up
7/71			Reorganisation in Nottingham resulted in closure of the Contracts depot in Comery Avenue, transfer of all services to the haulage depot in The Wells Road and conversion of this site to Contracts only. The KB general haulage series was discontinued as a result, all vehicles were renumbered into the KE series

East Anglia District (L)

8/65	Delete	LN	Bourne Branch transferred to East Midland District, becoming FJ
1965	Delete	LH	Bury St Edmunds Branch had been solely devoted to a contract with the British Sugar Corporation and when this contract passed to Silver Roadways the depot – and even some of the vehicles, till new ones arrived – passed to the new operator
6/66			Acquisition of the business of W H Sexton Junior Ltd, Elmstead. The 36 vehicles were attached to Colchester Branch as a sub-depot and given fleet numbers LE60 upwards, Colchester's own fleet having reached around LE45/50 by this time. At Colchester, in fact, numbering continued separately to reach LE63, thus duplicating the first few Elmstead numbers until continuing from LE150
6/67	Add	LF	Elmstead. After 12 months' independent trading the former Sexton's fleet was given its own Branch status, though vehicles continued to be numbered in the same series as Colchester's in a separate block of numbers, only the Branch codes varying. LF had been vacant since Chelmsford Office code became disused
12/69	Delete	LL	Whittlesey closed; fleet transferred to Peterboro' and renumbered in LK series
1970?	Add	LR	Felixstowe. A sub-depot set up for Ipswich Branch, using vehicles recoded from LD and additional vehicles numbered jointly in the same series as those at Ipswich
5/71	Delete	LP	Stevenage services ceased but premises regained for warehousing, controlled by Cambridge Branch
1971			Cambridge Branch converted to Contracts only work. General haulage LJ series discontinued
1971	Add	LS	Thetford. A new service set up largely using vehicles from Cambridge's former general haulage fleet
1/72			Felixstowe (LR) set up as a Branch in its own right. The vehicles were separated from Ipswich's LD series and numbered thereafter in their own distinct series. The same may also have happened at Elmstead (LF), believed to have been set up as a separate Branch from Colchester with distinct numbering sequence, but insufficient records are available to confirm this
1972	Delete	LS	The short-lived Thetford venture was closed down

South Midland District (M)

By 1968			Chesham Branch, MG, relocated to, and renamed, 'Amersham'
11/69	Add	MTS	A small fleet of vehicles operating a driver training school at Oxford
1/70	Add	MM	Castle Bromwich. This followed the acquisition of a fleet of vehicles operated by Stewart & Arden on car body transport, which was controlled by Oxford Branch. The vehicles were numbered in the same series as Oxford's (MA), only the Branch code varying
2/71?	Add	MP	Erdington. A further extension of specialist work for the motor trade in Birmingham, controlled from Oxford rather than by the West Midland District
3/71	Add	MKX	Code raised for small fleet of service and recovery vehicles at Oxford Repair Centre
6/71	Add	MAX	Similarly, raised to cover service and recovery vehicles at Reading Workshops
10/71			Castle Bromwich Branch separated from Oxford in its own right and a new series of numbers, MM1 upwards, began to be used distinct from the Oxford series
1971/72?	Delete	MF	Aylesbury Branch services ceased but premises retained

South Western District (R)

10/64	Delete	RK	Newton Abbot Branch closed
5/65	Add	RZ	Brentford Branch, services to South Western District
3/66	Delete	RP	Gloucester Branch transferred to South Wales District; fleet renumbered into new series and coded GQ
1/67			Unsuccessful proposal to include RZ, long distance services at Brentford, in Tufnell Park's activities. After being allocated NA numbers at the new independent Branch being set up, the plan was not followed through, and the vehicles returned to Brentford and regained their RZ numbers
12/67	Delete	RM	Barnstaple Branch closed
4/69	Add	RB	Avonmouth. New depot opened to replace the old depot in Days Road, Bristol, where vehicles had formerly been numbered in the RA series of Spring Street depot but were now renumbered in their own series RB1 upwards
By 1970?	Add	RAW	A small fleet of vehicles on Driver Training School duty at Bristol
1970?	Delete	RZ	Brentford vehicles dispersed among individual Branches where they worked
1/71			Four branches added, transferred in from South Eastern Division following boundary revision: Add RC Southampton (ex AS) – code vacant since office codes voided Add RJ Isle of Wight (ex AW) – code vacant since office codes voided Add RM Portsmouth (ex AT) – code vacant since closure of Barnstaple Add RR Poole (ex AV) - new code

London Contracts District (X)

Date n/k	Delete	XJ	Perivale closed
Circa 1968	Delete	XL	Overall code. Brentford General Haulage recoded to ZA in recognition of its unique position within the District; it later became responsible to the South Eastern District. Other individual Branch codes – XA, XE and XG – were reinstated, as applicable in 1965, instead of being universally lettered XL as had been the case until this time
12/70	Add	XP	Long Lane. This was formerly the BRS (Pickfords) Ltd Contracts depot in London, transferred to control of BRS (Contracts) Ltd following lengthy negotiations between both companies
1/71	Add		Two Branches transferred in from South Eastern District following reorganisation: XL Mid Kent Contracts (ex AP) XM Southampton Contracts (ex AY)
1971?	Delete	XF	Batemans Row sub-depot closed
1972?	Add	XH	Brentford General Haulage recoded yet again – previously ZA
5/72	Add		Two new Branches following takeover of Keymarkets operations: XS Burgess Hill XX Hainault
8/72	Add		Further new Branch following takeover of Mars Ltd distribution fleet: XT Bedfont – in this case the former operator's (Translloyd) fleet numbers were retained and BRS fleet numbers were not raised until 1975

Miscellaneous

1/67	New code NA – Tufnell Park Branch. All long distance services to the North East, Scotland and South Wales were recombined into one fleet but a proposal to include Brentford vehicles working to the SW at this Branch was refused. Tufnell Park did not belong to any District and reported to BRS Headquarters, the 'in' joke being that the code NA indicated 'Not Attached'

Circa 1968	New code ZA similarly introduced for General Haulage vehicles at Brentford. This fleet was later recoded yet again, to XH, as stated above
1/70	Revision to BRS (Contracts) Ltd vehicle numbering. A Head Office directive required the company letter 'C' to be applied as a suffix to all fleet numbers. This did not affect S E District (A), Yorkshire (D), West Midlands (E), South Wales (G), Northern (H), South Yorks & Lincs (J), South Midlands (M) or South Western (R) as they already did so. Other Districts that had placed the 'C' as a prefix – Scottish (B), East Midland (F), North Midlands (K) and East Anglia (L) were required to amend the 'C' to a suffix. Thus, for example, CB20 to become B20C; CFA25 to FA25C; CKE250 to KE250C; CLA50 to LA50C. Two Districts that had not previously used the Contracts letter at all were now obliged to do so. Thus, in North Western District CU750 would become CU750C and in London Contracts District XA1234 would become XA1234C

London District (N)

A new 'London District' was set up from January 1st 1970 combining the General Haulage services of the South Eastern District in the London area with the independent Branch Tufnell Park, coded NA since January 1967, and the other long distance depots controlled by North Western and West Midland Districts. The following codes were introduced:

NA	Tufnell Park	Independent since Jan 67
NB	Kentish Town	Ex West Midlands EZ
NC	Hampstead	Ex North Western CJ
ND	Mile End	Ex South Eastern AA
NE	Grays	Ex South Eastern AC
NF	Drummond Road	Ex South Eastern AZ
NG	Rochford	Ex South Eastern AD

No reference was made to the Tilbury Dock Office, latterly coded AB in S E District.

Early 1970	Add	NH	Dagenham, a satellite depot to Kentish Town using vehicles ex NB
6/70	Delete	NC	Hampstead closed

    The District was short-lived and was wound up after only 12 months' existence to be absorbed wholly within the South Eastern District from January 1st 1971. In order for that District to absorb the extra work, the Southampton portion of the old S E District was transferred to the South West, and the Home Counties and Southampton Contracts work to London Contracts. The new codes for all these alterations have been recorded elsewhere in this book.

Summary

By September 1972 the 14 new Districts formed in 1964/65 (15, if including the London District of 1970) had been reduced to 11. Also in the BRS Group within the National Freight Corporation, which had assumed responsibility for all the THC's road transport undertakings since January 1st 1969, were Cartransport and Mortons. There then came a further

1964–1972 Two-Letter Branch Codes

reorganisation of the entire fleet, effective from 10th September 1972.

For ease of comparison with the pages that follow, a summary of the codes in use at this time is given below:

S E District	AC, AD, AE, AF, AG, AK, AL, AM plus four uncoded offices
Scottish	BA, BB, BE, BF, BG including five sub-depots, BH, BJ, BK, BL, BM, BN, BP, BR, BS, BT, BV, BW, BX, BY, plus H & G S Bell uncoded, also 'B-C' for Contracts Spares
North Western	CA, CB, CD, CE, CF, CG, CH, CK, CL, CP, CQ, CR, CS, CT, CU, CV, CW, CX, plus Vere Street Warehouse and Salford Office uncoded
North Eastern	DA, DB, DC plus sub-depot, DE, DF, DG plus sub-depot, DH, DJ plus sub-depot, DK, DL, DN, DP, DQ, DS, DT, DU, DV, DY, plus Leeds Warehousing (formerly Castle Bros) uncoded
West Midland	EA, EB, EE, EH, EJ, EL, EM, ER, ES, EU, EW plus Dunstable premises, also E/DS
South Wales	GA, GB. GC. GD, GF, GG, GH, GJ, GK, GL, GM, GN, GP, GQ, GR, GS, GT, also GKW
East Midland	KA, KC, KE, KF, KG, KH, KJ, KK, KL, KM, KN, KP, KR, KS, KT, also 'K' for service vehicles
East Anglia	LA, LB, LC, LD, LE, LF, LG, LJ including Stevenage warehouse, LK, LM, LR, plus two uncoded offices
South Midland	MA, MB, MC, MD, ME, MG, MM, MP, plus Aylesbury premises, also MTS, MAX, MKX
South Western	RA, RB, RC, RD, RE, RF, RG, RH, RJ, RL, RM, RN, RR, plus three offices and three transfer depots all uncoded, also RAW
London Contracts	XA, XB, XC, XD, XE, XG, XH, XL, XM, XP, XS, XT, XX

5

1972-1979

With effect from 10th September 1972 the activities of BRS Ltd and BRS (Contracts) Ltd were combined and the eleven existing Districts of the two nationwide companies were reorganised into seven regional limited companies. With the abolition of the Contracts company the use of their letter 'C' as part of the fleet numbers was discontinued and, instead, two codes were now introduced for each Branch – one for General Haulage and one for Contracts. This allowed for expansion where any particular Branch did not operate both services at the time these codes were introduced.

The new companies were:

Southern BRS Ltd	HQ Potters Bar	Company letters A (General), X (Contracts), N (for later expansion)
Scottish Road Services Ltd	HQ Glasgow	Company letters B (General), H (Contracts)
North Western BRS Ltd	HQ Manchester	Company letters C (General), F (Contracts)
North Eastern BRS Ltd	HQ Harrogate	Company letters D (General), J (Contracts)
Eastern BRS Ltd	HQ Derby	Company letters K (General), V (Contracts)
Midland BRS Ltd	HQ Oxford	Company letters K (General), W (Contracts), T (expansion)
Western BRS Ltd	HQ Bristol	Company letters R&S (General), Y&Z (Contracts)

Compared with the list on the previous page, District Offices at Birmingham (West Midlands, letter 'E'), Cardiff (South Wales, letter 'G') and Norwich (East Anglia, letter 'L') were closed and the code letters discontinued. Letters F, H, J and N were reinstated, having been disused since January 1971, while letters S, T, V, W, Y and Z (apart from ZA) had not previously been used for two-letter codes at all. The use of letter 'T' was surprising as this was also used to prefix all trailer numbers and, as computerisation of records became increasingly adopted, the 'T' codes invariably tripped up computer printouts.

The recession of the early 1970s was still under way and the main reason for setting up these new limited companies was to enable each, and each of their individual Branches, to trade autonomously while profitability results were assessed. If any particular Branch did not attain a predetermined profit level it was earmarked for closure.

To further establish the separate identities of each company new liveries were introduced in February 1973, coinciding with a 'Trailer Vesting Day' on 24th February 1973, when all common-user trailers (mostly flats and platform skeletals), regardless of which Branch their fleet numbers indicated they belonged to, became the property of the Branch at which they were located on that day. Depot staffs had the task that day of painting the headboards of each trailer in their new colour and applying new fleet numbers to each trailer on the premises, claiming them as their own. The liveries adopted were:

Southern BRS	Marigold orange with white transfers for vehicle numbering
Scottish Road Services	Dark blue upper and lower with white waist
North Western BRS	Red with gold leaf transfers for triple arrowhead motif and lettering
North Eastern BRS	Marigold orange with black transfers for vehicle lettering, but white for the arrowhead logo. Blue transfers were used for Contracts vehicles
Eastern BRS	Red with yellow door panel and headboard carrying arrowhead motif
Midland BRS	Mid-blue ('French Blue') with white lettering
Western BRS	Red with arrowhead motif in yellow ochre

In addition, two companies – Southern and Eastern – discontinued the practice, established over 20 years earlier, of having the tailboards painted white carrying the fleet numbers in black. The new liveries were now extended over the entire vehicle or trailer, including the tailboards.

The livery was further revised in October 1976 when the size of the arrowheads motif was increased and two parallel lines were added to the logo extending around the sides and front of the cab. At this stage the opportunity was also taken to distinguish further between the three companies that had until then adopted a red livery. North Western BRS, whose M.D. had the longest period of service, was given first choice and elected to remain red, now with white transfers for arrowhead and lettering, as it had been originally; Eastern BRS adopted an all-over mid-brown livery (a cross between rust and chocolate, termed 'golden brown') and Western BRS became all-over yellow ochre, both now using white for all decals. A revision was also made to the livery of Scottish Road Services which became a slightly lighter shade of all-over blue, no longer with a white waist. The networks established from 1972 were as follows:

SOUTHERN BRS LTD (letters A and X)

Southern BRS arguably represented the most complicated reorganisation of former Districts. It combined the whole of the former South Eastern District; all the London Contracts District except the Southampton portion; the Bucks area of the old South Midlands District; the Beds area of the old West Midlands District; and the Suffolk and Essex portions of East Anglia District. Branch codes and identities were as below:

Existing:
General Codes Contracts Codes

NEW	OLD	NEW	OLD	IDENTITY
AC	Same	XC	AC-C	Grays
AD	Same	XD	AD-C	Rochford
AE	Same	-	-	Brighton
AF	Same	XF	XL-C	Canterbury
AG	Same	XR	AG-C	Tufnell Park
AH	MG	XY	MG-C	Amersham
AJ	-	XZ	-	Aylesbury (premises only)
AK	Same	XK	XL-C	Guildford
AL	Same	XJ	XL-C	Aylesford
AM	Same	XM	XL-C	Rochester
AN	AF	-	-	Dover
AP	LD	XH	LD-C	Ipswich
AQ	LR	XQ	LR-C	Felixstowe
AS	LE	XB	LE-C	Colchester
AT	LG	XN	LG-C	Stowmarket
AV	MD	XU	MD-C	High Wycombe
AW	LF	XW	LF-C	Elmstead
AX	XH	XG	XG-C	Brentford
		XA	XA-C	Newington Butts
		XE	XE-C	Victoria Park
		XL	XL-C	Maidstone (aka Mid-Kent)
		XP	XP-C	Long Lane
		XS	XS-C	Sussex Contracts (formerly Burgess Hill)
		XT	XT-C	Bedfont
		XV	-	Dunstable (premises only)
		XX	XX-C	Hainault

Additional:
General Codes   Contracts Codes

NEW	OLD	NEW	OLD	IDENTITY
AA	-	-	-	Kentish Town Workshops
AB	-	-	-	Tilbury Dock Office
AZ	-	-	-	Ipswich Repair Centre
AO	-	XO	-	Head Office Codes

New vehicle registrations continued to be raised from the GLC by the Potters Bar headquarters and then from the Central London LVLC after licensing centres were introduced in September 1974.

SCOTTISH ROAD SERVICES LTD (letters B and H)

The company was a merger of all BRS and BRS (Contracts) activities within the former Scottish District. The fleet of H & G S Bell, based in Edinburgh, continued to trade independently. The only significant change in vehicle numbering was the introduction of new Contracts codes. The network was as follows:

Existing:
General Codes Contracts Codes

NEW	OLD	NEW	OLD	IDENTITY
BA	Same	-	-	Glasgow, Lister Street
-	-	HB	BB-C	Glasgow Contracts, Townsend Street
BE	Same	HE	BE-C	Ardrossan
BF	Same	HF	BF-C	Grangemouth
BG	Same	-	-	Argyll (Warroch street, Glasgow, plus sub-depots at Campbeltown, Lochgilphead, Tarbert, Inverary and Dunoon)
BH	Same	-	-	Dunfermline
BJ	Same	HJ	BJ-C	Kirkcaldy
BK	Same	HK	BK-C	Alva
BL	Same	HL	BL-C	Dundee
BM	Same	-	-	Forfar
BN	Same	-	-	Arbroath
BP	Same	HP	BP-C	Perth
BR	Same	HR	BR-C	Aberdeen
BS	Same	HS	BS-C	Inverness
BT	Same	HT	BT-C	Elgin
BV	Same	HV	BV-C	Edinburgh
BW	Same	-	-	Bathgate
BX	Same	HX	BX-C	Haddington
BY	Same	-	-	Galashiels

Additional:
General Codes Contracts Codes

NEW	OLD	NEW	OLD	IDENTITY
BB	-	-	-	Forfar Repair Centre
BC	-	-	-	Glasgow Repair Centre
BD	-	-	-	Linlithgow Workshops
BO	-	HO	-	Head Office Codes
Uncoded				H & G S Bell, Edinburgh

The fleet of 'Contracts Spares' formerly numbered in the series B1C upwards was given the code HO, indicating control by Head Office, contracts services, from September 1972.

Head Office remained at Bothwell Street, Glasgow and the Linlithgow workshops continued to raise all new vehicle registrations from West Lothian CC until superseded by Edinburgh LVLC in 1974.

SRS underwent considerable change in subsequent years and from January 1975 it left the BRS Group, becoming instead a member of a new holding company, Tayscot Ltd, within the NFC, formed to administer all Scottish operations. However, as numbering systems continued to follow the established BRS format it will be considered alongside all the other BRS companies for the purposes of this study.

NORTH WESTERN BRS LTD (letters C and F)

This company was a merger of BRS Ltd and BRS (Contracts) Ltd in the whole of the former North Western District, the Cumbria area of North Eastern District and the Potteries area of East Midland District. Branch codes were now as follows:

Existing:
General Codes Contracts Codes

NEW	OLD	NEW	OLD	IDENTITY
CA	Same	-	-	Liverpool (Studholme Street)
-	-	FA	CX-C	Liverpool Contracts (Gt Howard Street)
CB	Same	-	-	Dockside Express (Liverpool)
-	-	FB	(CY)	Salford, Vere Street Warehouse
CC	DS	FC	DS-C	West Cumberland
CD	Same	FD	CD-C	Warrington
CE	Same	FE	CE-C	St Helens
CF	Same	-	-	Runcorn
CG	Same	-	-	Kitt Green
CH	Same	FH	CH-C	North Wales
CJ	KL	-	-	Stafford
CK	Same	FK	CK-C	Wrexham
CL	Same	-	-	Greenheys
-	-	FL	CU-C	Trafford Park Contracts
CM	KJ	FM	KJ-C	Stoke
CN	KK	-	-	Tunstall
CP	Same	-	-	Cheetham
CQ	Same	-	-	Bolton
CR	KM	FR	KJ-C	Sandbach
CS	Same	-	-	Preston
-	-	FS	CR-C	Preston Contracts (Bamber Bridge)
CT	-	-	-	Blackburn
-	-	FV	CV-C	Stalybridge Contracts
-	-	FW	CW-C	Stockport Contracts

Additional:
General Codes Contracts Codes

NEW	OLD	NEW	OLD	IDENTITY
CX	-	-	-	Manchester Repair Centre
CY	-	-	-	Stoke Repair Centre
CZ	-	-	-	Continental Operations
CO	-	FO	-	Head Office Codes

Head Office continued to be at 109 Corporation Street, Manchester 4. New vehicle registrations also continued to be raised at Branch level which required Stafford, Stoke, Tunstall and Sandbach also to conform to this policy. West Cumberland did not last long enough to do so, while Contracts continued to raise all registrations from the sub-office at Trafford Park.

NORTH EASTERN BRS LTD (letters D and J)

The formation of this company was a straightforward reconstitution of the former North Eastern District, excepting Cumbria which passed to North Western BRS Ltd. The North Eastern District had itself been a combination of three smaller Districts in 1970/71, which had now had some 18-24 months to settle down. The Branch network read as follows:

Existing:
General Codes   Contracts Codes

NEW	OLD	NEW	OLD	IDENTITY
DA	Same	JA	DA-C	Sheffield
DB	Same	JB	DB-C	Harrogate
DC	Same	JC	DC-C	Hull, plus Goole sub-depot
DE	Same	JE	DE-C	Leeds
DF	Same	JF	DF-C	Knottingley
DG	Same	JG	DG-C	Bradford, plus Dewsbury sub-depot
-	-	JH	DU-C	Selby Contracts
DJ	Same	JJ	DJ-C	Doncaster, plus Worksop sub-depot
-	-	JK	DK-C	York Contracts
DL	Same	JL	DL-C	Newcastle
DN	Same	JN	DN-C	Tees-side
DP	Same	JP	DP-C	Darlington
DQ	Same	JQ	DQ-C	Barnsley
DT	Same	-	-	Wakefield
DV	Same	JV	DV-C	Scunthorpe
-	-	JY	DY-C	Grimsby Contracts

Additional:
General Codes Contracts Codes

NEW	OLD	NEW	OLD	IDENTITY
DW	-			Leeds Warehousing (Lowfields Road, formerly Castle Bros)
DX	-			Newcastle Repair Centre
DY	-			Sheffield Repair Centre
DO	-	JO	-	Head Office Codes

The Head Office continued at Copthall Tower House, Harrogate, and to raise all new registrations from West Riding CC and then from Leeds LVLC after September 1974.

EASTERN BRS LTD (letters K and V)

Eastern BRS was a complex merger between almost all of the East Midlands District (excepting the Stoke area), the majority of the East Anglia District (excepting the Suffolk area) and the easternmost portion of the West

Midlands District, with the following network:

Existing:
General Codes Contracts Codes

NEW	OLD	NEW	OLD	IDENTITY
KA	Same	VA	KA-C	Derby
KB	LB	VB	LB-C	Kings Lynn (200 added to old LB numbers)
KC	Same	-		Alfreton
KD	LA	VD	LA-C	Norwich
-		VE	KE-C	Nottingham Contracts
KF	Same	-		Burton
KG	Same	VG	KG-C	Chesterfield
KH	Same	-		Newark
-		VJ	-	Driver Training School, Nottingham
KL	(LP)	-		Stevenage (warehouse only)
KN	Same	VN	KN-C	Leicester
-		VP	KP-C	Lincoln Contracts
KQ	LQ	-		Boston (100 added to old LQ numbers)
KR	Same	VR	KR-C	Loughborough
KS	Same	-		Corby
KT	Same	VT	KT-C	Melton Mowbray
KU	EU	VU	EU-C	Rugby (100 added to old EU numbers)
KV	LC	-		Beccles
KW	EW	VW	EW-C	Northampton
-		VX	LJ-C	Cambridge Contracts
KY	LK	VY	LK-C	Peterborough
KZ	LM	VZ	LM-C	Wisbech

Additional:
General Codes Contracts Codes

NEW	OLD	NEW	OLD	IDENTITY
KO		VO		Head Office codes

The former East Midland District office at Ashbourne Road, Derby was retained as the new HQ and the East Anglia District office at Norwich was closed. All new registrations were raised through Derby CBC until September 1974 and then Nottingham LVLC.

The Derby Office was always very precise in its fleet number allocations and took care to adjust the numbers held by vehicles at Kings Lynn, Boston and Rugby upon receiving their new Branch codes, to avoid numbers previously held at Nottingham, Bourne and Weldon which had reached KB200, KQ30 and KU70 respectively – thus, for example, Kings Lynn's LB42 became KB242 by adding 200.

Although the Driver Training School was allocated the code VJ in the initial allocations, the vehicles continued to be numbered in the overall series K1 upwards covering all non-revenue-earning vehicles (service vans, slave tractors, etc) until eventually being given a new series of numbers KO1 upwards, now using the Head Office code, from November 1974.

MIDLANDS BRS LTD (letters M, W and T)

The sixth company formed was a complex merger of most of the South Midlands District (excepting portions in Bucks and Berks), most of the West Midland District (excepting Beds, Northants and east Warwickshire) and the Gloucestershire and Hereford portions of the South Wales District. The resultant Branch network was as follows:

Existing:
General Codes Contracts Codes

NEW	OLD	NEW	OLD	IDENTITY
MA	Same	WA	MA-C	Oxford
MB	Same	WB	MB-C	Banbury
-		WD	ER-C	Birmingham Contracts (Bromford Mills)
ME	Same	WE	ME-C	Swindon
MF	EB	-		Birmingham (Bromford Lane)
-		WH	EH-C	Tamworth Contracts
MJ	EJ	WJ	EJ-C	Oldbury
MM	Same	WM	MM-C	Castle Bromwich
MP	Same	-		Erdington
MQ	GG	WQ	GL-C	Ross-on-Wye
MR	EA			Cheapside (originally to be MC)
-		WS	ES-C	Wolverhampton Contracts
MT	EM	WT	EM-C	Worcester
MV	GF	WV	GL-C	Hereford
MW	EE	-		Walsall
MX	GP	WX	GL-C	Forest of Dean
MY	GQ	WY	GL-C	Gloucester
MZ	EL	WZ	EL-C	Wellington (originally to be MG)

Additional:
General Codes Contracts Codes

NEW	OLD	NEW	OLD	IDENTITY
TA	-			Bromford Mills (property)
TB	MTS			Oxford Driving School
TC	E/DS			Birmingham Driving School
TD	MKX			Oxford Workshop
TE	-			Overnight Express
TF	-			Wolverhampton Repair Centre
MO		WO		Head Office Codes

The former South Midlands Office at Oxford was retained, obtaining new registrations from Oxford CBC and then Oxford LVLC after September 1974. The office in Birmingham was closed.

The merger of portions of three different former Districts combined a mixture of numbering systems used in the areas concerned and it was some months before they were satisfactorily correlated together. It was unfortunate that the timing coincided with staff absence, due to lengthy illness, by the very personnel responsible for raising fleet numbering and numerous variations of the established numbering systems, plus many inadvertent duplications of fleet numbers occurred, particularly at

Wolverhampton and Wellington. However, the system finally settled down into one in which, in general, all vehicles at each Branch were numbered in one joint series apart from Truck Rental introduced in 1975.

At least one trailer at Wellington is known to have been altered from 'TEL' to 'TMG' (consequently becoming 'lost' in the system) before the new code was revised to TMZ. Why these two last-minute alterations to the new codes at Wellington and Cheapside were made is not clear.

WESTERN BRS LTD (letters R and S. Contracts Y and Z)

The seventh and final regional company formed from September 1972. This was a merger of the former South Western District including Contracts vehicles in the Southampton area formerly controlled by London Contracts District, plus all of the South Wales District except the Gloucester and Hereford areas, and the Berkshire area from the South Midlands District.

Unlike all the other new regional companies new codes for the Contract vehicles were not introduced immediately – and in fact not until January 1974 – but for reference purposes they are shown alongside the 1972 General codes in the following summary. The old South Wales policy of numbering all their Contracts vehicles in the same joint series then continued but with the Branch codes now varying dependent on their base. The overall 'South Wales Contracts' code GL was no longer appropriate. All other Branches continued to number general and contracts vehicles in the same series at each Branch.

Existing:
General Codes Contracts Codes

NEW	OLD	NEW	OLD	IDENTITY
RA	Same	YA	RA-C	Bristol
RB	Same	YB	RB-C	Avonmouth
RC	Same	YC	XM-C	Southampton
RD	Same	YD	RD-C	Melksham
RE	Same	YE	RE-C	Wells
RF	Same	YF	RF-C	Exeter
RG	Same	YG	RG-C	Plymouth
RH	Same	YH	RH-C	Bridgwater
RJ	Same	YJ	XM-C	Isle of Wight
RK	MC	YK	MC-C	Reading
RL	Same	YL	RL-C	St Austell
RM	Same	YM	XM-C	Portsmouth
RN	Same	YN	RN-C	Yeovil
RP	GT?	-		Sharpness
RR	Same	YR	XM-C	Poole
RW	RAW	-		Bristol Driver Training School
RY	MAX	-		Reading Repair Centre
SA	GA	ZA	GL-C	Cardiff
SB	GB	ZB	GL-C	Newport
SC	GC	-		Ebbw Vale
SD	GD	-		Pontypool
SE	GS	-		Cardiff Docks
SF	GR	-		Newport Timber Terminal

SH	GH	ZH	GL-C	Swansea
SJ	GJ	ZJ	GL-C	West Wales
SK	GK	ZK	GL-C	Bridgend
SM	GM	ZM	GL-C	Port Talbot
SN	GN	-		British Tissues, Bridgend
SW	GKW	-		Bridgend Driver Training School

Additional:
General Codes   Contracts Codes

NEW	OLD	NEW	OLD	IDENTITY
RQ				Western Contracts
RZ				Brentford
SR				Southampton Contracts
SY				Cardiff Workshops
RO & SO				Head Office Codes

The former South Western District Office was retained at Bristol as the new company HQ and continued to raise all new vehicle registrations from Bristol CBC, then Bristol LVLC from September 1974. The Cardiff Office of the old South Wales District was closed.

The 'on-paper' code RQ is assumed to have related to internal matters concerning contracts activities for all former Branches except those at Southampton, Poole, Portsmouth and Isle of Wight, inherited from the London Contracts District, now covered separately by the 'on-paper' code SR.

Similarly, the 'on-paper' code RZ was apparently retained for matters relating to the trunk vehicles operating into the south west which, in practice, had long since been distributed among the Branches to which they worked.

MORTONS (BRS) LTD (letter W)

This company continued to operate independently within the Midlands BRS territory with a smart revised livery of light green, carrying the BRS triple arrowhead motif in white, but fleet numbering using serif-style characters in black. Vehicles from all bases continued to be numbered in a joint series with W prefix, at this time the depot network comprised:

Coventry:	Rowley Road, Baginton
Leamington:	LMR Goods Station, Milverton
Pitsea, Essex:	Marsh Road
Harwich:	c/o The Docks
Johnstone, Renfrew:	Thornbrae

Cartransport (BRS) Ltd (letter S)

The company also continued to function independently within the Midlands

BRS area. Its red livery was altered to a dark turquoise after the business of Lathams (Transporters) Ltd, already using that livery, was acquired and added to its fleet in 1974. Until then Cartransport's work had involved carrying for UK car manufacturers from inland depots; the addition of Lathams extended their operations to imported cars from their various ports of entry.

Cartransport itself operated from depots at Bathgate, Birmingham, Coventry, Ellesmere Port, Ipswich, Luton, Manchester, Oxford and Ramsgate around 1970/72, plus railhead agencies at Leeds, Lenham and Newcastle. The fleet continued to be numbered in a joint series with 'S' prefix and there was one subsidiary company, Leeds Car Collection Service at Garforth, whose vehicles were not numbered. After Lathams work was added, the network extended to include Bridgwater, Bridlington, Gateshead, Hooton, Immingham, Milton, Newhaven and also Larne (N.I.) by the subsidiary Autofreight (N.I.) Ltd.

At the end of 1976 the company was retitled simply Cartransport Ltd on removing it from the BRS Grouping and transfer to the 'Special Traffics Group' within the NFC. A further livery change then occurred, introducing a mainly orange base with black diagonal stripe across the front of the cab. The many vehicles operating under contract agreements adopted variations of this theme, all comprising a basic colour with diagonal stripe in a different colour. A revised numbering system was also introduced for all new vehicles – the 'S' series was discontinued and, instead, two-letter prefixes were used for different batches of vehicles in which the first letter indicated the year of delivery and the second the vehicle type. These new vehicles were mainly leased and licensed by their suppliers. Until this time new vehicles had been registered at Coventry through the company's head office.

Amendments

Just as was the case between 1964 and 1972, numerous alterations to the Branch network and the two-letter codes in use continued to occur from 1972 onwards until the next major alteration in lettering took place in 1979, when three-letter codes were introduced. Those in England and Wales will be considered first; the situation in Scotland was further complicated by the absorption of the Tayforth fleets after the 'Tayscot' grouping was established in 1975, and will be dealt with last. Other developments to affect fleet numbering during this period were the introduction of BRS Truck rental, generally from 1975 onwards, and the establishment of a specific Distribution Group within the BRS family of companies from around 1977.

SOUTHERN BRS (letters A and X)

A brief study of the codes outlined will reveal that apart from Southern

1972-1979 Two-Letter Codes - Regional Companies

BRS, each regional company had managed to devise Branch codes on General and Contracts service in which the second letter signified the same Branch, e.g. DA and JA at Sheffield, KD and VD at Norwich, etc. Within Southern BRS, however, this proved impossible owing to the multiplicity of services and the existence of so many Contracts-only Branches. One of the first things this company was obliged to do, therefore, was to introduce a third company letter 'N' for some of its services.

Southern BRS introduced Truck Rental in January 1975, with vehicles numbered in their own unique series at each Branch offering the service, using the Contracts codes and suffix letter 'R'. Using the new company letter 'N' a new series of initial codes was introduced as follows:

NA	Kentish Town Workshops (ex AA)
NB	Tilbury Terminal (ex AB)
NC	Ipswich Repair Centre (ex AZ)
ND	Burgess Hill (non-Keymarkets work)
NE	Hull Continental
NF	Canterbury Workshop
NO	Continental Services (TIR Tilt Trailers using this code introduced in 1974)
NQ	Felixstowe International
NT	Bedfont Driver Training School
NZ	ICS Freight Ltd

Codes AA, AB and AZ thus became available for reissue. Other early closures, freeing further codes for reissue, were:

AM/XM	Rochester closed
AS/XB	Colchester closed, services to Elmstead
AD/XD	Rochford closed
AE	Brighton closed Feb 73, services to Burgess Hill
XY	Amersham Contracts discontinued, converted to general only
AV	High Wycombe General haulage discontinued, converted to Contracts only

It then became possible to introduce the following new codes:

AB	Dunstable General Haulage, alongside XV (and numbered in same Contracts series)
XB	Dover Contracts, alongside AN
XD	Thamesmead. New, but short-lived contract with Matthews Butchers (4/75-9/75 only)
XM	Croydon Contracts, upgraded from sub-depot of Newington Butts
XX	Sunbury. Sub to Hainault, a second site following takeover of David Grieg fleet, merged into key markets activities.
XY	North London Freight Centre, based at the former Tartan Arrow terminal in Kentish Town, largely using vehicles drawn from the fleet of the former parcels and distribution company N Francis & Co

Later, again, the following deletions occurred:

| XJ | Following closure of Maidstone (XL), services relocated to Aylesford; code retained here and absorbed Existing Contracts fleet (XJ) which fell out of use |
| AG/XR | Amended. Tufnell Park, services relocated to North London Freight Centre. Code AG retained for haulage but XR merged into XY and fell out of use |

The BRS Reference Book

Other new codes continued to be raised, as follows:

AS	Dagenham. Numbered in same series as AC using vehicles drawn from their fleet
AZ	Tilbury. Numbered in same series as AC using vehicles drawn from their fleet
AU	Silvertown
AY	Enfield
XD	Welwyn Garden City. New Truck Rental Service introduced Jan 77
XJ	Cuckfield
NG	Bury St Edmunds
NH	Amersham, Ford Motor Co Distribution, using vehicles from AH fleet
NW	Milton Keynes. New Truck Rental Service introduced March 76
NX	Staines. Truck Rental introduced Nov 76

In 1975 the Keymarkets work was relocated to new bases in Norfolk and Wiltshire and their services at Hainault (XX) and Burgess Hill (XS) ceased. Other activities enabled XS to continue in existence, renamed 'Mid-Sussex Contracts', while XX was bow unique to Sunbury, lasting until 1979.

Southern BRS introduced so many adjustments between 1972 and 1979 that it became difficult to keep abreast of all the alterations. Insufficient data is available to place them in chronological order and it is possible others may have occurred that are unknown to the writer. The code XR was still in use, for an existing Truck Rental fleet, as late as May 78, though its title had changed from 'Tufnell Park' to 'North London' from January 78. The fleet at Bedfont (XT) was hugely expanded in June 75 upon allocating numbers to the large fleet of vehicles operated for Mars Ltd, acquired three years earlier.

NORTH WESTERN BRS (letters C and F)

Truck Rental was introduced late 1974 onwards, with vehicles numbered in the same series as Contracts at each Branch offering the service, and suffix letter 'R'.

10/72	Delete	CL	Greenheys Branch closed. Following this closure the following new codes were activated:
	Add	CL	Trafford Park – new general haulage service, vehicles numbered CL1-21
	Add	CV	Stalybridge – similarly, a new haulage service, vehicles numbered CV1-10 (these services were introduced to take up work diverted from Greenheys)
12/72	Delete	CC/FC	West Cumberland, Branch closed. Haulage fleet dispersed and/or mothballed. Contracts (FC) transferred to Preston (FS)
12/72	Delete	CA	Liverpool, Studholme Street branch closed. The fleet series had reached CA190. As a result a new much reduced haulage service was introduced from the contracts depot in Gt Howard Street, thus:
	Add	CA	Liverpool General, a new series CA1-16 alongside the contracts fleet
1/73	Add	FG	Contracts work introduced at Kitt Green
10/73	Add	FF	Contracts work introduced at Runcorn
2/74	Add	FP	Contracts work introduced at Cheetham
2/74	Add	FT	Contracts work introduced at Blackburn
7/74	Delete	CA	The new general haulage service at Liverpool was terminated. The series had reached CA24
9/74	Delete	CV	General service at Stalybridge ceased. The series had reached CV16

100

1/75	Delete	CL	General service at Trafford Park ceased. This series had reached CL32
1/75	Add	FB	Fleetwood. A fleet of artics with skeletal trailers introduced on container carriage for B+I Lines
3/75	Add	FJ	Contracts work introduced at Stafford
4/75	Delete	CB	Dockside Express service in Liverpool terminated
8/75	Add	FQ	Contracts work introduced at Bolton
10/75	Delete	CM	General Haulage at Stoke discontinued, all retained vehicles passing to Tunstall (CN). Stoke became contracts-only, using code FM
11/75	Delete	CT/FT	Blackburn, Branch closed
75 n/k			Stalybridge Branch (FV) relocated to Dukinfield and retitled 'Tameside Branch'
1/77	Add	CT	Longton. Fleet formerly operated by Road Services (Caledonian) Ltd made over to North Western BRS as a new Branch
6/77	Delete	CJ/FJ	Stafford. Road services ceased, retained as clearing house only. Vehicle fleets to Tunstall (CN) and Stoke (FM)
7/77	Delete	FB	Fleetwood's contract with B+I Lines terminated
11/77	Add	FT	Contracts work introduced at Longton
7/78	Delete	CG	General haulage at Kitt Green ceased, Branch became contracts-only as FG. Some vehicles retained as contract spares, renumbered FG
7/78	Delete	CS	Preston general haulage, Branch closed. Retained vehicles passed to Longton (CT)
12/78	Add	FB	Burnley. New Truck Rental service introduced

NORTH EASTERN BRS (letters D and J)

This company introduced Truck Rental in April 1975 at Leeds, gradually extending the service to other locations. It was regarded as an extension of the General Services and vehicles were numbered from 900 upwards at each Branch offering the service, with General codes, e.g. DE, DL and suffix letter 'R'.

10/72	Activate	DW	Formerly a warehouse code. Small vehicle fleet introduced to serve work for Hoover Ltd
10.72	Add	DH	Immingham. A small General haulage service using vehicles in the same series of numbers as those of Grimsby Contracts, nearby, was introduced. By Oct 73 eight vehicles were in use on this service; the four-figure contracts numbers were then altered to DH1-8 in a separate series that eventually reached DH12
2/73	Add	DD	Goole. Status restored, using vehicles taken from Hull Branch (DC)
8/73	Add	DK	York. A fleet of small self-drive vans was introduced as a forerunner to the forthcoming introduction of the Truck Rental service. This facility ended in 1979
1/74	Add	DR/JR	Worksop. Branch status restored, using vehicles drawn from Doncaster Branch (DJ & JJ)
4/74	Add	DS/JS	Dewsbury. Branch status restored, using vehicles from Bradford Branch (DG & JG)
Early 75			On paper a series of fleet numbers DO1 upwards was introduced by Head Office for vehicles placed in the company 'pool' or awaiting further duty. At least one vehicle, a new Seddon Atkinson tractor delivered in 1975, physically carried a number from this series while under evaluation as a demonstrator at different Branches, so the code merits a mention
Mid 75	Add	DM/JM	Consett. The fleet of Road Services (Tyne Tees) Ltd, renamed from Siddle C Cook Ltd in 1973, was made over to North Eastern BRS as a new Branch, as part of the dispersal of the 'Tayscot' group of companies

Early 77	Add	DX	Hexham. The fleet of the Road Services (Caledonian) Ltd depot at this site was transferred to N E BRS and set up as a new Branch. This move was short-lived, however, and the vehicles were transferred back to other former Caledonian depots late in 1978
11/77	Add	JT	Wakefield. Contracts work introduced
1/78	Add	DU	Hull Continental – a specialist additional service introduced at Hull
Late 78			A 'warehousing' service was introduced at Barnsley with vehicles coded DQW

Note: The earlier codes DX and DY, allocated to Newcastle and Sheffield Repair Centres, were used for a short while after first being raised in 1972 but soon discontinued in favour of the main respective Branches, DL and DA, so leaving DX to become vacant and available for reissue to Hexham in 1977.

EASTERN BRS (letters K and V)

Truck Rental was introduced from early 1975 onwards and regarded as an extension of General haulage work, with vehicles initially numbered in the same series as General vehicles at each Branch, plus suffix letter 'R'. The numbering system was varied to separate Rental vehicles into their own series in 1977, as explained below. Other alterations were:

9/72	Delete	KC	Alfreton Branch closed, fleet dispersed
1/73			Codes KE, KP and KX activated alongside existing contracts vehicles upon re-introducing General haulage at the three Branches: Nottingham, Lincoln and Cambridge
Early 73	Add	VH	Contracts introduced at Newark
11/74	Add	KO	Nottingham Driver Training School vehicles numbered in a new series, KO1 upwards, using company Head Office code instead of being numbered in former overall 'non revenue-earning series' of numbers simply lettered K1 upwards. The code VJ, originally allocated when Nottingham was 'contracts only', was never used
1975	Add	VK	Brandon Contracts. New Branch introduced for Keymarkets work (largely by relocating from Hainault (XX, Southern BRS)
5/75	Delete	KG/VG	Chesterfield and add KJ/VJ 'Heath Branch' following relocation of former Chesterfield Branch to new premises just off the M1 at Heath. The new site was purpose-built and included night stop-over facilities
Mid 75	Add	VF	Contracts introduced at Burton
9/75	Delete	KU	General Haulage ceased at Rugby; branch now contracts-only, using code VU
10/75			Within Eastern BRS territory a new service 'Overland Iran' was introduced at Northampton, using a fleet of Leyland Marathons numbered QN1 upwards, registered from Eastern BRS HQ at Derby
Late 1975	Add	KK	Brandon General Haulage. In practice all vehicles so numbered were shunt tractors; it was Eastern BRS policy for slave units to be numbered in each Branch's General series, but no General service had existed at Brandon for this to occur
5/76	Add	VS	Contracts introduced at Corby
10/76	Delete	KR/VR	Loughborough closed. Most vehicles transferred to Melton Mowbray (KT/VT)
1977	Add	KG	Nottingham Driver Training School given its own code in place of using HQ code (KO)
1/78	Add	VL	Wellingborough Contracts – new service introduced

At the beginning of 1977 three significant variations in fleet numbering occurred within Eastern BRS, thanks to their Derby HQ's penchant for precise vehicle identification, as follows:

1. With the establishment of the Distribution network referred to on previous pages, all other companies simply suffixed their Branch codes with the letter D as part of the vehicles' existing lettering. Eastern BRS, however, chose to renumber all their Distribution vehicles completely, introducing new series 2001 upwards for General Distribution and 3001 upwards for Contracts Distribution at each Branch offering either or both services. This had the effect of discontinuing General services altogether at two Branches, Boston (KQ) and Melton Mowbray (KT), where no vehicles remained in the original numbering series.
2. All Truck Rental vehicles, hitherto numbered in the same series as General haulage vehicles, were renumbered into new series from 701 upwards at each Branch involved, still utilising the General codes but with letter 'R' now suffixed to the Branch codes.
3. A new joint series of numbers specifically identifying vehicles working on the 'BRS Rescue' service was introduced, similar to the existing service and maintenance fleet simply numbered K1 upwards, which had now reached about K250. The new series incorporated the individual Branch code plus suffix 'E' in a communal series, this KHE1&2, KXE3, KYE4, etc.

MIDLANDS BRS LTD (letters M, W and T)

As at York (north Eastern BRS) a fleet of small self-drive vans was introduced in Birmingham in 1973, prior to introduction of the full Truck Rental service in 1974/75. Unlike York's, however, these were not given a unique series of numbers but were included in the overall Birmingham Contracts series 'WD'.

On introduction of Truck Rental in its own right, the vehicles were initially regarded as an extension of Contract Hire work and numbered in the individual Branches' contract series, e.g. at Swindon and Wolverhampton, with suffix letter 'R'. As the coverage expanded further new Rental vehicles began to be numbered in their own series from 1 upwards, at each Branch, still using the Contracts codes.

Other amendments:

9/72		MS	Activated at Wolverhampton for a small number of vehicles designated 'General Haulage'. The Branch had been contracts-only since May 71
Late 1972?	Delete	TB	Oxford Driver Training School discontinued
1/73	Add	MH	General haulage reintroduced at Tamworth

4/73	Delete	MW	Walsall Branch closed. Midlands BRS retained a clearing house facility at Walsall after this from different premises. Retained vehicles passed to Wolverhampton (MS)
9/73		MR	Cheapside Branch was relocated to Bromford Mills (the existing site of Birmingham Contracts, WD, north of Bromford Bridge) and retitled 'Birmingham Distribution Centre'. The Cheapside site was subsequently reoccupied by Mortons (BRS) Ltd.
6/74	Add	MC	Middlemore Branch, a new service based at Smethwick using a fleet of vehicles transferred in from Mortons (BRS) Ltd
7/74			Reorganisation at Birmingham Branch (MF) which was closed to General Haulage operations, the site (south of Bromford Bridge) being retained as a property offering extensive container storage. It was retitled 'Birmingham Containerbase' with just a small fleet of service vehicles to maintain the property, including slave tractors for the container trailers, still coded MF. Some 30 vehicles from the former Bromford Lane fleet were relocated to Bromford Mills and set up as a new 'Birmingham General' service, coded MD, operating alongside the existing contracts fleet (WD).
2/75	Add	WF	Truck Rental introduced in Birmingham, based at the Bromford Lane container site
1975	Delete	MQ/WQ	Ross-on-Wye Branch closed
11/75	Delete	MP	Erdington Branch closed. This specialist service, latterly also based at Bromford Mills, became superfluous alongside the other activities at this site
1/76	Delete	MD	'General' services of Birmingham Contracts at Bromford Mills discontinued
2/77	Delete	MX/WX	Forest of Dean Branch closed
6/78	Add	WN	New Truck Rental service introduced at Redditch

WESTERN BRS LTD (letters R & S, Y & Z)

Truck Rental was introduced from 1975 at selected sites using the General Haulage Branch codes and in separate series from 001 upwards at each Branch with suffix letter 'R'.

Western BRS underwent a period of rationalisation between 1972 and 1975, resulting in the discontinuation of numerous Branch codes, but no new or additional codes appear to have been introduced during this time. As with Southern BRS, lack of information prevents the details being shown chronologically. The following codes were discontinued, having only existed on paper:

RQ	Western Contracts (Head Office references only)
RY	Reading Repair Centre (incorporated into RK0
RZ	Brentford (not physically used since approx 1970)
SR	Southampton Contracts (formerly XM, separated into Branches since Sept 72)
SY	Cardiff Repair Centre (incorporated into SA)

The following codes were discontinued, apparently following closure of the Branches, but the fate of each is unknown:

RL/YL	St Austell
RN/YN	Yeovil

RP	Sharpness
RW	Bristol Driver Training School
SC	Ebbw Vale
SD	Pontypool

The following codes were discontinued following absorption into neighbouring Branches:

SE	Cardiff Docks absorbed into main Cardiff series, SA, certainly by May 74
SF	Newport Timber. Similarly absorbed into Newport series, SB
SN	British Tissues. Absorbed into main Bridgend series, SK, apparently during 1974

One new code raised during this period - precise date uncertain - was:

RQ	H S Morgan Distribution, Eastleigh – one of several former Tayforth Parcels Division Companies, latterly a member of the British Express Carriers group within the NFC, which were made over to the BRS Distribution Group after it was set up in 1977

It is unfortunate that details for Western BRS remain rather vague.

SCOTTISH ROAD SERVICES (letters B and H)

As with all the other regional BRS companies, some Branch code alterations took place after the formation of SRS. The following should be recorded:

2/73	Delete	BX/HX	Haddington Branch closed, fleet transferred to Edinburgh (BV/HV)
3/73	Add	BZ	New 'Glasgow Warehousing' service introduced at Townsend Street alongside the existing Contracts fleet (coded HB but later altered to HZ to match)
11/74	Add	BX	Coatbridge. New Distribution service offering Esso fuel deliveries
1974	Add	BQ	Continental Services (TIR trailers only)

Big changes were to follow, however. At the end of 1974 the activities of SRS and the Tayforth Group, acquired by the THC during the period of 'back door nationalisation' in August 1965 (75% interest) and allowed to trade as a separate grouping within the THC, and then by the NFC, were combined into a new 'Tayscot' grouping and separated from the BRS Group of companies.

From January 1975 Tayscot had the unenviable task of eliminating wasteful duplication of services. As a first move they split SRS into three smaller, more manageable, regional companies which necessitated recoding of Branches accordingly. The new network was now as follows:

SRS (WEST) LTD HQ Lister Street, Glasgow (letters B and H)

General Codes **Contracts Codes**

NEW	OLD	NEW	OLD	IDENTITY
BA	same	-	-	Glasgow, Lister Street

NEW	OLD	NEW	OLD	IDENTITY
BE	same	HE	same	Ardrossan
BG	same	-	-	Argyll (Warroch St, Glasgow)
BL	BG	-	-	Campbeltown – revised to BC, 1977
BV	BG	-	-	Dunoon – revised to BD, 1977
BW	BG	-	-	Oban – revised to BB, 1977
BX	same	-	-	Coalbridge
BZ	same	HZ	HB	Glsagow, Townsend St

For the first time in many years the former Argyll Branch sub depots received codes of their own, but whether any vehicles at the bases so coded ever physically held numbers using these codes is not known. Tarbert and Lochgilphead, though still listed, remained uncoded, apparently retained as 'outstations'.

The Glasgow Repair Centre, allocated code BC in 1972, did not feature in the 1975 listing.

SRS (NORTH) LTD (HQ East Dock St, Dundee, new letters G and O)

General Codes   Contracts Codes

NEW	OLD	NEW	OLD	IDENTITY
GL	BL	OL	HL	Dundee
GM	BM	-		Forfar
GN	BN	-		Arbroath
GP	BP	OP	HP	Perth
GR	BR	OR	HR	Aberdeen
GS	BS	OS	HS	Inverness
GT	BT	OT	HT	Elgin

The Forfar Repair Centre, coded BB in 1972, was not mentioned.

SRS (EAST) LTD (HQ Edinburgh, new letters L and U)

General Codes   Contracts Codes

NEW	OLD	NEW	OLD	IDENTITY
LF	BF	UF	HF	Grangemouth
LH	BH	-		Dunfermline
LJ	BJ	UJ	HJ	Kirkcaldy
LK	BK	UK	HK	Alva
LV	BV	UV	HV	Edinburgh
LW	BW	-		Bathgate
LY	BY	-		Galashiels

The subsidiary company, H & G S Bell Ltd of Edinburgh, which had traded independently since the early 1970s was finally absorbed into SRS operations during the middle of 1975. Specific contracts vehicles, mostly as Glasgow and Edinburgh, were merged into the SRS fleets and numbered in the HZ and UV series, while many of their general hire vehicles found further service with other regional BRS companies in England.

The former Scottish District workshops a Linlithgow, coded BD in 1972 and now within SRS (East) Ltd catchment area, was not mentioned in the 1975 listing. Vehicles at all three workshops (Glasgow, Forfar and Linlithgow) had, until this time, been numbered in a joint service vehicle series SB1 upwards, and how this series was affected by this three-way division is not known. Similarly, contracts spare vehicles, which had carried the Scottish Head Office code HO since 1972, must also have been split between the three new companies. It is most likely they were finally attached to the Branches at which they had been working.

Meanwhile, the Tayforth group at this time comprised the following companies:

Road Services (Caledonian) Ltd	HQ Dumfries. Bases at Dumfries, Glasgow, Lockerbie, Longton (Lancs), Hexham, Birmingham, London (Enfield) and Weybridge
Road Services (Forth) Ltd	HQ Falkirk. Bases at Falkirk, Alloa, Leven, Edinburgh and Coatbridge
Road Services (Tyne Tees) Ltd	HQ Consett. Renamed ex Siddle C Cook Ltd in 1973. Bases at Consett, Darlington and Newcastle.
D McKinnon (Transport) Ltd	HQ Kilmarnock. Bases at Kilmarnock and Nottingham
J & E Transport Ltd	HQ Haslingden, Rossendale. Bases at Haslingden, Dundee and Glasgow
Caledonian Bulk Liquids Ltd	HQ Immingham. Bases at Immingham, Leeds and Stanford-le-Hope, Essex

Two other Tayforth companies, A Smith (Darvel) Ltd and Bell & Co, Edinburgh (not to be confused with the BRS subsidiary H & G S Bell) had been phased out about 1969.

Put up alongside the three new Scottish Road Services companies, Tayscot started nationalising of their activities, particularly in areas south of the border. First to be affected was Caledonian Bulk Liquids which, as a specialist operator, was transferred to the control of Tankfreight Ltd, a grouping within the NFC set up in 1972 to administer the bulk liquids activities of Pickfords Tank Haulage Ltd and Harold Wood & Sons Ltd.

Road Services (Tyne-Tees) Ltd was also prepared for dispersal. The Darlington depot was closed and the Newcastle depot at Felling-on-Tyne was transferred to the control of Road Services (Caledonian) Ltd, their fleet being renumbered nos. 515-534 in the Caledonian series. The headquarters site at Consett was then transferred to North Eastern BRS and set up as their Consett Branch (Code DM) in mid-1975.

The Nottingham base of D McKinnon (Transport) Ltd was relocated to Long Eaton before being absorbed into the services operated by Eastern BRS at Derby.

The Edinburgh base of Road Services (Forth) Ltd was closed. The Coatbridge depot was transferred to SRS (West) Ltd, joining the fleet already coded BX, and the Leven depot was closed, this fleet moving to SRS (East) Ltd at Kirkcaldy and renumbered there as LJ58-79.

The Glasgow base of J & E Transport was closed. It is likely the work relocated to the Caledonian depot in Glasgow, at Hawthorn Street.

The Weybridge depot of Road Services (Caledonian) Ltd was closed, while the work at Enfield was transferred to Southern BRS (code AY); the Longton depot to North Western BRS, becoming their Longton Branch (coded CT) from January 1977; and the Hexham depot to North Eastern BRS, also early in 1977, becoming their Hexham Branch (code DX).

Meanwhile, the only change to affect the three SRS companies was the closure of the site at Ardrossan (code BE which became vacant).

As for the Tayscot grouping itself, this became a full member of the BRS Group once again from January 1976, after which time the pale blue Tayforth livery and J & E Transport's unique livery retained throughout, began to give way to the existing dark blue and white of the main SRS company. This, itself, was altered to an all-over shade of dark blue with white logo and lettering from October 1976.

The next change to affect Scottish operations came in February 1977 when the three regional SRS companies and the four remaining Scottish Tayforth companies were merged into four new companies, with HQ now relocated from Glasgow to Cumbernauld, as follows:

1. SRS (West) Ltd, which combined the existing SRS (West) network and the RS (Caledonian) operations in Glasgow, whose Hawthorn Street site was now coded BE/HE, vacant since Ardrossan had closed.
2. SRS (North) Ltd, which was a continuation of the existing SRS (North) network, with the addition of the Dundee fleet of J & E Transport, to whose site the old BRS fleet was relocated. The former J & E vehicles were renumbered GL170-191 (general) and OL34-41 (contracts) in the SRS system.
3. SRS (Forth) Ltd, which combined the existing SRS (East) network with the two remaining depots of RS (Forth) at Falkirk and Alloa. These were now encoded to match the existing Branches as follows: Falkirk – UP (contracts only) and Alloa – LT (general only). These codes were simply prefixed to the existing RS (Forth) fleet numbers. The Alva depot (LK) was closed during 1978.
4. SRS (Caledonian) Ltd, which combined the remaining RS (Caledonian) depots in Scotland and England, at Dumfries, Lockerbie, Newcastle and Birmingham, with the D McKinnon site at Kilmarnock and the J & E Transport depot at Haslingden. This caused the renumbering of the McKinnon and J & E fleets into the Caledonian series as they lost their identities – Nos. 559-587 (ex J & E) and 588-653 (ex-McKinnon) were added to the fleet from around April 1977.

Unusually, this new SRS company, like its predecessor, RS (Caledonian) Ltd persisted in not adopting Branch codes. The uncoded series eventually extended into the 680s.

Truck Rental, introduced from October 1976 onwards in Scotland, initially at Glasgow, was regarded as an extension of contract hire work and the Contracts codes were used for numbering, thus series such as UVR1 (at Edinburgh) and OLR1 (at Dundee) upwards, were introduced in SRS (Forth) and (North) areas. By this time, however, all vehicles of SRS (West) Ltd were being numbered in one joint series which appeared to be a continuation of the original Glasgow Contracts series, latterly recoded from HB to HZ and, when Rental was introduced for example at Glasgow (HZR), their vehicles were also numbered in this series, now well into the 400's.

Late in 1978, with the trading recession still badly affecting the Scottish lowlands, further contraction became necessary and the fleet of SRS (Caledonian) Ltd was absorbed into that of SRS (West) Ltd. This, for the first time, brought about Branch coding for the former Caledonian depots, as follows:

General Code	Contracts Code	Identity
BF	HF	Dumfries
BH	HH	Haslingden
BK	HK	Kilmarnock
BL	HL	Lockerbie
BN	HN	Newcastle
BP	HP	Birmingham

It also necessitated further fleet renumbering so soon after the 1977 exercise and the former SRS (Caledonian) vehicles now received new numbers, prefixed by the appropriate Branch code in the SRS (West) series, running from approx. No. 501 to around No. 685. Great care needs to be taken by enthusiasts in distinguishing between these two very similar series of numbers – in general, if the number does not carry a Branch code it is probably from the SRS (Caledonian) period; if it is Branch-encoded it will be from the SRS (West) series.

This was the situation in Scotland as 1978 ended. The next alteration imminent was the introduction of activity letters to all fleet numbering from the beginning of 1979. Some experience in this technique had already been gained in the Distribution, Rental and Engineering/service fleets from 1977 onwards, when D, R or E had been added to existing Branch codes, and the practice was now extended to all activities, as outlined in the next section.

6

1979-1983

From the beginning of 1979 the six regional BRS companies in England and Wales, and Scottish Road Services' three divisions, introduced yet another adjustment to their fleet numbering, whereby an 'activity' letter was suffixed to the Branch code forming three-letter codes for each item on their fleet. This had the effect of reverting to just one identification code for each Branch; the need for separate contracts codes was eliminated as the same codes could now be used with suffix 'C' to identify Contracts vehicles.

The Activity letters initially introduced were as follows:

G. General Haulage (e.g. MHG79 at Tamworth)

Originally the mainstay of BRS operations, general haulage and 'spot hire' work became less and less remunerative as the 1970s unfolded and there were determined efforts to reduce the company's commitment to such work. Rather than operate its own vehicles on such work, BRS instead set up its 'Datafreight' service – a freight brokerage agency enabling other hire or reward operators to avail themselves of return loads. Accordingly, activity letter 'G' in later years came to signify 'Freight Management'.

C. Contract Hire (e.g. XHC4455 at Ipswich)

Contract hire was by now the largest operation within the BRS group. The company's ability to supply anything from one local vehicle to a nationwide fleet at centres throughout the country, in customer's own livery, when required and spare vehicles always available when necessary, made good selling points. Also, vehicles could be supplied with or without drivers.

D. Distribution (e.g. KTD2020 at Melton Mowbray)

An increasing proportion of the BRS Group's work became devoted to Distribution, often by making use of the extensive warehousing facilities available at their more modern purpose-built depots. Certain Distribution work, such as that for the Grimsby Fish Merchants' Association, involved vehicles in customers' own livery, exactly as for Contract hire work, while other long-term distribution services used vehicles in the appropriate regional BRS livery. Several former 'British Express Carriers' group companies also joined the BRS Distribution network in 1977. A new livery of white with red and blue lettering for the arrowhead motif, similar to that used by BRS Truck Rental, was introduced in 1979 to market the service more effectively. The livery was further revised to a light shade of blue in 1981.

R. Truck Rental (e.g. DAR980 at Sheffield)

Following the successful pilot schemes using self-drive vans at York and Birmingham in 1973/74, BRS Truck Rental was introduced from January 1975, initially at three depots in the East Midlands and London. The service was gradually extended throughout the BRS Group to all areas of the country, seeing its maximum growth during 1977 and by 1979 was available from 50 strategically-sited depots in England and Wales. In Scotland the service was styled 'Scottish Truck Rental'.

Most depots operated a range of vehicles from small vans up to max cap articulated tractors and refrigerated vans were also available from many sites. Many new 'Contract Hire' agreements were made following initial periods of operation of Rental vehicles by satisfied customers. The Rental fleet adopted a standard livery of white with red and blue lining, often with the operating base and telephone number on the cab door but fleet numbers, if carried at all, were inside the cabs.

E. Engineering Services (e.g. LLE1100 at Dundee)

Every BRS depot had owned a service van since the earliest days, plus often a recovery vehicle, to service its fleet. Subsequent years saw expansion of BRS maintenance and engineering work which was duly identified as a separate activity. As well as servicing their own vehicles, contract maintenance was also undertaken for many other operators.

In Scotland the service was taken a stage further; all maintenance work offered by the Scottish Freight Group, for BRS Engineering, BRS Rescue and NCL Fleetcare, was merged in 1982 to provide one single maintenance network, marketed as 'Fleetcare', throughout Scotland using SRS as agent.

S. BRS Rescue (e.g. KNS52 at Leicester)

As a development of its established engineering services, BRS Rescue was launched in May 1977 offering a nationwide heavy vehicle recovery service, not only for its own vehicles but also to any other operators who were registered with the service. It was based in Birmingham and had at its disposal a fleet of radio-controlled heavy recovery vehicles based at over 60 BRS Branches nationwide. In subsequent years a link up was established between the AA and BRS Rescue, extending coverage even further.

K. Trailer Rental (Trailers only – e.g. TCDK125 at Warrington)

The BRS Truck Rental operation proved so successful that BRS identified a demand for a similar service offering trailer hire in certain areas of the country. Trailer Rental was duly introduced as a new activity from March 1979. Growth was such that some 500 trailers were available by the end of 1980, mostly of max cap types – flats, vans and curtainsiders. Livery was the same as that for Truck Rental.

Other Activity letters were introduced in some parts of the country where a specific service was provided. Among these the following should be mentioned:

T. (e.g. RZT15 at Bridgend)	Driver Training Schools
W. (e.g. DQW5 at Barnsley)	Warehousing, when regarded as a specialist activity
P. (e.g. MFP266 at Birmingham)	Property, an activity associated with sites having no working fleet
M. (e.g. KWM164 at Northampton)	Miscellaneous, relating to a local operation offered by a particular Branch rather than a nationally defined activity
A. (e.g. DKA1 at York)	Agency. BRS introduced a number of agencies offering engine supply and renovation

Still more Activity letters began to be added as the 1980s passed; the significance of many of these was never established among these were the following:

X. (e.g. TRBX at Avonmouth – trailers only)

Introduced to numbers of former General Haulage trailers in 1981 and, mysteriously, discontinued after less than a year at most locations, reverting to the former 'G' coding. It indicated Exchange Trailers.

L. (e.g. AKL0010 at Guildford)

Exclusively adopted by Southern BRS only; all their BRS Rescue vehicles were suddenly given this Activity letter instead of 'S' from late 1982

K. (e.g. LGK431 at Glasgow – vehicles only)

Already used for Trailer Rental, the letter 'K' also began to be used in 1983 by Scottish Road Services, at Glasgow only, for certain of its contracts vehicles. Its significance is unknown.

A. (e.g. LQA1811 at Portlethen)

Again, introduced in Scotland only, especially for a fleet of vehicles introduced at Portlethen in 1984 and nothing to do with the 'Agency' vehicles used in England and Wales. Again, significance unknown

Q. (e.g. DNQ003 at Tees-Side)
Used for some refrigerated Truck Rental vehicles but only by some BRS companies and not universally adopted. Also used by North Western BRS for certain 'Contract 12' vehicles – introduced for customers requiring only 12 months' hire

H. (e.g. CVH1 at Tameside)
Used by N W BRS for 'Powertrain' service, essentially another Agency

Y. (e.g. CQY1 at Middleton, sub of Bolton)
Washing plant. Code used by N W BRS

Z. (e.g. CDZ1 at Warrington)
Also used by N W BRS who light-heartedly referred to it as their code for 'odds and sods' not classified under any other heading

The Branch networks for the six BRS companies in England and Wales, and the three Scottish fleets, together with 'Activities' offered by each, are given in the following pages. The details comprise the Branch code as usual (the first two letters) and its identity, followed by the activities offered at each Branch (the third letter).

SOUTHERN BRS LTD

Three-letter codes introduced from January 1979, part-way through issue of YYE-T registration block. The new allocation was as follows:

Code	Branch	Activities
AC	Grays	G, C (ex XC), E
AH	Amersham	G, D (ex NH), E. Add: C 8/80. D finished 8/80
AK	Guildford	G, C (ex XK). Add: S 6/81 & L (ex S) 1/83
AQ	Felixstowe	G, C (ex XQ)
AS	Dagenham	G. Vehicle fleet finished 8/83 leaving trailers only
AT	Stowmarket	G, C (ex XN), D (ex XN), E
AU	Silvertown	G, D. Add: C 6/81
AW	Elmstead	G, C (ex XW), E
AY	Enfield	G. Add C 6/81 and D 4/83
AZ	Tilbury	G
XA	Newington Butts	C, R, S. Add: E 8/80 and L (ex S) 1/83
XB	Dover	G (ex AN), C. Add: E 8/80
XD	Welwyn Garden City	C, R, S. Add: G 6/81 and L (ex S) 1/83
XE	Victoria Park	C, R. R finished 8/80
XF	Canterbury, offices at Faversham & Minster	G (ex AF), C, R, E. R finished 7/81
XG	Brentford	C, D, G (ex AX), E, S, R. Add: K 7/79 (trailers). Add: M 6/81 (ex NX). Add: T 7/81 (ex M). Add: L 1/83 (ex S). R finished 8/80
XH	Ipswich	G (ex AP), C, E, R. Add: S 6/82 and L 1/83 (ex S) and D 1/83
XJ	Sussex (Cuckfield)	C, D, S
XL	Aylesford	G (ex AL), C, D, E, S, R. Add: D (ex G) and L (ex S) 1/83
XM	Croydon	C, R. Add: E 8 /82
XP	Long Lane	C

113

Code	Branch	Activities
XT	Bedfont	D, R. Add: E 8/80, C 6/81 and W 4/83
XU	High Wycombe	C, R, S. Add: E 8/80 and L (ex S) 1/83
XV	Dunstable	G (ex AB), C, D, S, R, E. Add: X 6/81 (trailers), D (ex G) 8/83 and L (ex S) 1/83. G and R finished 8/83
XY	North London	G (ex AG), C, D, R (ex XR). Add: E 7/79, D (ex G) 8/80, S 8/80, L (ex S) 1/83
XZ	Aylesbury	C. Add: E 8/80, G 6/81 (ex AH)
NG	Bury St Edmunds	C, S, R. Add: E 8/80, G & D 6/81 (ex AT), L 1/83 (ex S). R finished 8/80
NX	Staines	C, T (ex NT), R. Add: M (ex T) 8/80. R finished 8/80. M finished 6/81

Compared with the range of codes used between 1972 and 1979, several remain unaccounted for. Thus AJ, XS and ND, NA, NB, NC, NE, NF, NO, NQ, NZ and NW require further investigation.

The inevitable batch of further alterations to Branch codes occurred during the ensuing years, in addition to the variations in Activities already shown against the existing codes listed above, and the following should be recorded:

By 7/81	Delete	AQ	Felixstowe closed, services to Ipswich (XH)
	Delete	AT	Stowmarket closed, services to Bury St Edmunds (NG)
	Delete	XE	Victoria Park closed, services to Newington Butts (XA) and North London Freight Centre (XY)
	Delete	XJ	Cuckfield closed, services to Aylesford (XL)
	Delete	NX	Staines closed, services to Bedfont (XT) and Brentford (XG)
By 12/81	Delete	AH	Amersham closed, services to Aylesbury (XZ)
By 3/82	Add	XX	GDS Transport, Enfield (activity D). The local branch of a former N E BRS subsidiary Company, formerly coded JCD, transferred to S. BRS control
11/82	Add		Eight depots acquired from Whitbread brewers, with 90 vehicles set up under the name 'Bar Delivery Services' as a new subsidiary distribution company. Codes were as follows: NL – Chiswick (Activity D) NN – Dunstable (Activity D) NP – Hackney (Activity D) NS – Hornsey (Activity D) NT – Hoddesdon (Activity D) NV – Lewisham (Activity D) NW – Luton (Activity D) NZ – Manor Park (Activity D)
By 1/83	Delete	XX	GDS, Enfield – business returned to N E BRS control, reverting to code JCD
By 4/83	Add	XE	Watford, new Branch (Activities C, G, R)
By 7/83	Delete	XD	Welwyn Garden City, services to Watford

NORTH WESTERN BRS LTD

The company did not introduce three-letter codes until mid-September 1979, much later than all other companies, part way through their GVM-V block of registrations. Why they delayed so long is unknown. The resultant coding was as below:

Code	Branch	Activities
CA	Liverpool	C, D, E, S, R. Add: G (ex C) 1.80
CB	Burnley	R, C. Add: K (trailers) 6/81. K finished 3/82
CD	Warrington	G, C (ex FD), E, S, R. Add: K 7/81, and X 6/81
CE	St Helens	G, C (ex FE), E. Add: Z 6/82
CF	Runcorn	G, C (ex FF), E. Add: K 6/81, S 3/82, Z 1/83. K finished 8/82
CG	Kitt Green	C (ex FG), E, S. Add: G and K 7/79
CH	North Wales	G, C (ex FH), S, R. Add: D & E 8/80. C, R finished 2/81
CJ	Stafford	Clearing house only. No fleet
CK	Wrexham	G, C (ex FK), E. Add: D 8/80 and S 6/81
CL	Trafford Park	C and D (ex FL), E, R. Add: X 6/81, G, K & Z 8/82, S 3/84
CM	Stoke	C (ex FM), D, R. Add: G (ex CN) 3/81, K & X 6/81, E & S (ex CY) 1/83
CN	Tunstall	G, E. Add: C & D 12/79
CO	Head Office	E (Tyre Inspector's van only)
CP	Cheetham	G, C (ex FP), E. Add: K 10/84
CQ	Bolton	G, C (ex FQ), S. Add: R 8/80, X 6/81, E 8/82
CR	Sandbach	G, C (ex FR), E, S. G finished 8/81
CS	Preston	C (ex FS), R, S, G (residual trailers only)
CT	Longton	G, C and D (ex FT), E. Add: X 6/81, R (ex CS) 1/83
CV	Tameside	C (ex FV), D, R, E. Add: G (ex C) 8/80, S 12/81 G finished 12/80
CW	Stockport	C (ex FW), E, R. R finished 7/81
CX	Manchester R C	S
CY	Stoke R C	S. Add: E 12/81
Uncoded		Salford Dock Office; Manchester Containerbase (Barton Dock); Central Park (Warehousing, Trafford Park)

Branch amendments since this network came into use were as follows:

10/79	Add	CZ	Carlisle, new Truck Rental site opened. Activity R; later add: K (trailers) 6/81, C 9/81, S 3/82
3/81	Delete	CN	Tunstall Branch closed, services to Stoke (CM)
7/81			At Kitt Green (CG) all road services discontinued and transferred to Warrington; Premises retained for Engineering work only
By 3/82	Add	UA	Wm Cooper & Sons, Prestatyn, encoded after transfer to N W BRS from British Express Carriers. Activities D, E
By 8/82	Add	HA	Bridges Transport, Leyland, similarly transferred in from British Express Carriers. Activities D, C, E
By 1/83	Delete	CR	Sandbach Branch closed. Work passed to Stoke (CM) but operated from a new 'Mid-Cheshire' site at Middlewich, as an outstation
By 1/83	Delete	CS	Preston Branch closed. Contracts work passed to Longton. Rental placed under Longton Control but still out-based at Walton-le-Dale
By 1/83	Delete	CX	Manchester Repair Centre – Engineering services passed to control of Branch, recoded CL
By 1/83	Delete	CY	Stoke R C – Engineering services passed to control of Branch, recoded CM at Stoke
By 1/83	Add	CU	Identity not established. Activity M only

Notes: An on-paper code CI (Activity G only), used for computer purposes, was introduced from June 81 to refer to equipment temporarily located in a 'company pool' of reserve vehicles. This series was discontinued after March 82, after dispersal of the vehicles involved.

- Star Bodies Ltd was attached to NW BRS as a subsidiary company but no vehicle fleet is known.

- North Wales Branch (CH) had ceased operations by August 83, most retained vehicles passing to Wrexham (CK) but a residual fleet of surplus General haulage trailers continued to be administered by N W BRS as a 'reserve'.

NORTH EASTERN BRS LTD

Three-letter codes were introduced from January 1979, part-way through their DWU-T registration block. The network became:

Code	Branch	Activities
DA	Sheffield	G, C (ex JA), D (ex JA), R, E. Add: K (trailers) 6/81
DB	Harrogate	G, C (ex JB), E
DC	Hull	G, C (ex JC), R. Add: K 8/80, D 10/83
DD	Goole	G. Add: C 8/80, E 9/82
DE	Leeds	G, C (ex JE), D (ex JE) R. R transferred to DW 8/80
DF	Knottingley	G, C (ex JF). Add: E 1/83
DG	Bradford	G, C (ex JG), R. Add: E 4/83. G finished 1/83
DH	Selby	C (ex JH). Add: G 1979, finished later same year then reintroduced 3/82
DJ	Doncaster	G, C (ex JJ), R E. Add: K 8/80
DK	York	C (ex JK), D (ex JK). Add: G 9/81, A 1/83
DL	Newcastle	D (ex DL), C (ex JL), R, E. Add: G 8/80, K 8/80, X 6/81
DM	Consett	G, C (ex JM)
DN	Tees-side	G, C (ex JN), R. G finished 3/82
DP	Darlington	G, C (ex JP), D (ex JP), E. Add: R 8/80, S 4/83, K 8/83. R finished 1980
DQ	Barnsley	G, C (ex JQ), W, E
DR	Worksop	G, C (ex JR). G finished 3/82
DS	Dewsbury	G, C (ex JS)
DT	Wakefield	G, C (ex JT)
DU	Hull Continental	G
DV	Scunthorpe	G, C (ex JV), E
DW	Leeds Warehousing	D (ex JE). Add: M 8/80, R (ex DE) 8/80, W & K (trailers) 6/81
DY	Grimsby	D (ex JY), G (ex DH). Add: C 6/81, E 4/83
DO	Company Pool	O (on paper only). Add: A and D 6/81 (all on paper)

Subsequent Branch amendments continued to occur, as follows:

By 5/79	Add	DX	Watsons Carriers, Spennymoor encoded following transfer from British Express Carriers. Activity D
By 8/80	Delete	DM	Consett, Branch closed. Some vehicles to Newcastle (DL).
	Delete	DU	Hull Continental. Services added to existing work at Hull (DC)
By 2/81	Add	DM	Hexthorpe. Fleet of British Ropes Ltd (Bridon) acquired and operated on 'Contract Hire' Terms. Activities C, E
By 9/81	Add	DU	Basildon (Essex), Carreras-Rothman contract. A new service administered by NE BRS From their Darlington Branch. Activities C, later G (slave tractors) and E
	Add		Five depots with 96 vehicles trading as GDS Transport, the initials of the company, Group Distribution Services, set up by the confectioners Geo Bassett Ltd in 1969. Coded as follows: JA - Glasgow (Activity D) JB - Lutterworth (Activity D) JC - Enfield (Activity D)

1979-1983 Three-Letter Codes

			JD - Yate (Activity D)
			JE - Sheffield (Activity D and G)
By 12/81	Add	JG	GDS Transport, Sheffield, long distance services (Activity G, recoded ex JEG)
By 3/82	Delete		The three GDS Transport depots in England, transferred to control of local BRS Company, thus JB to KR (Eastern BRS); JC to XX (Southern BRS), JD to RN (Western BRS)
4/82	Delete	DE	Leeds (Bell Hill). All operational services transferred to Lowfields Road. Premises Retained for container storage only
4/82	Delete	DW	Leeds (Lowfields Road). All Leeds activities now centred on this site and given one single new code
4/82	Add	DR	Leeds. New code encompassing all work formerly carried out as DE and DW, now all at Lowfields Road. Activities G, C, D, E, R, also W and K (trailers)
By 4/82	Delete	DR	Worksop. Branch closed, services to Doncaster
By 1/83	Reinstate		GDS Transport codes JB, JC, JD. Branches returned to N E BRS control
By 4/83	Delete	DT	Wakefield. Branch closed
	Add	DE	Yorktruck, new Perkins engine agency opened at York. Activity A
	Add	DW	Darlington, Carreras-Rothman contract. New code introduced for specific duty, Contract already operating at Basildon. Activity C
	Add	DI	Hanson Haulage Ltd, Pudsey. Activity D. Encoded following transfer from Roadline (UK) Ltd

EASTERN BRS LTD

Three-letter codes were introduced from January 1979 during the BRR-T registration block. In order to accommodate the new numbering system, the former joint sequence of 'K' only for service vehicles was adjusted by substituting the individual Branch code in place of the single letter 'K' plus activity letter 'E', while the existing 'BRS Rescue' joint series, already using Branch codes plus letter 'E' since 1977, had their activity letter altered to 'S'.

The network was as follows:

Code	Branch	Activity
KA	Derby	G, C (ex VA), D (ex VA), R, E, S, K (trailers). Add: D (ex G) 6/81. K finished 8/83
KB	Kings Lynn	G, C (ex VB), E, S. Add: X (trailers) 6/81
KD	Norwich	G, C (ex VD), D (ex VD), E, S, R. Add: X (trailers) 6/81
KE	Nottingham	G, C (ex VE), D (ex KE & VE), R, E. Add: S 8/80, K & X (trailers) 6/81, T
KF	Burton	G, C (ex VF), E, S, W. Add: D (ex G) 8/82
KG	Nottingham DTS	T
KH	Newark	G, C (ex VH), D (ex VH), E, S. Add: X (trailers) 6/81
KJ	Heath	G, C (ex VJ), D (ex KJ & VJ), E, S. Add X 6/81. Renamed 'Chesterfield'
KK	Brandon	C (ex VK), G (slave units only), E. Add: S 8/82
KL	Wellingborough	C (ex VL), E, S
KN	Leicester	G, C (ex VN), E, S, R. Add: D (ex C) 8/82
KP	Lincoln	G, C (ex VP), D (ex VP), E, S, R. Add: D (ex KP) 12/81, X (trailers) 6/81
KQ	Boston	D (ex KQ), E. Add: C 8/80; R 8/80; S 12/81
KR	Langar	W (in service series) Warehousing facility for Melton Mowbray
KS	Corby	G, C (ex VS), E, S
KT	Melton Mowbray	D (ex KT & VT), C (ex VT), E. Add: S 4/83
KU	Rugby	C (ex VU), D (ex VU), E, S

117

Code	Branch	Activity
KV	Beccles	G, C (ex VV), E, S. Add: X (trailers) 6/81
KW	Northampton	G, C (ex VW), D (ex KW), E, S, R. Add: D (ex C) and M (ex G) 8/80
KX	Cambridge plus Stevenage	D (ex KX), C (ex VX), E, S. Add: R 8/83 Warehouse only (ex KL). No fleet
KY	Peterborough	G, C (ex VY), D (ex VY), E, S, R. Add: K (trailers) 6/81
KZ	Wisbech	G, C (ex VZ), D (ex VZ), E

There was no provision for the BRS Overland fleet, coded QN at Northampton, when the three-letter coding was introduced from 1979 and it ceased to receive any mention in Directories by 1978; consequently it appears to have been discontinued by this time.

Subsequent amendments were as follows:

By 8/80	Add	KC	Pinxton, Notts. New Branch. Activities C, D, E, S
	Delete	KR	No further reference
	Delete	KU	Rugby. Branch closed
By 3/82	Add	KR	GDS Transport, Lutterworth. Activity D. Branch transferred in from NE BRS control, Formerly JBD
By 1/83	Delete	KR	GDS Lutterworth, reverted to code JB under N E BRS control
	Delete	KC	Pinxton. Branch closed on establishing new premises for Nottingham Branch (KE) At Langley Mill nearby. The Nottingham fleet was later split between Langley Mill and a second, town centre site at Castle Meadow, the latter offering Rental and some contracts work while all other work remained at Langley Mill. These changes resulted from vacation of the Wells Road site. All services continued to use the code KE, still termed 'Nottingham'
	Delete	KG	Nottingham Driving School (KGT) recoded KET prior to this reorganisation

MIDLANDS BRS LTD

The company introduced three-letter coding from January 1979, during its PBW-T registration block.

The network was as follows:

Code	Branch	Activities
MA	Oxford	G, C (ex WA), D (ex WA), E,S, R (ex WA). Add: X (trailers) 6/81
MB	Banbury	G, C (ex WB), D (ex WB), E, S, R (ex WB). Add: X (trailers) 6/81
MC	Middlemore	D (ex MC), G
MD	Birmingham Contracts	C (ex WD), D (ex WD). Add: E 8/80
ME	Swindon	G, C (ex WE), E, S, R (ex WE). Add: K (trailers) 8/80; X (trailers) 6/81
MF	Birmingham Containerbase	P, G. Add: E 1/83, D 7/83
MH	Tamworth	G, C (ex WH), E, R (ex WH)
MJ	Oldbury	G, C (ex WJ), E, S. Add: K 8/80, X 6/81, R 12/81
MM	Castle Bromwich	G, C (ex WM), E, S. Add: D 8/80
MN	Redditch	R (ex WN). Add: C by 7/79, G by 8/80, G finished later
MR	Birmingham Distribution Cent.	D, E, R (ex WF). Add: S (ex MM) 6/81
MS	Wolverhampton	C (ex WS), G, E, R (ex WS). Add: S 12/81
MT	Worcester	G, C (ex WT), E, S. Add: R 1/83

1979-1983 Three-Letter Codes

Code	Branch	Activities
MV	Hereford	G, C (ex WV), E. Add: S 12/81
MW	Walsall	Clearing house only. No fleet
MY	Gloucester	G, D (ex WY), C (ex WY), S, R (ex WY). Add: E 8/80. S finished 1.83
MZ	Wellington	G, C (ex WZ), E, S, R (ex WZ). Add: X 6/81
TC	Birmingham DTS	T
TF	Wolverhampton R C	E, S

Certain residual equipment, mainly trailers, from extinct Branches – Erdington (MP), Ross-on-Wye (MQ), Walsall (MW), Forest of Dean (MX) and the Oxford Driving School (TD) – were still held in the company pool at this time but none were allocated activity letters.

Later adjustments:

By 3/79	Add	MK	Oxford – an additional code raised for a fleet of 30 Leyland Buffalo tractors, given the Truck Rental activity, code R, but in fact all leased to Cartransport Ltd and in their livery. At Oxford they were given the numbers MKR32-61 (matching the registrations TJO532-561T) and these numbers were also used by Cartransport Ltd, after which this company adopted an entirely new numbering system
By 8/80			Birmingham Driving School – code revised from TC to MI and Wolverhampton Repair Centre – code revised from TF to ML; uniformity thereby introduced to all Midlands BRS codes
By 7/81	Delete	MH	Tamworth. Branch closed
	Delete	MM	Castle Bromwich. Branch closed. Residual trailer fleet passed to company pool
By 1/82	Delete	ML	Wolverhampton R C closed, work transferred to nearby Branch (MS)
	Delete	MK	Termination of lease of Oxford vehicles with Cartransport Ltd
By 7/83	Delete	MC	Middlemore Branch closed
	Delete	MW	Walsall facility no longer mentioned

Within Midlands BRS territory, Mortons (BRS) Ltd continued its separate existence but was finally obliged to join the BRS Group's 'Activity Letter' coding system at the end of 1981. A new series of two-letter Branch codes using new company letter 'I' replaced the former 'W' company letter in fleet numbering, effective from XRW-X registration block onwards, as follows:

Code	Branch	Activities
1A	Coventry, Rowley Road	G, C, D, R, E, S, also K (trailers)
1B	Whitnash (Bishops Tachbrook)	No fleet
1C	Chipping Warden	G
1D	Pitsea	C, D, E, S, also K (trailers)
1G	Baginton, Coventry Airport	No fleet
1H	Baginton, Rock Farm	E
1K	Birmingham, Cheapside	D, E, S. Sub-depots at Cambridge and Leeds
1L	Coventry, Humber Road (Smiths)	No fleet

All sites were still listed in Directories by 1983 but only the five indicated had vehicle fleets.

WESTERN BRS LTD

As with most other companies, activity letter coding was introduced from January 1979, apparently during issue of the VTC-T registration block. The company took the opportunity of standardising on letter 'R' for all Branch codes at the same time, introducing new codes for all South Wales Branches formerly coded SA-SW. The new network now read:

Code	Branch	Activities
RA	Bristol	G, C (ex YA), E, S. Add: X (trailers) 6/81, R 8/82
RB	Avonmouth	G, C (ex YB), D (ex RB), S, R, E. Add: K (trailers) 8/80, X (trailers) 6/81
RC	Southampton plus Romsey sub-depot	G, C (ex YC), E, S, R. Add: D 7/79
RD	Melksham plus Trowbridge (Keymarkets)	G, C (ex YD), E, S. Add: X (trailers) 6/81
RE	Wells	G, C (ex YE), E, S
RF	Exeter	G, D (ex RF & YF) C (ex YF), S. Add: E 8/80, X 6/81, R 4/83
RG	Plymouth	G, C (ex YG), S. Add: R 4/83
RH	Bridgwater	G, C (ex YH), E, S, R. Add: X 6/81 R finished 6/81 reintro'd 4/83
RJ	Isle of Wight (T/A Islandlink Ltd)	D (ex RJ), C (ex YJ), E, S. Add: R 6/81
RK	Reading	G, C (ex YK), D (ex YK), R, E, S. Add: X 6/81
RM	Portsmouth	G, C (ex YM), S. Add: R & K 8/80, E 9/81
RQ	H S Morgan, Eastleigh	D
RR	Poole	G, C (ex YR), R, S
RS	Cardiff	G (ex SA & SE), C (ex ZA), R (ex SA), E, S. Add: X 6/81
RT	Newport	G (ex SB & SF), C (ex ZB), S. Add: R 8/80, X 6/81
RV	Swansea	G (ex SH), C (ex ZH), C, R (ex SH). Add: E 8/80, K 8/80
RW	West Wales	G (ex SJ), C (ex ZJ), S. Add: E 9/82, D (ex G) 4/83
RX	Bridgend	G (ex SK), C (ex ZK), D (ex SK), S. Add: X 6/81, E 8/82
RY	Margam	G (ex SM). Add: C 8/80
RZ	Bridgend DTS	T (ex SW)

Subsequent amendments:

By 8/80	Delete	RY	Margam, Branch closed, remaining work to Bridgend (RX). Also a code 'RP' for Company Pool was introduced, on paper only, to identify spare vehicles held in reserve
By 6/81	Add	RL	Merthyr Tydfil. Fleet of Hoover Ltd taken over to operate on contract-hire terms. Activities C, E, S
By 12/81	Add	SA	Power Western, Bristol. New dealership for Perkins Engines. (Activity M)
By 3/82	Add	RN	GDS Transport, Yate. Branch transferred from N Eastern BRS Activity D
By 1/83	Delete	RN	GDS Transport, Yate. Returned to control of N E BRS, reverting to code JD
By 4/83	Add	SD SH	Power Western, Perkins dealership, extended to Melksham and Bridgwater with codes matching existing Branches. (Activity M)

SCOTTISH ROAD SERVICES LTD

We have left this company till last again as it was still undergoing much reorganisation, as related already. It is unfortunate that detailed records for this fleet are not available between 1975 and 1980, and only brief details from 1980 onwards, so much of the following is conjecture.

Vehicle observations suggest that SRS introduced three-letter activity-coded lettering from the beginning of 1979, in common with most other BRS fleets. At this time the fleet still operated in three divisions – West, North and Forth – each now responsible for its own vehicle licensing, and the new codes were introduced during issue of respective registration blocks FGA-T, XES-T and RMS-T. The brief records seen from 1980 suggest that SRS misconstrued the intent of the new codes and in fact continued to use both previous codes (haulage and contracts) along with appropriate activity suffix as well, rather than to realise just one code would now suffice. Accordingly we believe the new 1979 network and codes were as follows:

SRS (WEST) LTD

Branch	General Code & Activities	Contracts Code & Activities
Glasgow General	BA – G, E, S	
Oban	BB – not known if ever used	No data
Campbeltown	BC – not known if ever used	No data *
Dunoon	BD – not know if ever used	No data
Glasgow Distribution	BE – D, E	HE – C
Dumfries	BF – G, E, S	HF – C
Argyll (Warroch St)	BG – G	No data *
Haslingden	BH – G, E	HH – C
Kilmarnock	BK – G, E, S	HK – C
Lockerbie	BL	HL – C
Newcastle (Felling)	BN	HN – C, D
Birmingham	BP – no fleet (sub of Dumfries)	
Coatbridge	BX – D, E	HX – C, later add R
Glasgow Contracts		HZ – C, R
Lochgilphead & Tarbert		

* One contract hire vehicle is known for the former Argyll Branch, based at Campbeltown but whether this held a number in HC or HG series is not known.

SRS (NORTH) LTD

Branch	General Code & Activities	Contract Code & Activities
Dundee	GL – G, E, S	OL – C, R
Forfar	GM – G, E, S	OM – C
Arbroath	GN – G, E	ON – C
Perth	GP – G, E	OP – C
Aberdeen	GR – G, E	OR – C, R
Inverness	GS – G, E	OS – C, R
Elgin	GT – G, E	OT - C

SRS (FORTH LTD)

Branch	General Code & Activities	Contract Code & Activities
Grangemouth	LF – G, E	UF – C
Dunfermline	LH – G, E	UH – C
Kirkcaldy	LJ – G, E	UJ – C
Falkirk	LP – E, S	UP – C, R, M
Alloa	LT – G, E	UT – C
Edinburgh	LV – G, D, E	UV – C, R
Bathgate	LW – G	UW – C
Galashiels	LY – G, E	UY - C

By July 1979 all three companies had been combined as one single 'Scottish Road Services' all over again, but with a hugely altered network from that established in September 1972. With the Head Office now relocated from Cumbernauld to Falkirk, the SRS (Forth) codes and company letter 'L' used in this area were retained, and 'B': the Scottish identification letter ever since its first introduction in 1949/50, was discontinued. One code per Branch was utilised, plus activity letter, as had been intended at the beginning of the year.

The new network was as follows:

New Code	Old Code	Branch	Activities
LA	BA, HZ	Glasgow (Lister St)	G, C, R, E, S. Add: K (trailers) by 8/80. G&K finished by 8/80
LB	BH, HH	Haslingden	G, C, E
LC	GT, OT	Elgin	G, C, E. Add: R (ex LS) 7/81
LD	BF, HF	Dumfries	G, C, E, S. Add: R, also X (trailers) 6/81. R finished 8/83
LE	GP, OP	Perth	G, C, E
LF	LF UF	Grangemouth	G, E
LG	BE, HE, BG	Glasgow Distrb.	G, D, C, E. Add: R (ex LA) 1/83, K (ex C) 4/83
LH	LH, UH	Dunfermline	G, E. Add: C 6/81
LI	BP, HP	Birmingham	No fleet (sub of Dumfries)
LJ	LJ, UJ	Kirkcaldy	G, C, R, E. R finished by 8/80
LK	BK, HK	Kilmarnock	G, C, E, S. Add: X (trailers) 6/81. C finished by 8/80
LL	GL, OL	Dundee	G, C, R, E, S. Add: X (trailers) 6/81, D 12/81. G finished 1/82, R finished 7/83
LM	GM, OM	Forfar	G, C, E, S
LN	GN, ON	Arbroath	G, C, E. Add: X (trailers) 6/81
LP	LP, UP	Falkirk	C, R, E, S, M. Add: G (ex LF) 6/81, X (trailers) 6/81
LQ	BN, HN	Newcastle	C, D. Add: E 6/81
LR	GR, OR	Aberdeen	G, C, R, E. Add: X (trailers) 6/81, D 12/81
LS	GS, OS	Inverness	G, C, R, E
LT	LT, UT	Alloa	G, C, E. Add: X (trailers) 6/81, S 8/81, R 1/83. R finished 7/83
LV	LV, UV	Edinburgh	C, D, E, R. Add S 6/81
LW	LW, UW	Bathgate	G, C
LX	BX, HX	Coatbridge	D, C, R, E

| LY | LY, UY | Galashiels | C, G, E. G finished 8/81 |
| LZ | BL, HL | Lockerbie | C. Add E 7/83 |

A code 'LO' was also used by Head Office for one vehicle, possibly an inspector's van, with activity letter 'O' (Other). The repair centres at Glasgow, Forfar and Linlithgow remained uncoded.

A particularly sad closure that occurred around the time of this reorganisation in mid-1979 was the unique Argyll service that BRS had operated ever since its inception in 1949/50, carrying anything from livestock and hay bales to boats and even a piano. It was reported that services to Argyllshire were in future to be administered by sister NFC company National Carriers, from their Sighthill depot in Glasgow, and in August 1979 it was announced that Roadline (UK) Ltd was to relocate to the Warroch Street premises formerly used by SRS Argyll Branch. By coincidence the resultant loss of four Branch codes (BB, BC, BD and BG) left just sufficient remaining Branches to occupy one alphabet – viz, new codes LA to LZ – without the need to introduce a second overspill letter.

A small residue of vehicles from SRS Warroch Street ended up at Hawthorn Street to be recoded along with their own vehicles but what became of any residual vehicles at the outlying Argyllshire depots is unknown. After the final cessation of the general services to Argyllshire in July 1980, a single new Branch was established at Campbeltown to pursue new work specifically for the Scottish Milk Marketing Board (see below).

Up until mid-1979, SRS (North) and (Forth) had continued to use the individual series of fleet numbers for each activity at each Branch, from No.1 upwards, first introduced from 1965 onwards, apart of course from the two Road Services (Forth) depots at Falkirk and Alloa which simply continued from the old Forth series. SRS (West), meanwhile, had introduced a joint series for all activities at all Branches since at least 1976, as mentioned on earlier which had reached No.927 by this time (mid-way through MYS-V registration block).

After the three regional companies were merged into one single company again, the new Falkirk HQ chose to introduce a new joint series now covering all Branches and activities throughout Scotland, similar to that established by SRS (West), commencing from No.1000. in the event of future transfers of older vehicles from one Branch to another, the opportunity was taken to allocate a number in this new series on each occasion this took place, rather than simply recode or otherwise adjust the old numbers. Vehicles numbered in the new four-figure series 1000+ then only required branch recoding in the event of transfer between Branches.

Amendments

The recession was particularly badly felt in Scotland and a large number of fleet reductions and Branch closures continued to occur. These can be outlined as follows:

By 8/80	Delete	LI	Birmingham Branch code never activated; traded as a sub-depot to Dumfries
	Delete	LM	Forfar. Branch closed, services to Arbroath (LN). Residual vehicles stored.
	Delete	LW	Bathgate. Branch closed. Some vehicles to Grangemouth (LF), remainder 'pooled' and recoded LM on computer alongside Forfar vehicles to leave code free for re-issue
	Add	LW	Campbeltown. New service introduced in Argyllshire. (Activities C, G)
8/80	Delete	LE	Perth. Branch closed. Contracts work to Dundee (LL). Haulage fleet dispersed
By 6/81	Add	LU	Apparently an 'on paper' code only, issued to a whole range of vehicles placed in company pool as significant fleet reductions continued to occur at numerous Branches, particularly Dumfries, Aberdeen and Elgin and, later, Dundee and Kilmarnock. All activities were accommodated (G, C, E & D), al in series from 001 upwards and, in the event of a vehicle being returned to service, if it had previously held a fleet number in the new four-figure series, this was reinstated at the new base
By 7/81	Delete	LF	Grangemouth. Branch closed, services to Falkirk (LP) necessitating introduction there of activity 'G' for the first time
	Delete	LJ	Kirkcaldy. Branch closed, services to Dunfermline (LH)
	Delete	LS	Inverness amended to sub-depot of Elgin; all equipment recoded LC but still at Inverness
By 1/82	Delete	LK	Kilmarnock. Branch closed. Fleet dispersed, particularly to Alloa, and remainder 'pooled'
By 3/82	Add	LE	Believed to be Cumbernauld (activity C) which operated an exclusive contract for Woolworths formerly carried out by National Carriers Contracts Division all Woolworths' work in England, however, continued to be carried out by NCL
By 8/82	Add	LF	Glasgow Repair Centre, Kilbirnie Street, encoded at last. (Activities E, S). Some vehicles already recoded ex LM
	Add	LI	Edinburgh Repair Centre, St Marks Place, Portobello, similarly encoded for the first time.(Activity E)
	Add	LJ	Kirkcaldy. Code reinstated for Workshops on St Clair Industrial Estate. (Activity E)
	Add & Delete	LM	Unidentified, possibly Stranraer Workshop, now listed as a subsidiary of Glasgow Repair Centre. (Activities E, S)
	Add	LS	Inverness. Code reinstated for maintenance and engineering work only. (Activities E, S)

These last five Branches appear to have resulted from fully incorporating the Fleetcare work into the SRS organisation. There was no further mention of the old Divisional Workshop at Linlithgow which had presumably fallen out of use.

By 1/83	Delete	LA	Glasgow, Lister Street closed. Services to Hawthorn Street (LG)
	Delete	LQ	Newcastle. Branch at Felling closed. Services passed to North Eastern BRS and renumbered into DL series at Branch on Team Valley Estate
By 4/83	Add	LM	East Tullos Workshop, Aberdeen. Additional Fleetcare base. (Activity E)

By coincidence there continued to be sufficient closures, vacating codes, for them to be reissued straightaway to new services, so care needs to be taken in identifying which Branch any particular code relates to at different times.

From July 1982, Scottish Road Services was separated once again from the BRS Group within the NFC and transferred to a new 'Regional Group' which also accommodated Scottish Parcels Ltd (the recent merger of Roadline UK Ltd and National Carriers in Scotland), and Northern Ireland Carriers Ltd (the former Ulster Transport Authority Freight division, added to the THC's interests from 1965 and renamed). This had no effect on fleet numbering.

In September 1983, the six regional BRS companies in England and Wales were reorganised into four new companies with revised boundaries. This did cause further alterations in Branch codes, of course, as outlined in the next section.

7

1983-1991

September 1983 saw a reorganisation of BRS in England and Wales that combined the six regional companies into four with revised boundaries and the closure of two further regional offices. As many of the vehicles involved now carried inappropriate liveries from their various former companies, the opportunity was taken to standardise the livery of the remaining General Haulage vehicles and a common livery of white with red and blue arrowhead motif and lining, and fleet numbers in serif-style black lettering, was adopted throughout the fleet, very similar to that already held by the Truck Rental fleet.

Scottish Road Services continued its separate existence within the 'Regional Group' at this time and was not affected by this reorganisation. Instead it continued to use its existing dark blue and white livery but now with a stylised 'S' logo on the cab sides in place of the triple arrowhead. It will continue to be described alongside the BRS companies, however, for chronological purposes.

Branch networks and titles of the new regional companies were as follows:

BRS SOUTHERN LTD (letters A, X and N)

This was a merger of the whole of Southern BRS Ltd, the East Anglian portion of Eastern BRS Ltd and the Berkshire portion (Reading) from Western BRS Ltd. Head Office continued to be at Potters Bar and new registrations from Central London LVLC, though increasing quantities of new vehicles were now on short term leases and licensed by suppliers by this time.

New Code	Old Code	Branch	Activities
AC	Same	Grays	G, C, E
AD	KV	Beccles	G, C, E, L (ex S)
AE	KK	Brandon	C, G, E, L (ex S)
AF	KB	Kings Lynn	G, C, E, L (ex S)
AG	KD	Norwich	G, C, D, E, R, L (ex S)
AK	Same	Guildford	G, C, L. Add: R 3/85
AL	RK	Reading	G, C, D, R, E, L (ex S)
AS	Same	Dagenham	G (two trailers only) (sub of Grays)
AT	NG	Bury St Edmunds	G, C, D, E, L
AU	Same	Chadwell Heath	D, G, C. Relocated from Silvertown)
AW	Same	Elmstead	G, C, E
AY	Same	Enfield	G, C, D. Add: R 3/84
AZ	Same	Tilbury	G
XA	Same	Newington Butts	C, R, E, L
XB	Same	Dover	G, C, E
XE	Same	Watford	C, G, R
XF	Same	Canterbury	G, C, E. Add: A 10/84
XG	Same	Brentford	C, D, G, E, L, K (trailers), T
XH	Same	Ipswich	C, G, E, R, L, D
XL	Same	Mid-Kent	C, D, G, E, L, R
XM	Same	Croydon	C, R, E
XP	Same	Long Lane	C. Add: E 3/85
XT	Same	Bedfont	D, R, C, E, W
XU	Same	High Wycombe	C, R, L, E
XV	Same	Dunstable	C, D, L, R, E
XY	Same	North London	C, D, G, R, E, L
XZ	Same	Aylesbury	C, G, E

Having recoded Bury St Edmunds from NG to AT, letter 'N' was now exclusive to the subsidiary company, Bar Delivery Services, with network still as before:

NL	Chiswick	Activity D only
NN	Dunstable	Activity D only
NP	Hackney	Activity D only
NS	Hornsey	Activity D only
NT	Hoddesdon	Activity D only
NV	Lewisham	Activity D only
NW	Luton	Activity D only
NZ	Manor Park	Activity D only

BRS NORTHERN LTD (letters C, D and J, also codes HA and UA)

The company was a merger between the whole of North Eastern BRS Ltd and all of North Western BRS Ltd except the Branches at Stoke, Stafford and Wrexham. The former N E BRS office at Harrogate was retained as HQ and the Manchester office of N W BRS was closed, though a local sub-office was introduced at Trafford Park to assist with 'West Pennine' activities, the area covered now being so large. The Harrogate office continued to raise new vehicle registrations from Leeds LVLC.

WEST PENNINE DIVISION

New Code	Old Code	Branch	Activities
CA	Same	Liverpool	C, D, G, E, S, R
CB	Same	Burnley	R, C
CD	Same	Warrington	G, C, E, S, R, K (trailers). Add: Q 1986, Z by 8/89, L by 9/91
CE	Same	St Helens	G, C, E, Z
CF	Same	Runcorn	G, C, E, S, Z. Add: M by 10/89
CG	Same	Kitt Green	E
CH	Same	North Wales	G (residual trailers only – Branch now closed)
CL	Same	Trafford Prk	C, D, G, E, R, Z, K (trailers). Add: S 3/84, L by 9/91
CO	Same	Head Office	E (inspector's van only). Add: O ('other') 3/84
CP	Same	Cheetham	G, C, E. Add: K (trailers) 10/84
CQ	Same	Bolton	G, C, S, R, E. Add: Y by 11/89, Z by 11/91
CT	Same	Longton	G, C, D, E – plus R at Walton-le-Dale
CU	Same	Unidentified	M
CV	Same	Tameside	C, D, R, E, S. Add: K (trailers) by 10/86, H by 10/87, Z by 11/91
CW	Same	Stockport	C, E
CZ	Same	Carlisle	R, C, S, K (trailers)
HA	Same	Bridges, Leyland	D, C, E
UA	Same	Coopers, Prestatyn	D, E

EAST PENNINE DIVISION

New Code	Old Code	Branch	Activity
DA	Same	Sheffield	G, C, D, R, E, K (trailers). Add: Y by 11/91
DB	Same	Harrogate	G, C, E
DC	Same	Hull	G, C, R, D, E, K (trailers). Add: Q by 11/89
DD	Same	Goole	G, C, E
DE	Same	Yorktruck, York	A. Add: Y by 10/87
DF	Same	Knottingley	G, C, E
DG	Same	Bradford	C, R, E
DH	Same	Selby	C, G
DI	Same	Hansons, Pudsey	D
DJ	Same	Doncaster	G, C, R, E, K (trailers)
DK	Same	York	C, D, G, E. Add: R 3/85, A (ex DEY) by 11/89
DL	Same	Newcastle	D, C, G, R, E, K (trailers). D finished by 11/89
DM	Same	Hexthorpe	C, E. Add: G & R 12/83
DN	Same	Tees-side	C, R. Reinstate G & E 3/85. Add: Q by 11/89
DO	Same	Company Pool	O, D, A (on paper only)
DP	Same	Darlington	G, C, D, E, S, K (trailers). Add: L by 10/87. K finished by 11/89
DQ	Same	Barnsley	G, C, W, E. Add: R by 11/89, K (trailers) by 5/90. G&W finished
DR	Same	Leeds	G, D, C, R, E also W & K (trailers). Add: L by 11/91
DS	Same	Dewsbury	G, C
DU	Same	Carreras Rothman, Basildon	C, E, G (slave tractors)
DV	Same	Scunthorpe	G, C, E. Add: R by 11/89, H by 5/90, Q&L by 11/91

1983-1991 Revised Regional Network

New	Old	Branch	Activity
DW	Same	Carreras Rothman, Darlington	C. Add: G (slave tractors)
DX	Same	Watsons, Spennymoor	D
DY	Same	Grimsby	D, G, C, E. Add: R by 10/86 but finished by 11/91

Subsidiary Company, GDS Transport

New Code	Old Code	Branch	Activity
JA	Same	Glasgow	D
JB	Same	Lutterworth	D
JC	Same	Enfield	D
JD	Same	Yate	D
JE	Same	Sheffield Distribution	D
JG	Same	Sheffield long distance	G

BRS MIDLANDS LTD (letters K, M and I)

This was a complex merger of all Eastern BRS Ltd Branches except those in East Anglia, the majority of Midlands BRS Ltd (excluding areas to the furthest south and west), the North Staffs portion of North Western BRS Ltd and Mortons (BRS) Ltd.

The following BRS offices at Derby were retained as HQ; the Oxford office of Midlands BRS was closed and Coventry, former HQ of Mortons, also lost its controlling power. Derby continued to raise the few new registrations from Nottingham LVLC but most new vehicles received by this company were now registered by their suppliers.

Branch network and activities were as follows:

New Code	Old Code	Branch	Activity
KA	Same	Derby	G, C, R, D, E, S/ K (trailers) reinstated 2/85
KC	CM	Stoke	C, D, G, R, S, E, K (trailers)
KE	Same	Nottingham	C, D, E, S at Langley Mill plus R, G, K (trailers) at Castle Meadow, also T
KF	Same	Burton	G, C, D, E, S, W. Add: R 3/84
KH	Same	Newark	G, C, E, S, D
KJ	Same	Chesterfield	G, C, E, S, D (renamed ex 'Heath')
KL	Same	Wellingborough	C, E, S
KN	Same	Leicester	G, C, E, S, R, D
KP	Same	Lincoln	G, C, D, E, S, R
KQ	Same	Boston	D, E, C, S, R
KR	CJ	Stafford	No fleet (clearing house only)
KS	Same	Corby	G, C, E, S
KT	Same	Melton Mowbray	D, C, E, S
KW	Same	Northampton	G, C, D, E, S, R, M, K (trailers). Add B 3/85
KX	Same	Cambridge	D, C, E, S, R - including Stevenage
KY	Same	Peterborough	G, C, D, E, S, R, K (trailers)

The BRS Reference Book

New	Old	Branch	Activity
KZ	Same	Wisbech	G, C, D, E
MB	Same	Banbury	G, C, D, E, S, R
MD	Same	Birmingham Contracts	C, D, E. Add: R (ex MF) 3/85
MF	Same	Birmingham Containerbase	G, P, E, D. Add: R (ex MR) 3/84 but transfer to MD 3/85
MI	Same	Birmingham DTS	T
MJ	Sake	Oldbury	G, C, E, S, R, K (trailers). Add: D 3/84
MN	Same	Redditch	C, R. Add: E 3/85
MR	Same	Birmingham Distribution	D, E, R, S. (aka Bromford Mills). Delete: R 3/84 – to MF
MS	Same	Wolverhampton	C, G, E, R, S
MZ	Same	Wellington	G, C, E, S, R
IA	Same	Coventry	G, C, D, R, E, S, K (trailers)
IB	Same	Leamington (Tachbrook)	No fleet (warehousing only)
IC	Same	Chipping Warden	G
ID	Same	Pitsea	C, D, E, S, K (trailers)
IH	Same	Rock Farm	E
IK	Same	Cheapside	D, E, S

BRS WESTERN LTD (letters R, S and T)

The fourth new company combined all of Western BRS Ltd except Reading, with the southern and western portions of Midlands BRS Ltd and Wrexham from North Western BRS Ltd. The Western BRS office at Bristol continued as HQ, using Bristol LVLC for new registrations.

Network as follows:

New Code	Old Code	Branch	Activity
RA	Same	Bristol	G, C, E, S, R
RB	Same	Avonmouth	G, C, D, S, R, E, K (trailers)
RC	Same	Southampton (Chandlers Ford)	G, C, E, S, R, D
RD	Same	Melksham plus Trowbridge	G, C, E, S. Add: R 10/84 C (in 300s) for Keymarkets
RE	Same	Wells	G, C, E, S, R
RF	Same	Exeter	G, D, C, S, E, R
RG	Same	Plymouth	G, C, S, R
RH	Same	Bridgwater	G, C, E, S, R. Add: D 10/84
RJ	Same	Islandlink, Isle of Wight	D, C, E, S, R
RL	Same	Merthyr Tydfil	C, E, S
RM	Same	Portsmouth	G, C, S, E, R, K (trailers)
RP	Same	Company Pool	C (spare vehicles – on paper code only)
RQ	Same	Morgans, Eastleigh	D, E
RR	Same	Poole	G, C, R, S
RS	Same	Cardiff	G, C, R, E, S
RT	Same	Newport	G, C, S, E
RV	Same	Swansea	G, C, S, R, E, K (trailers)
RW	Same	West Wales	G, C, S, E, D
RX	Same	Bridgend	G, C, D, S, E
RZ	Same	Bridgend DTS	T
SA	Same	Power Western, Bristol	M. Add: E 10/84
SD	Same	Power Western, Melksham	M

1983-1991 Revised Regional Network

New Code	Old Code	Branch	Activity
SH	Same	Power Western, Bridgwater	M
TA	MA	Oxford	G, C, D, E, S, R
TE	ME	Swindon	G, C, E, S, R, K (trailers). Add: D 10/84
TK	CK	Wrexham	G, C, E, S, D
TT	MT	Worcester	G, C, E, S, R
TV	MV	Hereford	G, C, E, S
TY	MY	Gloucester	G, C, D, R, E

SCOTTISH ROAD SERVICES LTD (letter L)

There was no change to this company at this time but because so many changes had occurred in the previous four years, this is an opportune moment to summarise the current network for direct chronological comparison. Most new registrations continued to be raised by the Falkirk HQ, from Stirling LVLC.

Code	Branch	Activities
LB	Haslingden	G, C, E
LC	Elgin	G, C, E, R
LD	Dumfries	G, C, E, S
LE	Cumbernauld (?)	C
LF	Glasgow Repair Centre plus Stranraer Workshop	E, S
LG	Glasgow Freight Centre	G, D, C, E, R, K (vehicles)
LH	Dunfermline	G, E
LI	Edinburgh Repair Centre	E
LJ	Kirkcaldy Workshop	E
LL	Dundee	C, E, S, D (sub of Arbroath)
LM	East Tullos Workshop	E
LN	Arbroath	G, C, E
LO	Head Office	O
LP	Falkirk	G, C, R, E, S, M
LR	Aberdeen	G, C, R, E, D
LS	Inverness	E, S (sub of Elgin)
LT	Alloa	G, C, E, S
LU	Company Pool	C, G, E, D (on paper codes only)
LV	Edinburgh	C, D, E, R, S
LW	Campbeltown	C, G
LX	Coatbridge	D, C, R, E
LY	Galashiels	C, E (sub of Edinburgh)
LZ	Lockerbie	C, E (sub of Dumfries)

Amendments

Branch closures and the introduction of new sites especially operating Truck Rental, where a demand was identified, and contract hire for customers, continued to take place after the 1983 reorganisation, necessitating constant raising of new codes and reissues of codes as they became vacant. Unfortunately, the series of internal directories that were issued regularly since 1977 was discontinued in 1986, in favour of less freely available guides, and our access to these alterations was severely affected and we began to lose track of such events. Computerised fleet lists for the entire fleet that had given at least brief identification for all vehicles and trailers operated also ceased to be produced in 1985, which further hampered our efforts to keep abreast of current developments. The alterations that are known are recorded below but there are many matters that remain unresolved.

BRS SOUTHERN

Bar Delivery Services:

By 10/83	Add	NN	Relocated at Dunstable from Eastern Avenue to Church Street
By 12/83	Delete	NT	Hoddesdon site closed, relocated to Dunstable (NN)
By 3/84	Add	NQ	Kentish Town. The former site of North London Freight Centre (XY), vacated at the end of 1983, was redeveloped as the main London centre for BDS
	Delete	NL,NP NS,NV,NZ	All relocated to new site at Kentish Town (NQ)
	Add	NU	Dunstable – the former site at Eastern Avenue, now redeveloped
	Delete	NN	Old site at Dunstable in Church Street relocated to Eastern Avenue (NU)
By 3/85	Delete	NW	The final original BDS site at Luton, basically a repair centre, relocated to Kentish Town (NQ)
10/85	Delete	NQ & NU	Bar Delivery Services transferred to SPD as part of NFC Distribution Group

BRS Branches:

By 1/84	Relocate	XY	North London Freight Centre from Kentish Town to Kings Cross
By 3/84	Add	XC	Radlett (activity D). New base operating for Argyll Foods supermarket services
By 3/85	Add	AH	Stevenage (activities C, D). Formerly designated a sub-site for Cambridge Branch by Eastern BRS Ltd, latterly BRS Midland Ltd, it was reallocated to BRS Southern Ltd and services were duly reintroduced, using several former Cambridge (KX) vehicles to do so
10/85	Delete	XC	Radlett. Distribution services transferred to SPD, along with BDS
	Delete	XT	Bedfont. Distribution services transferred to SPD, along with BDS
3/86			The entire Contracts fleet, until now numbered in a joint series that had reached well into the 6000s, was renumbered into separate series from 001 upwards at each Branch
By 10/86	Add	XQ	Brighton, offering Rental
	Add	XW	Dartford, offering Rental and Contracts
	Add	XX	Leyton, offering Rental
	Add	?	Chelmsford, offering Rental
	Expand	AK	Guildford, by addition of sub-office at Ditchling and repair centre on Cathedral Hill Estate
	Delete	AU	Chadwell Heath. No further reference, assumed closed
	Delete	AZ	Tilbury. No further reference, assumed closed
	Delete	XP	Long Lane. No further reference, assumed closed
	Reduce	XV	Dunstable. Services wound down and offering Rental only
Late 1986	Add	NB	Harlow Engineering. Added on transfer from NCL Fleetcare service as maintenance and engineering centre

	Add	ND	Ipswich Truck Sales. Added on transfer from NCL Fleetcare service as maintenance and engineering centre
	Add	NE	Watford Engineering. Added on transfer from NCL Fleetcare service as maintenance and engineering centre
	Add	NL	Kings Cross Engineering. Added on transfer from NCL fleet care service as maintenance and engineering centre
	Add	NM	Leyton Engineering. Added on transfer from NCL Fleetcare services as maintenance and engineering centres
6/87			Head Office relocated from Potters Bar to Stevenage. London LVLC continued to be used for new vehicle registrations

By 3/88: Access to a computerised fleet list (detained by accident) showed vehicles numbered in various series, including many that remain unidentified as they receive no mention in directories of 1986 or 1989. Along with other sites that are identified, note the following:

By 3/88	Add	AA	Dunstable (activities C, R, E). But no further reference to code XV, the inference being this must have closed after 10/86 but subsequently been re-opened later
	Add	AN	Milton Keynes (activity R)
	Add	XN	Newbury (activity R)
	Add	NF	Park Royal (activity E)
	Add	NP	Croydon Engineering (activity E)
	Add	NS	Aldershot (activity E)
	Add	NX	Tonbridge (activities C, R, E)
	Add	?	Ashford, Kent, offering Rental and Contracts
	Add	?	Letchworth, services unclear
	Add	AV	Unidentified (activities R, Q) *
	Add	XD	Unidentified (activity C) *
	Add	XK	Unidentified (activities C, R) *
	Add	XS	Unidentified (activity C) *
	Add	NC	Unidentified (activities C, E) *

* Three of the 'Unidentified' above could be Chelmsford, Ashford and Letchworth.

Also by 3/88 add the following 'Unidentified' branches, AB, XJ, NH, NJ, NN, NV and NZ, all Activity 'E' and which all appear to extend the network of Fleetcare engineering centres.

By 6/89	Add	AP	Cambridge (ex BRS Midlands KX), activities C, R, W, E
	Add	XP	Guildford workshop (formerly part of AK), activity E
	Add	XS	Clearfreight, Brentford (formerly part of XG)
	Delete	AE	Brandon. Keymarkets work discontinued
	Delete		Ditchling office of Guildford Branch (AK)
1989	Add	AX	Kelloggs contract, Watford
By 9/91	Add	XT	Sittingbourne
	Amend	XX	Code for Leyton from to XC, reason unclear
	Relocate	AW	From Elmstead to new premises and retitle 'Colchester'
	Expand	AC	Grays by addition of Trailer Rental from new site at Brentwood
	Add	AS	Basildon, additional sub-depot of Grays Branch
	Delete	AN	Milton Keynes
	Delete	XN	Newbury
	Delete	XS	Clearfreight, Brentford

	Delete	ND	Ipswich Truck Sales
	Delete	NS	Aldershot
	Delete		Ashford and Letchworth (codes unknown)

At September 1991 BRS Southern was trading in six defined areas covering the following Branches, the first-named being designated 'Area Office' in each case:

1. Brentford (XG), plus XA (Newington Butts), XM (Croydon), NF (Park Royal), NP (Croydon Engineering).
2. Leyton (XC), plus AC (Grays & Brentwood), AS (Basildon), AY (Enfield), XY (Kings Cross), NB (Harlow)
3. Maidstone (XL), plus XB (Dover), XF (Canterbury), XT (Sittingbourne), XW (Dartford), NX (Tonbridge)
4. Reading (AL), plus AK (Guildford), XP (Guildford Engineering), XQ (Brighton), XU (High Wycombe)
5. Norwich (AG), plus AD (Beccles), AF (Kings Lynn), AT (Bury St Edmunds), AW (Colchester), XH (Ipswich)
6. Stevenage (AH), plus AA (Dunstable), AP (Cambridge), XE (Watford), XZ (Aylesbury), NE (Watford Eng)

All other sites not already described as deleted and not mentioned here were presumably finished. Of those listed here, Bury St Edmunds was closed later in 1991.

BRS NORTHERN LTD
WEST PENNINE DIVISION

By 12/83	Add	CR	Mid-Cheshire Branch (based at Middlewich), formerly an outstation for Stoke Branch, now in BRS Midlands territory, was raised to Branch status using equipment taken from Stoke (KC). Activities C and E. Add: G by 11/85
	Delete	CH	All North Wales residual trailers disposed of
	Delete	UA	Coopers, Prestatyn, closed. Most vehicles dispersed to Roadline (UK)
By 7/84	Add	CS	Fort Sterling, Bolton (activity G), fleet acquired to operate for customer. This service was discontinued shortly afterwards and the fleet merged into the main Bolton fleet (CQ)
By 7/85	Delete	HA	Bridges, Leyland, closed down. Residual vehicles sold at auction
By 11/85	Add	CG	Chester, new Rental service. Activity R. C (largely ex CR) and E by 11/91
	Reinstate	CS	Fort Sterling, Bolton. All 'General' work at Bolton now devoted to this service and entire CQG fleet renumbered into CSG series
By 10/86	Reinstate	CQG	Fort Sterling work returned to Bolton's general fleet for a second time, ex CSG. Astonishingly yet again, this did not last and service reverted to CSG later, for the third time.
		CR	(Mid-Cheshire). Delete 'C' – contracts work split between Chester (CG) & Tameside (CV)
By 6/87	Add	CK	Kelloggs work, Trafford Park. Separate code introduced for specific

By 10/87			duty, previously included in CL. Activities G and C, later add Z and W
			New 'Powertrain' service introduced at Tameside Branch, given Activity letter 'H'

EAST PENNINE DIVISION

By 12/83	Delete	D1	Hansons, Pudsey, transferred to control of National Carriers Parcels
By 3/85	Delete	DH	Selby – Branch closed. Final four vehicles transferred to Goole (DD)
	Add	DH	Huddersfield. New Rental Service (activity R). Add: C by 10/86 but finished 11/91 and contract work passed to Bradford (DG)
	Add	JP	Peaudouce, Hoddesdon (associate of GDS Transport). Activities D & G, ex JCD, relocated from Enfield
By 11/85	Delete	DB	Harrogate. Branch closed
By 10/86	Delete	DU	Basildon base for Carreras-Rothman contract finished
	Delete	DX	Watsons, Spennymoor, transferred to SPD within NFC Distribution Group
	Delete		GDS Transport and Peaudouce (codes JA, JB, JC, JD, JE, JG & JP). Business passed to SPD
By 10/87	Add	DT	J Lyons contract, Barnsley (trailers and a shunt unit only: vehicles coded DQ)
	Add	DX	Leeds, Bell Hill. Former Leeds Branch site, latterly used for container storage now offering trailer rental (activity K)
	Amend	DJ	To 'Doncaster Engineering'. All other services at former Doncaster site relocated to Hexthorpe (DM) and renumbered there, taking new title 'Doncaster Branch')

Fast running out of alphabetical combinations for new development, BRS Northern introduced a third company letter 'F' from the end of 1987. The following additional codes were duly raised:

By 10/87	FA	Star Bodies, Oldham – activity M
	FC	Central Park, Trafford Park – warehousing only, no fleet
By 5/90	FE	Kirklees – activity E
By 8/89	FG	Oldham Road, Manchester – activities E, R (former NCL site)
	FH	Rochdale – activities R, C & E and, later, S ('Contract 12' for Fuel Link) and Z
	FJ	Barton Dock, Trafford Park – activities E (ex CLE), Q (18 month contract for Royal Mail) and L
By 11/91	FS	Unidentified – activity G
By 5/90	FV	Shearbridge, Bradford – activity C (council fleet acquired to operate on contract) and E
	FZ	Barrow-in-Furness – activity C (council fleet acquired on contract), later E & R. Code FZC was later altered to CYC

Codes in the original 'West' and 'East Pennines' series also continued to be amended and the following are known:

WEST PENNINE

By 8/89	Add	CM	Stonehouse contract, Trafford Park (activity C) – later finished and absorbed into CLC fleet

By 6/89			At Middlewich, reintroduce code CRC (ex CGC) and later add activities R & K (trailers)
By 11/89	Delete	CP	Cheetham, Branch closed
	Delete	CSG	Fort Sterling work returned to main CQG fleet at Bolton yet again
	Delete	CE	St Helens demoted to sub-depot of Warrington (CD)
1/91	Delete	CK	Kelloggs work transferred to Exel Distribution
By 11/91	Add	CH	Rochdale Branch recoded from FH (activities C, R, E)
	Add	CY	Barrow-in-Furness, non-council work recoded from FZ (activities C, E)
			At Bolton, delete CQQ/CQR. All Rental work transferred to Trafford Park as CLR
	Delete	CF	Runcorn, Branch closed. Most of fleet transferred to Warrington (CD); small residue of contracts work, still coded CFC, now termed 'Widnes'
	Delete	CG	Chester, Branch closed

EAST PENNINE

By 6/89	Delete	DS	Dewsbury, Branch closed. Services to Huddersfield (DH)
	Delete	DX	Leeds (Bell Hill). Trailer Rental fleet relocated to Knottingley (DF)
By 11/89	Delete	DD	Goole. Fleet pruned, site relegated to sub-depot of Scunthorpe (DV)
	Delete	DW	Carreras-Rothman work at Darlington transferred to main Branch fleet (DPC)
By 9/91	Delete	DH	Huddersfield, services transferred to Bradford (DG)
	Delete	DJ	All 'Doncaster' services relocated from Hexthorpe to original Engineering site in London Road, Doncaster, retaining code DM
	Delete	DE	Yorktruck activity added to main York Branch control (DK)
By 11/91	Delete	DF	Knottingley, Branch closed, services to Barnsley (DQ)
	Add	DB	Chesterfield, Br transferred from BRS Midlands Ltd (KJ) (activities C, R)
			Code DCR now termed 'Scunthorpe' and DMR now 'Barnsley' on Truck Rental fleets, indicating joint control of combined fleets with Hull and Doncaster respectively

BRS MIDLANDS LTD

By 1/84	Add	KG	Burnaston, new development work
	Add	MW	New code introduced for Nottingham Branch. Castle Meadow site, formerly part of KE, which now became specific to the Langley Mill site only
	Delete		IC, ID, IH, IK – all former Mortons services curtailed, residual work passed to Coventry (IA)
	Delete	KR	Stafford site no longer mentioned
By 10/86	Delete	KL	Wellingborough, Branch closed. Services to Northampton (KW)
	Delete	KE	All work at Nottingham based on Castle Meadow (MW). Langley Mill finished
	Delete	MF & MR	All work at Birmingham concentrated on Bromford Mills. Largest of the fleets based here used the code MD so this code was retained for all three series
	Delete	KG	Burnaston site no longer mentioned
By 6/89	Amend	MJ	To West Bromwich, relocated from Oldbury
	Delete	IB	Leamington (no operational fleet involved)
	Delete	KX	Cambridge, Branch transferred to BRS Southern, recoded AP

1983-1991 Revised Regional Network

No further adjustments reported by 9/91. The transfer of Chesterfield Branch (KJ) to BRS Northern, becoming DB (see above), came later.

BRS WESTERN LTD

By 1/84	Delete	RQ	Morgans, Eastleigh. Fleet added to Southampton's activities and recoded RCD
	Amend	RC	From Southampton to Chandlers Ford following relocation and add sub-branch at Romsey
	Add	Unknown	Yate, new Distribution centre, working for Sainsburys
By 10/84	Add	SE	Powertrain, Wells. Activity M
	Add	YN	Identity unknown. Activity D
10/85	Delete	RCD	Morgans. Services transferred to SPD of NFC Distribution Group
	Delete	Unknown	Yate. Services transferred to SPD of NFC Distribution Group
By 10/86	Add	TB	Basingstoke. Activities R, C, W. Also K (trailers)
	Add	TC	Kidderminster. Activities R, C, E
	Amend	RC	Add further sub-depot at Eastleigh for Keymarkets work. No further ref to Romsey sub-branch
By 6/89	Add	RN	Yeovil. Activities R, C
	Add	RY	Par, Cornwall. Activities R, C and K (trailers)
	Add	TD	Abingdon. Activities R, C, E, W
	Add	TF	Winchester. Activity E
	Add	TH	Barnstaple. Activities R, C, E
	Add	TR	Ross-on-Wye (sub of Hereford, for Gateway supermarkets work). Activity C
	Add	TS	Tredegar (sub Cardiff for National Coal Board contract). Activity C
	Add		Boscombe. Sub-depot of Poole (RR)
	Add		Colwyn Bay. Sub-depot of Wrexham (TK)
	Add		Taunton. Engineering sub-depot of Bridgwater (RHE)
	Add	Unknown	Andover. Activity R
	Amend	RC	Eastleigh sub-depot now trading for Gateway, renamed from Key Supermarkets
	Amend	RD	Trowbridge, sub-depot of Keymarkets finished, work relocated to Eastleigh
By 9/91	Amend	RC	Gateway sub-depot relocated from Eastleigh to Hamble
	Amend	RY	Relocated from Par to St Austell
	Delete		RE (Wells), RN (Yeovil, closed 10/90 but still listed in 9/91 Directory), TF (Winchester), TS (Tredegar) and Andover (code unknown). All assumed closed

SCOTTISH ROAD SERVICES LTD

By 3/84	Delete	LI	Edinburgh Repair Centre, services transferred to Edinburgh Branch (LV)
By 10/84	Add	LA	Glasgow Power Centre. Sales of Perkins and Rolls-Royce engines, based at Kilbirnie Street. Activities E, B
	Add	LQ	Portlethen. New temperature-controlled services in Aberdeen. Activities A, E
	Delete	LH	Dunfermline. Branch closed

By October 1986 at Glasgow, Hawthorn Street (LG) was now termed 'Glasgow North' and Kilbirnie Street (LF) 'Glasgow South'. A number of new services had been introduced and by 1987 many of these had been encoded using SRS's second company letter 'B' as follows:

By 10/86	Add	BG	Glasgow Distribution, additional services at Hawthorne Street.	Activities D, W
	Add	BJ	Inverness Distrib., second site at Longman Road	Activities D, W, Temp controlled
	Add	BL	Renfrew Distribution, new site at Wright Street	Activities D, W, Temp controlled
	Add	BM	Belfast Distribution, Mallusk Road, Newtonabbey, N.I.	Activities D, W Temp controlled
	Add	BP	Falkirk Engineering, specialist services at Burnbank Road	Activity E
	Add	BR	Clydesdale Distribution, new service at Rutherglen	Activity D
	Add	BV	Edinburgh Engineering, specialist services at Granton	Activity E
	Add		Aberdeen Distribution, second site at Quay Road (code unknown)	
	Add		Carstairs Workshop, additional site, sub to Glasgow South (LF)	
	Add		Perth Wkshp, additional site, sub to Dundee (LL)	
	Delete		LB (Haslingden), LT (Alloa), LX (Coatbridge).	Branches appear closed

Also, Cumbernauld (believed to have operated Woolworths Distribution Services with code LE since at least 1982 but always listed as a National Carriers Contracts activity in directories) may, by this time have been physically returned to NCCS, in common with the losses of other BRS Distribution work to NFC subsidiaries at the end of 1985. Code LE may now also be considered deleted.

The expansion into Belfast followed the addition of Northern Ireland Carriers to the NFC Regional Group set up in 1982, which traded as a subsidiary of SRS.

By June 1989 the NFC Regional Group set up in 1982 had been discontinued. Scottish Road Services had transferred to the BRS Group once again, along with Northern Ireland Carriers, while Scottish Parcel Services had been added to the new Lynx parcels network, as observed later in 1987.

By 6/89	Add	LH	East Kilbride. Two sites, one offering contract services for Gateway Supermarkets, the second a separate workshop
	Delete		Kilbirnie Street base in Glasgow. All services now centred on Hawthorne Street (LG). However, both former codes were retained – LA for Glasgow Power Centre and LF for the former sub-base at Stranraer which, along with a new workshop a Kilmarnock, now traded as subs to Dumfries
By 9/91	Add	LB	Kilmarnock. Uprated to full Branch now also offering Contracts and Rental
	Add	LE	Additional site at Edinburgh, services for Halls Contract
	Add	LX	Cumbernauld, new Contracts service for the Co-op
	Add	BX	Power Services, Aberdeen

NORTHERN IRELAND CARRIERS LTD

Upon being set up as a Division of Scottish Road Services within the

Regional Group, NIC was operating from the following bases in October 1986 and these had additionally been encoded by 1987 using SRS's third company letter 'G' as follows:

GA	Belfast International Airport	Activity, Airfreight	From 1989 – BB
GB	Ballymena	Activities, G, D, W, E	From 1989 – BD
GC	Craigavon	Activities, G, P, E	From 1989 – BF
GD	Londonderry	Activities, G, P, W	
GE	Enniskillen	Activities, G, P, E	From 1989 – BI
GG	Belfast, Grosvenor Road plus Airport Road	Activities C, E, R, D, W Activity, Petroleum Distrib.	From 1989 – BQ
GM	Belfast, Milewater Road	Freight Forwarding	From 1989 – BS

The activities included Parcels (P) as the NFC's existing Parcels companies had no presence in Northern Ireland at this time.

By June 1989 the Branches had been recoded using the letter 'B' in common with other existing SRS bases, the new codes being shown to the right of the above listing. The site at Londonderry was no longer mentioned, presumably closed, and that at Airport Road was now attached to a further NFC subsidiary, the Caledonian Oil Co, which did not adopt Branch codes and whose other bases were all in Scotland, at Ayr, Berwick, Girvan and Grangemouth.

By September 1991 the only further amendment was to delete the Belfast base of Caledonian Oil Co.

8

1991-1998

The final major reorganisation of the BRS fleet came in September 1991. As all distribution work had already passed from BRS to various other NFC Groups, including SPD and National Carriers, from 1986 onwards the BRS Group now offered mainly Contract Hire, Truck and Trailer Rental, Engineering and Rescue services and a small amount of work still regarded as 'General Haulage' but now termed Freight Management (basically a clearing house agency). The new trading name, Exel Logistics, adopted for all Distribution activities from June 1989, was in due course applied to all NFC work including NFC Distribution, SPD, Carrycare, GDS Transport, SPD Contract Distribution, Bar Delivery Services and Alpine Refrigerated Services, plus Fashionflow, Newsflow, NCCS and this latter company's specialist work for numerous specific customers including Argos, Boots, Currys, Vogue and Woolworths, and many smaller accounts.

The NFC promoted the Exel name as its primary function in successive years, while the BRS empire continued to recede. Early in 1991, for example, such long-established contracts as those with Kelloggs and the Grimsby Fish Merchants' Association (now trading as Britfish) were redefined as 'Contract Distribution' and transferred to Exel, thus losing BRS further valuable business. Then in September the remaining regional BRS companies were combined into one single 'British Road Services' organisation all over again, with a network of 23 'Hub-and-Spoke' areas, many remarkably similar to the regions covered by many of the 25 Districts of BRS Ltd formed in 1957. The business had done a full circle!

As the regional offices of the separate former limited companies were closed, we unfortunately lost our local contacts for access to fleet information, all operations eventually being based at a new Head Office established in Milton Keynes.

1991-1998 National Hub-and-Spoke Network

The 23 new areas of the combined company were initially defined with Branches identified as follows (the codes believed to be involved included in brackets):

South West	Exeter (RF); Plymouth (RG); Bridgwater & Taunton (RH); St Austell (RY); Barnstaple (TH)
Avon	Bristol (RA, SA); Avonmouth (RB); Melksham (RD)
South Wales	Merthyr Tydfil (RL); Cardiff (RS); Newport (RT); Swansea (RV); Carmarthen (RW); Bridgend (RX, RZ)
South	Chandlers Ford (RC presumably including Hamble); Isle of Wight (RJ); Portsmouth (RM); Poole (RR); Basingstoke (TB)
South East	Guildford (AK, XP); Maidstone (XL); Croydon (XM, NP); Brighton (XQ); Sittingbourne (XT); Tonbridge (NX); also Ashford (unknown) and Greenwich (see note). No further reference to Canterbury (XF), Dover (XB) or Dartford (XW)
N. London	Grays (AC presumably including Brentwood); Basildon (AS); Newington Butts (XA); Leyton (XC); Watford (XE, NE); Kings Cross (XY); Park Royal (NF). No further reference to Brentford (XG), Enfield (AY) or Harlow (NB)
East Anglia	Beccles (AD); Kings Lynn (AF); Norwich (AG); Stevenage (AH); Cambridge (AP); Colchester (AW);Ipswich (XH); Boston (KQ); Peterborough (KY); Wisbech (KZ)
Chilterns	Reading (AL); High Wycombe (XU); Oxford (TA); Abingdon (TD); Swindon (TE). No further reference to Dunstable (AA) or Aylesbury (XZ)
West	Ross-on-Wye (TR); Worcester (TT); Hereford (TV); Gloucs (TY);
Birmingham	Bromford Mills (MD presumably including Driving School) West Bromwich (MJ); Wolverhampton (MS); Wellington MZ);
West Midlands	Kidderminster (TC); Stoke (KC)
East Midlands	Leicester (KN); Corby (KS); Northampton (KW); Banbury (MB); Coventry (IA)
North Midlands	Derby (KA); Burton (KF); Newark (KH); Lincoln (KP); Melton Mowbray (KT); Nottingham (MW presumably including Driving School)
S. Yorkshire	Sheffield (DA); Scunthorpe (DV); Chesterfield (KJ revised to DB); plus Immingham and South Killingholme (see note). No further reference to Doncaster (DM) or Grimsby (DY)
Yorkshire & Humberside	Hull (DC); Bradford (DG presumably including FV); York (DK); Barnsley (DQ); Leeds (DR) No further reference to Kirklees (FE)
Manchester	Trafford Park (CL, FJ); Middlewich (CR); Tameside (CV); Rochdale (FH); also Urmston (see note) No further reference to Oldham Road (FG) or Bolton (CQ)
Merseyside & N. Wales	Liverpool (CA); Warrington (CD); Widnes (CF); Wrexham (TK); also Ellesmere Port (see note) No further reference to Chester (CG)
Preston	Burnley (CB); Preston (CT including Walton-le-Dale CTR); Barrow (CY, FZ)
North Scotland	Newcastle (DL); Tees-side (DN); Darlington (DP); plus Billingham (see note)
W. & S. Scotland	Stranraer (LF); Glasgow (LG, LA); East Kilbride (LH);

141

N. & E. Scotland	Campbeltown (LW) Galashiels (LY); Lockerbie (LZ); Carlisle (CZ); Dumfries (LD); Kilmarnock (LB). No further ref. to Rutherglen (BR) Elgin (LC); Kirkcaldy (LJ); Dundee (LL); Falkirk (LP); Portlethen (LQ); Aberdeen (LR, BX); Inverness (LS); Edinburgh (LV); Cumbernauld (LX); plus Broxburn and Grangemouth (see note). No further reference to East Tullos (LM) or Arbroath (LN)
N. Ireland	Aldergrove (BB); Ballymena (BD); Enniskillen (BI); Mallusk (BM); Belfast (BQ, BS). No further reference to Craigavon (BF)
Caledonian Oil Co.	Ayr, Berwick, Girvan and Grangemouth (not coded)

The additional bases shown as 'see note' in the above summary were said to be Engineering depots from sister NFC company Tankfreight Ltd, which were to be operated alongside the existing BRS network. What became of the sites not referred to in this summary is unknown. As the list appears quite comprehensive their omission suggests they were closed, or due to close, and so not involved in the reorganisation.

One depot within each Area was duly selected as main centre, or 'Hub'. The West Midlands area was the first to become operative in August 1991, with West Bromwich as Hub, in order to gain experience in the technique before it was applied to all the other Areas from around November onwards. In the Yorkshire & Humberside Area, Leeds was selected as 'Hub' and brief computerised fleet records for this Area's fleet could be obtained from Leeds Branch.

I never found out the hierarchy of the others, nor did any opportunity to pursue events through the Milton Keynes HQ ever arise, and have no knowledge of any further Branch code alterations that would inevitably have followed. It was understood that when the 'Hub-and-Spoke' areas were originally set up the existing Branch codes would not be altered as they no longer indicted attachment to any particular regional company and were now parts of a nationwide network. However, there would have been further additions and deletions.

Our late colleague, Michael Houle, was probably the only person who would have had details of events after 1991. From snippets that he made available we learnt that the next two Areas to be set up, in December 1991, were the 'North' with Hub at Tees-side and the 'Manchester' with Hub at Trafford Park. All areas were fully converted by July 1992. Numerous areas were subsequently combined and, for example, 'S West' and 'S Wales' areas were all combined with the 'Avon' area and jointly controlled from Bristol. A further development was to concentrate the operation of Truck Rental fleets in each area on the Hub centres, which resulted in wholesale renumbering of all such vehicles during 1992. Trailer Rental fleets were then placed under HQ control and located at strategic sites, often in adjoining areas to where they had previously operated necessitating still further fleet renumbering.

In October 1993 a new managing director was appointed with responsibility for 'UK Transport and Logistics, NFC', the remit being to oversee the integration of all BRS and Exel logistics work and administer the combined business. In the event, this resulted in the absorption of much BRS work within the Exel organisation, though this was a gradual, almost insidious, process which scarcely received our attention while it took place throughout 1994 and 1995. Indeed, BRS was successful in gaining some large new Contract Hire deals during 1994, including one with Hall & Co (formerly part of the RMC Group) with vehicles based at 60 locations in the South and South West, and several Town Councils. So all appeared to be going well. However, this year also saw the Truck Rental fleet reorganised yet again, by bulk renumbering exercises, to operate from just four centres – at Birmingham Bristol, Kings Cross and Leeds only – Kings Cross now responsible for all East Anglian activities and Leeds for all those as far away as Scotland, while the Trailer Rental fleet was concentrated on Trafford Park, into whose numbering sequence all such trailers were now renumbered in a series that attained TCLK2331, which bore little relation to the actual fleet strength, now reducing as there had been little investment in the service since 1988 and much of the equipment was now nearing the end of its lease period.

1995 saw the closure of selected Branches and transfer of their remaining work to nearby locations and by the end of that year 'O' licences carried by many vehicles were lettered 'NFC UK Ltd' rather than 'BRS Ltd', confirming the transformation of BRS into Exel was nearing completion. In the event, Exel appears to have absorbed mainly work that would involve retaining staff within the NFC family, i.e. with-driver contracts and what little general haulage remained, leaving just Truck Rental and 'driver-excluded' contract work to be administered by BRS. What happened to the Trailer Rental fleet and the AA-BRS Rescue network was never established, while the Engineering fleets presumably passed to Exel as part of the overall service.

During 1996 the allocation of fleet numbers to new vehicles on the remaining BRS fleet was discontinued. As observed above, Contract Hire agreements had been of two types for many years: 'Complete with Driver' (termed CD, later TC) or 'Excluding Driver' (XD, later TX) and, with the allocation of Cost Centre codes to each Branch, vehicles now began to be recognised by the Cost Centre code plus code TC or TX indicating contract type, followed by a five-figure contract number. Fleet numbers were now only raised for inter-branch transfers of existing vehicles. In effect they had become 'Asset numbers' in latter years and were raised for such items as tail-lifts and spare bodies as well as powered vehicles and, furthermore, to the casual observer the discontinuation of fleet numbers went unnoticed as few, if any, vehicles now carried external fleet numbers anyway. It was my experience in the north of England that few Contracts vehicles carried numbers inside the cabs either, as they were supposed to do, while Rental vehicles never did.

No new vehicles joined the fleet from P-registration onwards (August 1996) and, indeed, there had been instances where second-hand vehicles were purchased to augment a particular Branch's requirements in backing up Contract work. By 1997 only a small number of Hub-and-Spoke Areas remained, following further Branch closures and mergers of Areas. Indeed the NFC's Accounts for 1998 report that 62 sites had been closed during the previous 12 months but this is probably throughout the NFC and not solely due to BRS contraction.

In May 1998 the final BRS Hub Offices were closed and the remaining business, covering Truck Rental and certain driver-excluded contract services, was purchased by Volvo Trucks to operate as an independent company titled 'BRS Truck Rental' within their organisation. This was now simply a registered company name and nothing to do with the 'British Road Services' organisation to which the initials had always referred; and so our beloved BRS fleet was effectively finished. A new logo, incorporating single lower-case lettering for the 'brs' emblem instead of the previous interlinked herring-bone motif, was duly introduced for this fleet.

Exel was a difficult fleet for the observer to follow as it functioned in so many different sections and failed to adopt a fleet numbering system after SPD's metal plate numbers were discontinued, so there was no continuity here; and Volvo Trucks inherited a Rental fleet whose fleet numbering system had already been discontinued, with no need to introduce another. As the enthusiasts' interest in BRS had always been to follow the fleet numbering systems used, nothing was left for us to pursue in these new operators. All we have left is our collection of nearly fifty years of historical records to process at leisure, while Michael is the only one who would have knowledge of any further Branch code amendments over the final six years since 1991.

To those attempting to follow the fate of particular former BRS vehicles once Exel had assumed responsibility for most of the fleet in 1995/96, this was further hampered in February 2000 when the Exel Logistics business and that of the Ocean Group were merged. Ocean Transport & Trading, to give it its full name, had substantial marine and shipping interests as well as a transport division, latterly entitled McGregor Cory Cargo Services, (largely based upon the former business of Robertson, Buckley & Co of Liverpool, to which the Henry Long Group in Bradford had been added, following its acquisition in 1974). A separate company Cory Distribution Services, which included the business of Archbold Storage Ltd, taken over in 1970, had by coincidence passed from The Ocean Group to SPD in 1982, before the NFC took SPD under its wing from January 1st 1985.

Surprisingly, although NFC and Ocean proposed the combined business as an equally-owned partnership, it was to trade under the name 'Exel plc' following the merger.

This Group was then acquired by Deutsche Post in September 2005 and merged into their operations, trading under the DHL brand name, so completing the elimination of Exel and BRS before it. The DHL business (the initials of Dalsey, Hillblom & Lynn) had been acquired by Deutsche Post two years previously and the addition of the Exel business created the world's largest logistics company. Sadly, it failed to adopt any form of fleet numbering for its fleet and, as a result, holds little interest to the enthusiast.

9

BRS Parcels 1955-56

As observed at various points during the earlier allocation of Group codes used by BRS, control of all the Parcels Groups passed to a new company, BRS (Parcels) Ltd, that had been set up specifically with a view to disposing of the entire parcels network as a going concern during denationalisation. It was registered in September 1954 to become operational from January 1st 1955. The company continued to operate in the same eight geographical regions as those established by BRS, though they were now termed 'Areas' and the former Groups were now termed 'Branches'. They retained the same BRS-style fleet numbers but now preceded by the letter 'P' signifying the new ownership. They continued to report through the same lines of management to BRS Divisional level but as the BRS network was reduced from eight to six Divisions early in 1955, two of the Parcels Areas became responsible to other Divisions, which necessitated altering the colours of the BTC crest roundels in the vehicle livery.

Under the summary of BRS Group codes the Groups that passed to BRS (Parcels) Ltd have already been mentioned. For convenience they are now repeated together below for ease of reference:

South Eastern Area (A) reporting to S E Division:
Crest colour initially royal blue, but revised to Road Haulage green on adoption of new crest design in 1956

       P33A – Metropolitan smalls
       P34A – City Area Parcels
       P35A – Parcels – South of Thames (continued to be lettered P34A)
       P36A – Parcels – North of Thames (continued to be lettered P34A)
       P37A – Shipping, Trunk Pool and Cartage (continued to be lettered P34A)

Scottish Area (B) reporting to Scottish Division:
Crest colour remained Traffic Blue

    P6B – Aberdeen
    P25B – Dundee
    P41B – Edinburgh
    P61B – Glasgow

North Western Area (C) reporting to NW Division:
Crest colour remained Sea Green

    P9C – Liverpool
    P20C – Lancaster
    P63C – Manchester

North Eastern Area (D) reporting to NE Division:
Crest colour remained Road Haulage Red

    P10D – Tyne/Tees
    P29D – Leeds, York and East Riding
    P50D – West Riding (formed 1.1.55)
    P67D – South Yorkshire

Midland Area (E) reporting to Midland Division:
Crest colour originally Nut Brown, revised to Turquoise upon introduction of new BTC crest in 1956

    P7E – Birmingham
    P42E – Leicester
    P43E – Northants
    P60E – Nottingham

South Western Area (F) now without the S W Division to report to, this now reported to S E Division, which initially required a change in BTC crest colour from Road Haulage Green to Royal Blue, but the colour reverted to Road Haulage Green when the new crest was adopted in 1956

    P7F – Bristol
    P25F – Eastleigh
    P83F – Exeter

Western Area (G) as there was no specific Parcels Groups in this BRS Division, selected vehicles and depots were taken from the existing network to establish a parcels service. It continued to report to BRS Western Division, with crest colour initially Lead Grey, amended to Deep Cream when the new crest was introduced in 1956

    P2G – bases at Cardiff, Newport and Cheltenham (the former Carter Paterson Western Unit)

P20G – base at Skewen
P31G – base at Welshpool
P42G – section of Hereford depot separated for Parcels work
P44G – base at Oxford, Ferry Hinksey Road

Eastern Area (H) with no BRS Eastern Division to report to, this now reported to S E Division which required a change in crest colour from Turquoise to Royal Blue. A further change in crest colour, to Road Haulage Green, came with the new crest adopted in 1956.

P8H – 'Eastern Parcels', centred on Norwich

While a small quantity of individual Parcels depots was sold during de-nationalisation, no acceptable tender was received for the entire business and the BTC was obliged to retain it, contrary to the intention of the Disposals process, thereby further increasing the eventual size of the 'Retained Fleet' when de-nationalisation was terminated in September 1956.

10

BRS (Parcels) Ltd 1956-64

Some adjustments to Branch codes were made to the 'Retained Parcels' fleet from 1957, many demonstrating the close link between the Parcels company and the existing general haulage fleet and a complete listing of the retained Branches and depots can now be shown as follows:

South Eastern Area

The same Branch codes were retained:

P33A Metropolitan – depots at Waterden Road, Epworth Street, Welwyn Garden City, Seward Street, Coppetts Road, Richardson Street, Mandrell Road
P34A City – Macclesfield Road, Whitecross Street
P35A South of Thames – Willow Walk, Surbiton, Croydon, Brighton, Eastbourne, Eltham, Tunbridge Wells, Margate, Chatham, Canterbury
P36A North of Thames – Acton, Slough, High Wycombe, Harrow, Southend, Stratford, Tottenham, Chelsea
P37A Shipping – Central Street

Codes P35A-P37A remained non-existent; all vehicles were lettered P34A

Head Office was at Goswell Road, London EC1, later relocated to City Road. All new vehicles continued to be registered by S E Division, including those for the Parcels Area. Batches of registration numbers, usually of 100, were obtained from the London council and issued jointly to General, Contracts or Parcels vehicles as required. After September 1957, S E Division also assumed responsibility for licensing new vehicles in the Eastern and Southern Parcels Areas as well (see below):

Scottish Area

The Dundee Branch (P25B) had been wound up and split between

Aberdeen and Edinburgh in 1955. From 1957 the Aberdeen Branch retained the code P6B but the others were given consecutive codes to match:

P6B Aberdeen – depots at Aberdeen, Elgin, Inverness, also Dundee and Perth (ex P25B)
P7B Edinburgh (ex P41B) – Edinburgh, Earlston, also Methil (formerly P25B)
P8B Glasgow (ex P61B) – Glasgow, Ayr

Area office, initially at Portman Street, Glasgow later relocated to Hope Street. Exactly as for BRS Ltd, whilst vehicles were administered from the Area Office, vehicle registrations were raised by the BRS Divisional Workshops at Linlithgow, from West Lothian CC, as this was where new vehicles were prepared for service. Batches of registration numbers were at first shared jointly with BRS Ltd but in later years the Parcels company obtained its own blocks of numbers.

North Western Area

The BRS Districts having now been numbered in series 1C-3C the Parcels Area Branches were duly given new codes P4C-P6C:

P4C Manchester (ex P63C) – White City, Mayfield, Radium Street, Macclesfield, Belfast
P5C Liverpool (ex P9C) – Vulcan Street, Great Howard St, Lightbody Street, Lower Milk Street, Seacombe
P6C Lancaster (ex P20C) – Burnley, Bamber Bridge, Blackburn, Carlisle, Lancaster

Area Office was at 74 Corporation Street, Manchester. Each Branch of the N W Area, however, was responsible for its own vehicle licensing through the Branch Offices – at Manchester, Old Trafford used the Lancs CC authority, at Liverpool the local city authority and at Lancaster, Burnley CBC. From January 1st 1963 the Manchester Branch began to use Manchester CBC rather than Lancs CC and, from mid-1963, new vehicles for all three Branches were being administered from the Area Office and registered from Manchester.

North Eastern Area

The same Branch codes were retained in this Area:

P10D Tyne/Tees – Gateshead, Stockton, Hartlepool, Darlington
P29D Leeds, York & East Riding – Whitehall Road, Brown Lane, Fleece Lane, Grant Mount, all in Leeds plus Hull
P50D West Riding – Wakefield Road and Legrams Lane in Bradford; Milnsbridge and Nile Street both in Huddersfield; Dewsbury, Halifax, Ripponden
P67D South Yorkshire – Penistone Road and Worthing Road in Sheffield; Newark, Scunthorpe

Area Office was at 57 Clarendon Road, Leeds. The majority

of registrations in the north east were raised in blocks by the Divisional HQ from Leeds CBC and used by both the haulage and the Parcels fleets, as required from 1957 onwards. However, high proportions of parcels vehicles, particularly in the Tyne/Tees and South Yorkshire Branches, had been registered locally at Gateshead and Sheffield during 1955 and 1956 and the use of local authority centres continued to be the norm in the west Riding Branch both before and after 1956, with registrations obtained from Bradford, Halifax, Huddersfield and Dewsbury.

Midland Area

Like North Western Area, Midland Area chose this opportunity to follow the new odes 1E-6E with a Parcels series P7E-P10E, with the following results:

> **P7E** Birmingham (no change) – Walter Street, Vauxhall and South Yardley, all in Birmingham, plus Willenhall (Staffs) and Coventry
> **P8E** Leicester (ex P42E) – Belgrave Road, Gipsy Lane, Great Northern, all in Leicester, plus Burbage nr Hinckley
> **P9E** Northants (ex P43E) – Rushden, Compton Road & Croyland Road, both in Wellingborough, Northampton, Rothwell, Bedford, Luton
> **P10E** Nottingham (ex P60E) – Nottingham, Derby, Stoke

Area Office was set up at London Road, Leicester which was responsible for raising all new registrations from Leicester CBC from early 1956 onwards. Prior to this they had been raised by the BRS Divisional Office at Birmingham. Leicester continued to be used for all new registrations and indeed in February 1964, when the further renumbering exercise was due to be introduced, an extensive vehicle replacement programme was under way with particularly large quantities of new vehicles coming on fleet, many still unknown.

South Western Area

The existing Branch codes were retained:

> **P7F** Bristol – Bristol, Yeovil
> **P25F** Eastleigh – Southampton, Bournemouth, Southampton Docks Office
> **P83F** Exeter – Exeter, Plymouth

Area Office originally at Bournemouth relocated to Bristol (Albert Road) after September 1957. Until this time vehicles continued to be licensed from the Bournemouth Office using Bournemouth CBC as they had done for the entire former South Western Division since 1952.

After September 1957, on transfer of the S W Area from S E Division control to Western Division, an unusual situation arose whereby, although the Area Office was now Bristol, vehicles continued to be licensed from

Bournemouth CBC for the network (now comprising Bristol, Exeter and Oxford but not Eastleigh, as explained later). Presumably it was felt unnecessary to interfere with existing procedure.

Western Area

The interim codes derived from the former BRS Groups were standardised from 1957 onwards but unusually, rather than introduce codes concurrent with the new BRS Ltd codes 1G-6G they chose to introduce codes more reminiscent of the pre-1956 Group series such as 20G+, 40G+ Accordingly new codes were as follows (still un-named):

P60G (ex P2G) – Cardiff, Newport, Cheltenham
P61G (ex P20G) – Skewen
P62G – Welshpool (ex P31G), Hereford (ex P42G)
P63G (ex P44G) – Oxford

Area Office was established at Queen Street, Cardiff. During 1955 vehicles continued to be licensed at local level by the appropriate Branch. Thus at Cardiff, Newport and Cheltenham, Cardiff CBC was used; at Skewen, Swansea CBC; at Welshpool, Montgomery CC; at Hereford, the local authority; at Oxford, the local city council. From 1956 onwards the responsibility for licensing passed to the Area Office and from that time onwards all were registered from Cardiff until 1964 .

Eastern Area

The single existing code was retained:

P8H 'Eastern Parcels' – Surrey Street and Mountergate Street, both in Norwich; Ipswich, Cambridge, Chelmsford, Clacton, Kings Lynn, Boston

Area Office was at Surrey Street, Norwich. New vehicle registrations were raised by the Area Office from Norwich CBC until September 1957, the time of formation of the new (ninth) Southern Parcels Area. After this time new registrations for both the Eastern and the Southern Areas began to be raised through the S E Divisional HQ in London and Norwich CBC ceased to be used.

With regard to the BRS (Parcels) Ltd fleet in general, unlike the BRS Ltd fleet which had required complete renumbering following massive reduction during de-nationalisation, the Parcels fleet had remained almost unchanged in size with still around 4400 vehicles. Consequently the existing fleet numbers remained in use, subject only to altering some of the Branch codes as outlined above.

Subsequent Amendments

In September 1957 a ninth Parcels Area was added to the network by forming a new 'Southern Area' merging the Eastleigh Branch (now renamed 'Southampton') from the South Western Area with six Home Counties Branches from the South Eastern Area. Given the new Area letter 'J', the network became:

P25J – Southampton, Bournemouth and Docks Office (ex P25F)
P26J – Brighton ('ex non-existent' P35A)
P27J – Eastbourne (ex 'non-existent' P35A)
P28J – Tunbridge Wells (ex 'non-existent' P35A)
P29J – Margate (ex 'non-existent' P35A)
P30J – Chatham (ex 'non-existent' P35A)
P31J – Canterbury (ex 'non-existent' P35A)

The old P25F numbers were retained and simply recoded P25J, the series having attained around P25F180 by this time. New vehicles took the series to P25J192 and the Home Counties Branches vehicles were given new numbers following on from this point, in Branch-by-Branch order, from P26J193 to P31J267. The series then continued from this point, all Branches using this joint sequence.

This new Area reported to BRS S E Division and the appropriate BTC crest colour therefore remained 'Road Haulage Green'. Area Office was retained at Bournemouth (the former S W Area Office) but all new vehicle registrations were raised by the S E Division HQ in London, in the same blocks of numbers as those used by Haulage, Contracts and Parcels vehicles already.

The boundary of the South Western Parcels Area was adjusted at the same time by transferring Oxford Branch in from the Western Area which was duly recoded from P63G to P63F. Responsibility for the South Western Area, now comprising P7F, P63F and P83F (P25F having gone to the Southern Area) passed to BRS Western Division, necessitating a change in BTC crest colour from Road Haulage Green to Deep Cream.

Other amendments to the Parcels network from 1957 onwards are detailed below, Area by Area:

South Eastern

P33A – Richardson Street depot finished 1958
P36A – Southend transferred to Eastern Area P8H in 1958. Also Paddington depot reintroduced having previously been vacated in 1956

In August 1959 the remaining Branches were reorganised into a new 'London Area' and completely new Branch codes and fleet numbers were raised for the entire fleet which did away with the unwieldy former

Carter Paterson numbers in four- and five-figure series. The new network was now as follows:

P38A City & Suburban – Macclesfield Road, Whitecross Street, Surbiton, Croydon, Eltham, Harrow, Stratford, Tottenham, Chelsea, Slough, High Wycombe
P39A Shipping – Central Street
P40A North West London – Coppetts Road, Acton, Paddington
P41A North East London – Waterden Road, Seward Street, Welwyn Garden City, Epworth Street, Mandrell Road
P42A South London – Willow Walk

Early in 1961 Acton depot was transferred from P40A to P38A.

Rationalisation and vacation of selected sites resulted in several other closures: P38A lost Whitecross Street in 1961; P40A lost Paddington in 1962; P41A lost Mandrell Road at the end of 1959, then Epworth Street and Welwyn, both in 1961 and, finally, Seward Street in 1962, leaving just the Waterden Road site.

The business of N Francis & Co Ltd, Dalston, with a 97-vehicle fleet, was acquired by the BTC in 1960 and attached to the London Area of BRS (Parcels) Ltd, continuing to trade as an independent subsidiary.

Scottish (B)

P6B – During 1958 the bases at Dundee and Perth were transferred to Edinburgh Branch (P7B)
P7B – By 1963 the depot at Methil had been relocated to Kirkcaldy

North Western (C)

P4C – The Belfast depot was transferred to the control of P6C in 1958
P5C – In Liverpool the depot at Lower Milk Street was closed in 1958. All other Liverpool depots were closed in 1960 after purpose-built new premises were opened in Townsend Lane. A new sub-depot was opened at Colwyn Bay during 1963
P6C – The Bamber Bridge depot was renamed 'Preston' but by 1961 had relocated to Leyland. The Blackburn depot had closed by 1963

The company Wm Cooper & Sons Ltd, Prestatyn, was acquired by the THC in October 1965. The 21-vehicle fleet was allowed to continue trading as an independent member of the Parcels grouping, attached to N W Area.

North Eastern (D)

P10D – Following the earlier closure of the Hartlepool depot, the fleets at Stockton and Darlington were combined during 1960 and relocated to new premises at Middlesbrough
P29D – The Leeds depot at Grant Mount closed in 1959 and Fleece Lane closed in 1960
P50D – The Dewsbury depot was closed to BRS (Parcels) Ltd traffic and made over to BRS Ltd. Parcels work at Legrams Lane in Bradford was similarly terminated, the work passing to Wakefield Road in 1958, following which Legrams Lane also returned to BRS Ltd. The Ripponden depot was closed in 1958.
P67D – A new site at Boston was added in 1957, transferred in from Eastern Area (P8H)

The Sheffield site at Worthing Rd was relocated to Langsett Rd in 1960 but later closed.
The Newark and Scunthorpe depots were closed, the work passing to a new site at Lincoln in 1959

Several additional Branch codes were introduced by N E Area in successive years:

P4D – Introduced from Jan 1st 1959 upon formation of a new 'West Riding District' of BRS Ltd, coded 4D to which Parcels activities were also attached. Existing vehicles at Bradford, the two sites in Huddersfield and Halifax, were altered from P50D to P4D and, unusually, General and Parcels vehicles added after this date were jointly administered and numbered in the same series. The depot at Nile Street, Huddersfield, had closed by 1963

P11D – Middlesbrough, new Branch separated from Tyne/Tees (P10D) approximately June 1961

P12D – Lincoln, new Branch separated from South Yorkshire (P67D) in September 1961

P13D – Boston, also separated from South Yorkshire (P67D) in September 1961

P14D – Hull, new Branch separated from Leeds, York & East Riding (P29D) in September 1961

P15D – York, new service set up from January 1962

Midland (E)

P8E – The depot at Burbage was closed by 1960

P9E – The Compton Road depot in Wellingborough had also closed by 1960

As in the N E Area, numerous new Branch codes were introduced as selected depots were separated from their parents and set up as individual Branches. They were given codes from P12E onwards, code 11E being unavailable as it had already been used by BRS Ltd for its new Birmingham Contracts District series C11E

P12E – Coventry, separated from Birmingham (P7E) approximately February 1961

P13E – Stoke, separated from Nottingham (P10E) June 1961

P14E – Northampton, separated from Northants (P9E) June 1961

P15E – Wolverhampton, retitled ex-Willenhall, separated from Birmingham (P7E) Dec 1961

P16E – Derby, separated from Nottingham (P10E) December 1961

P17E – Bedford, separated from Northants (P9E) December 1961

P18E – Luton, separated from Northants (P9E) December 1961

South Western (F)

P63F – A second site was introduced at Reading in 1959 and a third at Swindon in 1963

P83F – A new base at Perranporth was opened in 1958

The company James Express Carriers Ltd at Bristol, with a 90-vehicle fleet and a network of about a dozen depots in the south west, was acquired by the THC in June 1965. It continued to trade as an independent member of the Parcels grouping within the S W Area.

Western (G)

P61G – A second base at Carmarthen was introduced in 1961

Eastern (H)

P8H – The Boston depot was transferred to South Yorkshire Branch of the N E Area during 1957. The Southend depot was added during 1958, transferred in from S E Area. The Mountergate depot in Norwich had closed by 1963

Southern (J)

P25J – Additional bases were opened at Portsmouth and Salisbury in 1958. The office at Southampton Docks received no further mention after 1961
P29J – Margate Branch was closed in 1963

11

BRS Parcels Ltd 1964-76

With the passing of BRS (Parcels) Ltd to the THC, following the winding-up of the BTC in 1963, new fleet numbering was introduced, just as had been the case with the BRS general haulage and contracts fleets. But a completely different coding system was adopted for the network from February 1964. Instead of alphabetical District letters, as used by BRS Ltd, the Parcels Areas adopted simply an individual number of each Branch, plus their own abbreviated Area identification letters, as detailed below. Branch codes were 1-98, following which the first new Branch to be opened (Bridgwater in the S W Area) was given the number 99. After this any further new Branches received numbers within the series that had been vacated by earlier closures.

London Area
Area Office remained in London, responsible for all new registrations from London CBC and, later, from the GLC from January 1966 and then the Central London LVLC from September 1974.

1LN – N W London (Coppetts Road) ex P40A
2LN – N E London (Waterden Road) ex P41A
3LN – S London (Willow Walk) ex P42A
4LN – City (Macclesfield Road) ex P38A
5LN – Shipping (Central Street) ex P39A
6LN – Surbiton ex P38A
7LN – Croydon ex P38A
8LN – Eltham ex P38A
9LN – Stratford ex P38A
10LN – Tottenham ex P38A
11LN – Harrow ex P38A
12LN – Acton ex P38A
13LN – High Wycombe ex P38A
14LN – Slough ex P38A
15LN – Chelsea ex P38A

Code 16 was not used then but was eventually raised for a new Branch 16LN titled 'London Airport' which relocated to new premises at Heathrow Cargo Centre in May 1973. Harrow (11LN) and Chelsea (15LN) were closed and the premises disposed of during 1972. The Hackney Branch (2LN), formerly the base of the famous Bouts Tillotson company, also closed. N Francis continued to function as an independent company within London Area control.

Scottish Area

Head Office Glasgow, which began to raise all new vehicle registrations from Glasgow CBC from 1971 onwards, a notable change in policy.

17SC – Glasgow ex P8B	22SC – Dundee ex P7B
18SC – Ayr ex P8B	23SC – Perth ex P7B
19SC – Edinburgh ex P7B	24SC – Aberdeen ex P6B
20SC – Earlston ex P7B	25SC – Elgin ex P6B
21SC – Kirkcaldy ex P7B	26SC – Inverness ex P6B

Ayr traded as a sub-depot of Glasgow, Perth a sub to Dundee and Elgin and Inverness as subs to Aberdeen and the sub-depot codes 18, 23, 25 and 26 were only used for a short time; vehicles later resorted to use of their main Branches' codes. Pruning of small sites had resulted in the closure of both Elgin and Inverness by mid-1972.

North Western Area

The Area Office in Manchester continued to raise all new registrations from Manchester CBC.

27NW – Liverpool ex P5C	33NW – Belfast ex P6C
28NW – Colwyn Bay ex P5C	34NW – Burnley ex P6C
29NW – Mayfield ex P4C	35NW – Preston ex P6C
30NW – White City ex P4C	36NW – Lancaster ex P6C
31NW – Radium Street ex P4C	37NW – Carlisle ex P6C
32NW – Macclesfield ex P4C	

Code 38 was voided and never used

The Macclesfield vehicles were only lettered 32NW for a short time. As a sub-depot to White City the fleet came under direct control from Manchester and is believed to have closed shortly afterwards. The Belfast depot (33NW) was transferred to the control of the Ulster Transport Authority in 1965. The Lancaster depot (36NW) was closed in 1972 and Mayfield (29NW) in 1971. Wm Cooper & Sons continued its separate existence at Prestatyn, controlled by the NW Area.

North Eastern Area

Head Office remained at Leeds and was still responsible for raising all new registrations.

39NE – Leeds, Whitehall Road ex P29D	46NE – Newcastle ex P10D

40NE – Leeds, Brown Lane ex P29D
41NE – York ex P15D
42NE – Hull ex P14D
43NE – Bradford ex P4D
44NE – Halifax ex P4D
45NE – Huddersfield ex P4D
47NE – Middlesbrough ex P11D
48NE – Sheffield ex P67D
49NE – Lincoln ex P12D
50NE – Boston ex P13D

The code 39NE was never activated – the premises at Whitehall Road were vacated and all Leeds vehicles centred on Brown Lane before the new network became functional. It remained unused.

The Halifax Branch (44NE) was closed in 1967 following the opening of new premises in Bradford, to which the existing fleets of both 43NE and 44NE were relocated, retaining the 43NE code. Most of Huddersfield's vehicles (45NE) were later also transferred to the Bradford site and recoded 43NE. A small residual service remaining at Huddersfield was retitled 'Transpennine Parcels' and given the vacant code 44NE in March 1971. This service was later discontinued in 1975.

The Hull depot relocated from Reform Street to new premises adjoining the BRS Ltd depot in Leads Road in August 1968.

Midland Area

The Area Office at Leicester continued to raise all new registrations from Leicester CBC.

51M – Nottingham ex P10E
52M – Derby ex P16E
53M – Stoke ex P13E
54M – Wolverhampton ex P15E
55M – Walter Street, Birmingham ex P7E
56M – Vauxhall ex P7E
57M – South Yardley ex P7E
58M – Coventry ex P12E
59M – Belgrave Road, Leicester ex P8E
60M – Gipsy Lane, Leicester ex P8E
61M – Gt Northern, Leicester ex P8E
62M – Rothwell ex P9E
63M – Rushden ex P9E
64M – Wellingborough ex P9E
65M – Northampton ex P14E
66M – Bedford ex P17E
67M – Luton ex P18E

In Birmingham the Vauxhall depot closed in 1966 leaving code 56M vacant. Later, when the South Yardley depot closed (57M) and was relocated to Droitwich, this new Branch took the vacant code 56M in July 1968.

In Leicester the Great Northern Branch closed in 1968, leaving code 61M vacant. A new service introduced for a short time at Groby, Leics, was given this vacant code 61M. Later, in 1968, the remaining Leicester depots at Belgrave Road and Gipsy Lane were relocated to new premises in Western Boulevard which took the code 59M, leaving 60M vacant.

The Branches at Rothwell and Rushden were also closed, leaving codes 62M and 63M vacant.

South Western Area

The Area Office at Bristol became responsible for all new registrations for the first time and the old procedure of using Bournemouth CBC for new vehicle licensing was discontinued.

68SW – Oxford ex P63F
69SW – Reading ex P63F
70SW – Bristol ex P7F
71SW – Yeovil ex P7F

72SW – Exeter ex P83F
73SW – Plymouth ex P83F
74SW – Perranporth ex P83F
75SW – Swindon ex P63F

The first new depot to be opened after the schedule of codes was drawn up, at Bridgwater, was given the code 99SW in 1966. James Express Carriers continued to operate independently under the control of the S W Parcels Area.

Western Area

Area Office at Cardiff continued to raise all new vehicle registrations from Cardiff CBC.

76W – Welshpool ex P62G
77W – Cheltenham ex P60G
78W – Hereford ex P62G
79W – Newport ex P60G

80W – Cardiff ex P60G
81W – Skewen ex P61G
82W – Carmarthen ex P61G

77W was relocated from Cheltenham to Gloucester and renamed.
The Skewen depot moved to new premises late in 1971.

Eastern Area

The Area Office at Norwich became responsible for raising all new vehicle registrations from Norwich CBC. It no longer reported to the old BRS S E Division, this level of management having now been discontinued.

83E – Cambridge ex P8H
84E – Norwich ex P8H
85E – Kings Lynn ex P8H
86E – Ipswich ex P8H

87E – Clacton ex P8H
88E – Chelmsford ex P8H
89E – Southend ex P8H

The depot at Clacton was closed shortly afterwards, leaving code 87E vacant. The Ipswich depot relocated to new premises in Hadleigh Road in October 1970

Southern Area

Area Office at Bournemouth, no longer reporting to BRS S E Division, began raising new vehicle registrations for this Area but ceased doing so for the South Western Area at the same time, as observed on the previous page.

90S – Southampton ex P25J
91S – Bournemouth ex P25J

94S – Brighton   ex P26J
95S – Eastbourne ex P27J

92S – Salisbury ex P25J
93S – Portsmouth ex P25J
96S – Tunbridge Wells ex P28J

97S – Chatham ex P30J
98S – Canterbury ex P31J

At 92S the Branch was relocated to, and renamed, Basingstoke in October 1970

Four of the new Areas (Scottish, NW, NE and Western) chose this opportunity to assign completely new series of fleet numbers from No.1 upwards – these were now joint series for the entire Area, only the Branch codes varying, unlike BRS Ltd which instead raised numbers from 1 upwards at each Branch. The other five Areas simply retained the earlier numbers and altered the Branch codes, thereby permitting a variety of former series to continue in use. Midland Area then erred by commencing series numbered from 1 upwards for new vehicles at each of their Branches from 1964 onwards, which soon caused great difficulty in the event of later inter-Branch transfers occurring; they later reverted to a further new joint series covering all Branches.

Over succeeding years a number of adjustments were made to the Parcels company and its fleets, some of which affected fleet numbering while others caused no alteration. In October 1964 the company was retitled BRS Parcels Ltd, now without the brackets, in an attempt to signify that it was now an independent company in its own right and not simply a subsidiary of BRS Ltd as the brackets might have implied. This had no effect on vehicle numbering.

Reference has already been made briefly to the Holding Company, British Express Carriers Ltd and this is an opportune point at which to outline its significance in greater detail. As will be seen, its member companies all became involved with the Parcels network in later years. Initially set up in September 1968 its remit was to co-ordinate all the THC's parcels interests which, at this time, comprised BRS Parcels Ltd, its three subsidiaries N Francis, Wm Cooper and James Express, the Tayforth Parcels Division and also the British Rail sundries road fleet which was due to come under the wing of the new National Freight corporation set up by the Government to acquire all THC activities from January 1st 1969.

The Tayforth Parcels Division, acquired by the THC along with their Haulage Division in August 1965 comprised the following companies:

Scottish Parcel Carriers – at Glasgow and Aberdeen, plus subsidiary Robert Ower Ltd, Dundee
Watsons (Carriers) Ltd of Spennymoor
H S Morgan (Transport) Ltd of Southampton, later moving to Eastleigh
Hanson Haulage Ltd, with bases at Huddersfield, Pudsey, Liverpool and London and which had only been acquired by Tayforth a few months earlier, in January 1965. It is not to be confused with the separate company Hanson Transport Ltd, also of Huddersfield, which was engaged mainly in Contract Hire work for ICI and remained in the Hanson family's ownership
Bridges Transport Ltd with two depots in Preston plus other sites at Liverpool and Salford. This was attached to the Tayforth Parcels grouping after its acquisition by the THC in April 1966

The British Rail sundries fleet, meanwhile, was given the name National Carriers Ltd from January 1st 1969. Much of its work was in the same domain as that of BRS Parcels and the sudden addition of a fleet of 10,000 vehicles and 26,000 trailers, with a 200-depot network, virtually in direct competition, was clearly not good news. Even after separating certain specialist activities as Contract Hire and dedicated distribution services for such companies as Marks & Spencer and Woolworths, an 80-depot network with over 6000 vehicles still existed in 1979 and much rationalisation of both companies' activities was necessary to avoid wasteful duplication of resources in efforts to return either business to profitability.

A further business attached to the British Express Carriers grouping in 1971 was that of Tartan Arrow Ltd which had originally been acquired by the THC in August 1966 and allowed to trade as yet another direct subsidiary. This had been a specialist service offering long-haul services by rail, with railhead distribution at its two terminals in London and Glasgow. The London base was in Kentish Town and had one subsidiary, Deans Transport Ltd of Tottenham. The Glasgow base also had a subsidiary, A Ritchie Ltd, and a sub-depot at Edinburgh.

A major change to affect the BRS Parcels fleet occurred in 1972 when the nine Parcels Areas were reduced to seven and the Area Offices at Bristol and Norwich were closed. The former Midland Area Office at Leicester became responsible for all former Eastern Area Branches and after losing five Branches in the West Midlands to the North Western Area at the same time, was retitled 'Eastern Area'. It also took responsibility for two N E Area Branches in Lincolnshire. In the South West, control of all Branches passed to the Western Area at Cardiff while one Western Branch, at Welshpool, passed to N W Area.

North Western Area:	Add 53NW, 54NW, 55NW, 56NW, 58NW – ex Midland Area And add Branch 76NW ex Western Area
New 'Eastern Area' (Leicester control):	Recode 51E, 52E, 59E, 61E, 64E, 65E, 66E, 67E – ex Midland Area Add 83E, 84E, 85E, 86E, 88E, 89E – former Norwich control Add 49E, 50E – ex N E Area
Western Area:	Add 68W, 69W, 70W, 71W, 72W, 73W, 74W, 75W, 99W – ex S W Area

Following this reorganisation, further adjustments continued to occur. In the new Eastern Area, Groby (61E) was closed and in the enlarged Western Area, Yeovil (71W) also closed.

The business of James Express Carriers was closed on December 31st 1973, with vehicles being absorbed into other Parcels Branches. Many of them ended up in the Midlands, in Eastern Area's control: several of the larger Bedford boxvans were converted to light recovery units.

In London the three Branches 1LN, 2LN and 3LN had been renamed Muswell Hill, Hackney and Bermondsey respectively from January1st 1966, giving them regional names on a par with all other London area Branches, Hackney closing later as has already been observed. In November 1974 the Eltham depot of London Area (8LN) was relocated to Dartford. Also in London, a new 'Shoppers Express' home delivery service was introduced in 1975, jointly with the GLC, using vehicles in a new orange and white livery based on Lewisham.

A new depot at Barton Dock, Trafford Park, was opened by N W Area in 1975, replacing former sites at White City and Radium Street. It used the code 30NW for both former fleets and was said to be the largest Parcels depot in Europe.

12

ROADLINE (UK) LTD 1976-1987
NATIONAL CARRIERS - ROADLINE 1986-1987
(Including Scottish Parcel Services 1981-1987)

The company was given a new image in February 1976 when its name changed from BRS Parcels Ltd to Roadline (UK) Ltd. This caused no alteration to existing fleet numbering but did result in the introduction of a new brighter green livery with a lower case letter 'r' motif on a yellow ground as a new logo. It was said that prospective customers for either BRS or the Parcels services were still frequently approaching the wrong company and hence a completely new name for the Parcels fleet was required to differentiate between them.

In May 1976 the first new site to be introduced by Roadline was opened in Northampton, replacing older sites at Northampton (65E) and Wellingborough (64E). The new Branch was given the code 60E, code 60 having been vacant since Gipsy Lane closed in 1968.

From 1976 onwards strenuous efforts were made to market Roadline as a high-speed overnight carrier, leaving the sister company National Carriers to deal with routine movements at regular frequencies. At the end of 1976 Roadline's fleet comprised 2200 rigid vehicles plus 900 artic units using 3000 trailers.

The Parcels Areas were renamed 'Regions' from January 1st 1977 and there was a reduction in the number of Regions, from seven to six, by merging the North Western and North Eastern Regions to form a new 'Northern Region' using letter 'N', with HQ at Manchester; the Leeds office was closed. This also caused boundary changes and consequent recoding of Branches again and the 'Midland Region' title was revived for the Branches controlled from Leicester, termed 'Eastern' since 1972, upon regaining the Branches in the West Midlands from the N W Region, which had controlled them from the same time.

The new Northern Region controlled: 27N, 28N, 30N, 34N, 35N and 37N (ex N W) and 40N, 41N, 42N, 43N, 46N, 47N, 48N (ex N E)

The revamped Midland Region controlled: 49M, 50M, 51M, 52M, 59M, 60M, 66M, 67M, 83M, 84M, 85M, 86M, 88M, 89M (all previously 'Eastern') plus 53M, 54M, 55M, 56M, 76M (all ex N W Region)

One success was the opening of a second Branch in Bristol in February 1978 at Feeder Road, augmenting the existing site at Albert Road, following a considerable expansion in Roadline's 'Relay Express' work. It is believed to have been coded 63W though this was never confirmed.

Apart from this, the general trend was for continuing reductions in demand. In April 1979, proposals were put forward to close the Branches at Stratford, London Airport, Slough, Leeds, Kings Lynn, Luton and Newport and, that August, drastic fleet reductions were also proposed for Birmingham, Liverpool and Glasgow, which duly relocated from the large site at Dixons Blazes to the smaller premises at Warroch Street, recently vacated following the closure of SRS' Argyll services.

The Holding Company, British Express Carriers, was dissolved in 1979. There had been further changes in this grouping since its formation in 1968 which should now be outlined. During the early 1970s the two Preston sites of Bridges Transport were relocated to new premises at Leyland and H S Morgan moved to new premises at Eastleigh. A more dramatic reorganisation then occurred, causing the partial demise of Tartan Arrow whose long-haul services had largely become superfluous with the growth in the motorway network and resultant reduction in road journey times. At the London end the subsidiary, Deans Transport, was closed down while, in Scotland, the Edinburgh depot was closed and the Glasgow operations were merged with those of Scottish Parcel Carriers, the resultant new business being given the name North British Carriers.

At the end of 1973 the BRS Parcels subsidiary, Wm Cooper, Prestatyn, was transferred to the control of BEC, retaining the same independence as the existing member of the Group. The final BRS Parcels subsidiary, N Francis of Dalston, followed suit in 1975, having by now extended its coverage to introduce a second base at London Airport. Now within BEC, Francis absorbed the remaining work of Tartan Arrow and the fleets were merged, Francis moving into the Tartan Arrow site at Kentish Town; the London work of Hanson Haulage was also subsequently moved to this site.

Upon dissolution of BEC in 1979 businesses were mostly defined as 'Distribution' rather than 'Parcels' and were therefore transferred to the control of the appropriate BRS companies: Bridges and Wm Cooper to N W BRS; Watsons and Hansons (now based at Pudsey only) to N E BRS; H S Morgan to Western BRS; while N Francis was split between Southern BRS, their base becoming the 'North London Freight

Centre' (which later absorbed the remaining work at Tufnell Park) and Roadline's Bermondsey Branch, which gained several of their vehicles and where a new specialist service carrying valuable goods was established, with code 3LNX. What became of the Scottish subsidiary, North British Carriers, was never resolved – it appears to have ceased operations altogether and many former Scottish Parcel Carriers and Tartan Arrow vehicles later found their way on to the fleets of Bridges Transport and Watsons.

In November 1979 Roadline announced a major restructure of its services by proposing to set up 17 of its 70 remaining Branches as 'Hubs', with other depots feeding into these main centres, and a pilot scheme was introduced using Gloucester as such a 'Hub'.

March 1980 saw the establishment on Jersey of a new subsidiary company for Roadline which had developed steady growth in traffic to this location during the previous two years. It was named Islandlink (Jersey) Ltd – not to be confused with the similarly-named BRS company Islandlink Ltd, the title that had been given to their Isle of Wight Branch.

In December 1980 all the NFC's Scottish activities – Scottish Road Services, Roadline (UK) and National Carriers – were brought together and combined as the 'Scottish Freight Company', effective from January 1st 1981. Plans were announced for the Roadline and National Carriers activities to be combined to form a single new company, Scottish Parcel Services, and by May a new blue and white livery had been introduced for the former Roadline vehicles. Further complicated negotiations with the different unions then followed until, in March 1982, agreement was reached for the merger to go ahead even though it meant combining duplicated depots at Aberdeen, Inverness, Dundee and Edinburgh, though two sites were retained in Glasgow. Former National Carriers vehicles were then repainted. The new company retained links with Roadline in England and continued the existing fleet numbering that had been introduced by BRS (Parcels) Ltd in 1964 but with a revised network now as follows:

175C	Glasgow Anderston – Warroch Street.	Former Roadline fleet moved from Dixons Blazes
185C	Glasgow Distribution – Dixons Blazes	Former NC fleet moved from Sighthill
195C	Edinburgh – Marine Gardens	Former Roadline site. NC site at Brunswick Pl closed
205C	Earlston – Westfield Road	Former Roadline site
215C	Kirkcaldy – Hayfield Ind Estate	Former Roadline site
225C	Dundee – Maryfield Goods Yard	SRS site combining Roadline fleet from East Dock St & NC fleet from South Union St Former NC site,
235C	Inverness – Falcon Square	Roadline site already closed
245C	Aberdeen – Hillview Road, East Tullos	Former NC site. Roadline site at King St closed

Of these locations Kirkcaldy was closed in 1982 and Glasgow Warroch Street in 1983. All Glasgow Services were then combined at Dixons Blazes using the code 17SC, and 18SC was discontinued. By 1986 the Dixons Blazes site had closed (it was duly reoccupied by

Pickfords Ltd) leaving SPS no base in the Western Scotland conurbation except a new service 'Citispeed' based at the SRS depot in Renfrew, the code for which is unknown.

The removal of the Scottish Region left Roadline (UK) Ltd with a network including 15 Hub Centres in England and Wales from 1981. In efforts to improve profitability the number of operating Regions was reduced from five to three by merging the London, Southern and Western Regions to form an enlarged 'Southern Region', at the same time proposing the closure of up to 30 unprofitable Branches including Birmingham, Bournemouth, Eastbourne, Hull, Leicester, Middlesbrough Oxford, Reading and York. By reprieving some of these sites and reorganising others to form a number of 'outstations' not meriting full Branch status, but simply providing back-up to remaining Branches, the proposals were finally accepted.

Further additions to the list of closures included Surbiton, Chatham, Perranporth, Hereford, Droitwich, Nottingham, Lincoln, Liverpool and Preston. This was not a good time for the company. The Cardiff and Bournemouth offices were also closed but a sub-office was introduced at Bristol to aid administration of the newly enlarged Southern Region.

By March 1981 the new streamlined network comprised just 33 Branches – 14 Hubs (excluding Gloucester which had now been downgraded), 17 offering c&d work only and two offering specialist services – plus ten 'outstations'. They can be summarised as follows:

Region	Main (Hub) Branch	Sub-branch (c & d only)	Outstation (c & d back-up)
Northern	46N Newcastle	37N Carlisle	–
	43N Bradford	34N Burnley	–
	30N Manchester	28N Colwyn Bay	–
	48N Sheffield	42N Hull	41N York
Midland	59M Leicester	–	50M Boston 52M Derby
	54M Wolverhampton	53M Stoke 58M Coventry	76M Welshpool
	60M Northampton	68M Oxford 83M Cambridge	13M High Wycombe
	86M Ipswich	84M Norwich 88M Chelmsford	89M Southend
Southern	4S London City	–	–
	1S London Muswell Hill		–
	7S Croydon	94S Brighton	–
	8S Dartford	98S Canterbury	–
	90S Southampton	92S Basingstoke	91S Bournemouth
	70S Bristol	72S Exeter 73S Plymouth 75S Swindon 81S Skewen	77S Gloucester 82S Carmarthen 99S Bridgwater
Specialist Branches	3S London Bermondsey (valuable goods)		
	16S London Airport (Air Cargo)		

In practice it is believed the former London and Western Region Branches in the new Southern Region continued to use the old Regional letters 'LN' and 'W' in their fleet numbers even though they were regarded as 'S' on paper.

After this much-reduced network settled down it remained substantially unaltered in subsequent years. However by 1983 Swindon Branch (75S) had been closed and the 'outstations' at Welshpool (76M), High Wycombe (13M), Southend (89M) and Gloucester (77S) had been raised to Branch status again as c & d depots serving their Hubs. The London Airport service (16S) had also been discontinued. By 1984 High Wycombe had also closed and the outstations at York, Derby and Bridgwater were no longer mentioned. The three remaining outstations at Boston, Bournemouth and Carmarthen, were no longer coded having assumed the codes of their Hub Branches, Leicester, Southampton and Bristol.

Mention should be made at this point of the National Carriers Parcels network working alongside Roadline UK during this period. This fleet never held the same appeal to enthusiasts, its fleet numbering system being more concerned with vehicle specifications rather than identifying a particular vehicle's home base, which had always been the attraction in BRS numbering systems.

The former BEC company, Hanson Haulage, had been transferred from control of North Eastern BRS to that of National Carriers Parcels in 1983, duly becoming an NCL depot. By 1984 the Parcels Division was operating in North, South and West Areas, from a total of 14 depots. There was also a separate 'Freight Services' Division operating from a further 14 sites, making a total of 28 bases working in parallel with the Roadline UK fleet. While some of these were in locations that Roadline had already withdrawn from, such as Birmingham, there were still many towns where both companies still had a presence, so wasteful duplication remained a problem for the NFC.

With falling profitability still causing difficulty the beginning of 1985 saw trials combining the services of the two companies in selected areas of England, such as Devon/Cornwall and Norfolk/Suffolk/Essex, following the successful merger of the two businesses in Scotland in 1982. Eventually the two Parcels companies were fully integrated but not without considerable further reductions in the Branch network and fleet totals. Early in 1986 the combined business, now trading under the name 'National Carriers-Roadline' was established, now operating a fleet of just 850 c&d vehicles, 250 tractors and 800 trailers operating in four regions from 46 depots, 16 defined as 'Hubs' and the remaining 30 as c&d outstations. Still further contraction clearly occurred as the business settled down for, by October 1986, the first date for which we have a depot network, only 34 Branches were listed:

Region	Main Branch (Hub)	Outstations (c & d work only)
Northern	Gateshead (46N)	-
	Preston (NC)	Carlisle (37N)
	Manchester (NC)	Colwyn Bay (28N)
	Pudsey (Hansons NC)	Hull (42N, Sheffield (NC), Scarborough (NC)
Midland & Eastern	Derby (NC)	Stoke (NC), Lincoln (NC)
	Birmingham (NC)	Welshpool (76M)
	Ipswich (86M)	Norwich (84M), St Neots (NC), Harlow (NC)
South East	Watford (NC)	Northampton (60M)
	London, Kings Cross (NC)	-
	Dartford (8S)	Brighton (94S)
	Reading (NC)	Coulsdon (NC)
South West	Eastleigh (90S)	Bournemouth (91S)
	Bristol (70S)	Gloucester (77S)
	Exeter (NC)	Redruth (NC)
	Neath (81S)	Cardiff (NC), Carmarthen (82S)

The new business no longer used Branch codes; former Roadline Branches are shown with their old codes in brackets, former National Carriers Branches are shown as 'NC'. Only seven of Roadline's former Hubs remained and one of those had been demoted. Three sites were renamed – Gateshead, Eastleigh and Neath – and the Preston site was actually at Leyland, at the former Bridges Transport depot.

It was clear from roadside observations that fleet numbering for both fleets had been discontinued from around March 1986. During July decals and lettering began to be removed from the vehicles and from August the new 'National Carriers-Roadline' details began to appear on the vehicles. For almost a year the surviving vehicles continued to operate in their different green, yellow or white liveries with no apparent direction and becoming increasingly neglected in appearance until, in June 1987, vehicles in the new black livery of the successors, Lynx Express Delivery Service, began to appear on the road.

13

LYNX 1987-2005

Lynx Express Delivery Service, set up in June 1987, was the new name adopted for the fleet of 'National Carriers-Roadline' that had operated with perceptible neglect since mid-1986 following the merger of these two former businesses. The NFC closed its Regional Group at the same time and the Scottish Parcel Services fleet was also absorbed into the Lynx operations, so giving full coverage throughout England, Wales and Scotland once again.

National Carriers-Roadline had already discontinued the use of fleet numbers and the Scottish Parcels vehicles also lost their fleet numbering upon joining the Lynx network. Consequently it became very difficult for observers to attempt to follow the fortunes of any particular vehicles in subsequent service with Lynx and, as parcels companies remained loath to allow enthusiasts access to their depots with the obvious risk of pilfering always on their mind, pursuit of the fleet was hopeless. Not until September 1993 did fleet numbers begin to be applied to the vehicle fleet. By this time some six years had passed since the company was set up – more than the book life of most vehicles in use – so the fleet had by now almost completely turned over since the company had been formed and any prospect of recording the intervening period was lost.

The introduction of fleet numbering was obviously very helpful but the system adopted was not as useful as that of the earlier BRS empire. Different blocks of numbers were allocated, sub-dividing vehicles into categories by gvw, the smallest vans carrying the lowest numbers and max-cap artics the highest. However, upon becoming vacant they were reissued, a procedure always disapproved of by BRS. Two-letter codes preceding the number indicated the depot, usually the first and last letters of the location.

For record purposes we do have a 1991 list of Lynx Branches to work from. This shows a network divided into five operating regions and continuing to use Hubs and Outstations, with a Head Office at Halesowen in the W. Midlands, which raised some of the new registrations;

other new vehicles were licensed by their suppliers, as had become the norm. The known codes raised in 1993 are shown in the summary below:

Region	Main Branch (Hub)	Outstations (c&d work only)
Scottish	? Aberdeen	-
	AE Airdrie	-
	DE Dundee	-
	EH Edinburgh	? Dumfries; ? Earlston
	IS Inverness	-
Northern	GD Gateshead	-
	LS Leeds (Pudsey)	HL Hull; SD Sheffield
	LD Leyland (Preston)	CE Carlisle
	MR Manchester	CY Colwyn Bay
Midland & Eastern	BM Birmingham	WL Welshpool
	DY Derby	LC Lincoln
	IH Ipswich	NH Norwich; ? St Neots
South East	DD Dartford	BN Brighton
	LN London (Muswell Hill)	-
	RG Reading	CN Coulsdon
	WD Watford	? Harlow
South West	BL Bristol	-
	ER Exeter	-
	GR Gloucester	-
	SN Southampton (Eastleigh)	? Bournemouth
	SA Swansea (Skewen)	-
Specialist Services	EX Euro Express, Dartford	
	JY Islandlink (Jersey) Ltd	

Driving schools at Peterborough and Pudsey, inherited from National Carriers and still listed in 1991, were not referred to by the time coding was introduced in 1993.

The network was remarkably similar to that in 1986, indicating it had finally stabilised. Subsequent years saw further changes. The sites at Aberdeen, Airdrie, Derby, Hull, Ipswich, St Neots, Sheffield and Welshpool either closed or relocated and that at Manchester also relocated from Oldham Road to Barton Dock (the former Roadline site) showing this had remained in the company's use but presumably not at Branch status. Four of the depots defined as outstations, Bournemouth, Dumfries, Earlston and Harlow, also received no further mention.

Other sites known to have been used since 1993 are as follows:

BY Barnsley
CD Chelmsford
KX London, Kings Cross
?? Luton
NN Northampton
NU Nuneaton
SE Stoke
?? Hellaby (new location for former Sheffield fleet)
BW Bothwell (new location for former Airdrie fleet)
?? Alfreton (new location for former Derby fleet)

Other known codes have been:

FC Franchise (mostly Mercedes Sprinter vans)
BS Body Shop (believed to be at Leyland)
SY Systems (believed to be at Birmingham)

The Lynx network functioned as an NFC subsidiary with cab door lettering indicating as such for another ten years, though recording losses for much of this time. In 1997, however, following three successive years during which operating profits had been returned, it underwent a management buyout. Long-serving enthusiasts of the BRS organisation, having been obliged to study other related companies within the NFC as they affected BRS operations over the years, required little persuasion to continue following the Lynx fleet even though it had now left the NFC empire as the livery and, more importantly, the numbering system continued unaltered though the application of fleet numbers did become rather haphazard towards the end – and were able to do so for a further eight years.

In early 2005, almost 18 years after its formation, Lynx was purchased by the UPS Organisation (United Parcels Services), an American parcels carrier that had commenced European operations in West Germany in 1976 and duly expanded throughout Europe, gaining a foothold in the UK in 1992 upon acquiring the business of Carryfast and introducing the drab plain brown livery of UPS to their smaller vans from that time, though the blue livery was retained for the bigger artics.

Carryfast had been set up in October 1970 by GKN to merge the parcels work of its existing subsidiaries, H B Everton of Droitwich and A Packham Ltd of London and the South West. The fleet was expanded by adding the businesses of Hallett Silbermann Parcels, Feltham in June 1971, followed by the Dean Group, Manchester in June 1972 and Harrisons of Dewsbury in September 1972, to build a fleet exceeding 300 vehicles. In July 1976, GKN sold the company to Unilever who attached it to their SPD business as a subsidiary but it later underwent a management buyout, following which it was sold to Tibbett & Britten, finally passing to UPS in 1992.

The demise of Lynx was clearly the end of the line for BRS enthusiasts. UPS allocated their own fleet numbers, in simple six-figure serial numbers commencing 126xxx and 127xxx, and then their plain brown livery to all vehicles retained after the takeover. Mustoe, Ingram and Pearson report in their book 'BRS Parcels Services' that Lynx had a fleet of 2000 vehicles at the time UPS took over but this sounds unlikely on recalling the earlier report, in 1986, that the fleet totalled 1100 vehicles and Lynx's own fleet numbering system only allowed for numbers to reach the 1500s, including gaps between different blocks of vehicles –

although the series eventually extended into the 1700s as some blocks were used up.

As was usually the case with parcels carriers it was not possible to obtain information or lists from UPS relating to the renumbering. For similar reasons, no record exists of the Lynx Branch network at the time of takeover either, though Mustoe, Ingram and Pearson do indicate they were down to just 20 main depots by 1999. Thus our pursuit of the BRS Parcels fleet since 1955 and its successors under NFC control, which had given nearly 50 years' entertainment, came to an end – it was 'game over'.

APPENDIX A

GROUP CODES 1950-56

Code	Group Name	Currency
1A	East Kent	1950-52
2A	Mid Kent	1950-52
3A	North West Kent	1950-52
4A	Medway	1950-52
5A	Blackwall Tunnel	1950-56
6A	Bermondsey	1950-56
7A	Camberwell	1950-52
7A	South East London	1952-55
8A	Rother Valley	1950-52
9A	Newington Butts	1950-56
20A	Brighton	1950-52
23A	Croydon	1950-52
24A	Kingston	1950-51
25A	Battersea	1950-52
25A	SouthWest London	1952-54
26A	Guildford	1950-52
27A	Lambeth	1950-51
28A	Borough	1950-52
33A	Metropolitan Smalls	1952-55
34A	Parcels - City	1952-55
35A	Parcels - South of Thames	1952-55
36A	Parcels - North of Thames	1952-55
37A	Shipping	1952-55
40A	St Albans	1950-51
41A	High Wycombe	1950-51
42A	Shoreditch	1950-54
43A	Islington	1950-56
44A	Tottenham	1950-51
45A	Brentford	1950-54
46A	Slough	1950-51
46A	Slough & St Albans	1951-56
47A	(City?)	1950-
48A	Hayes	1950-51
49A	Finsbury	1950-56
50A	Muswell Hill	1950-52
51A	Chiswick	1950-55

Appendices

Code	Group Name	Currency
52A	Perivale	1950-55
53A	West London	1950-56
60A	Bow	1950-51
61A	Thurrock	1950-56
62A	Bishopsgate	1950-54
63A	Hackney Marsh	1950-55
64A	Monument	1950-52
64A	East London	1952-55
65A	Millwall	1950-51
66A	Stratford	1950-56
67A	(Plaistow?)	1950-
69A	Poplar	1950-
70A	Victoria Park	1950-56
71A	East Ham	1950-51
72A	Stepney	1950-52
74A	Edmonton	1950-51
99A	Covent Garden	1952-56
1B	Aberdeen General	1950-54
2B	Old Ford Road	1950-54
3B	Peterhead/Fraserburgh	1950-52
3B	North East Scotland	1952-54
4B	Buckie	1950-52
5B	Inverness	1950-54
6B	Aberdeen Parcels	1952-55
7B	Aberdeen	1954-56
20B	Dundee General	1950-54
20B	Dundee	1954-56
21B	Angus	1950-56
22B	Perth	1950-54
23B	North Fife	1950-54
24B	South Fife	1950-54
25B	Tay	1950-51
25B	Dundee Parcels	1951-55
26B	Fife	1954-56
40B	Edinburgh General	1950-54
40B	Edinburgh	1954-56
41B	Leith	1950-51
41B	Edinburgh Parcels	1951-55
42B	Waverley	1950-54
43B	West Lothian	1950-55

Code	Group Name	Currency
44B	East Lothian	1950-51
44B	East Lothian & Borders	1951-56
45B	Borders	1950-51
60B	Douglas	1950-56
61B	Scottish Parcels	1950-55
61B	Glasgow Parcels	1955-
62B	Clyde	1950-54
63B	London-Scottish	1950-54
63B	Glasgow	1954-56
64B	Wallace	1950-54
65B	Taylor	1950-54
66B	Argyll	1950-56
67B	Central Scotland	1950-55
68B	Caledonian	1950-54
69B	Ayrshire	1950-55
1C	North Liverpool	1950-54
2C	Central Liverpool	1950-54
3C	South Liverpool	1950-54
4C	East Liverpool	1950-54
5C	Warrington	1950-56
6C	St Helens & Widnes	1950-56
7C	Wigan	1950-56
8C	North Wales	1950-56
9C	Liverpool Parcels	1950-55
10C	(Wrexham?)	1950-
10C	Merseyside	1951-55
11C	Mid Cheshire	1950-56
12C	Liverpool Port Control	1952-?
13C	City of Liverpool	1954-56
20C	Lancaster Parcels	1950-55
21C	Burnley	1950-54
22C	Preston	1950-56
23C	Carlisle	1950-56
24C	West Blackburn	1950-56
25C	Morecambe Bay	1950-54
26C	Rossendale	1950-56
27C	East Blackburn	1950-52
40C	?	1950-
41C	Burslem	1950-
42C	Tunstall	1950-

Appendices

Code	Group Name	Currency
43C	?	1950-
44C	?	1950-
45C	Longton	1950-
60C	Kearsley	1950-55
61C	North Manchester	1950-54
62C	Manchester Contracts	1950-56
63C	Manchester Parcels	1950-55
64C	Greenheys	1950-56
65C	Salford	1950-51
66C	Central Manchester	1950-51
67C	Trafford Park	1950-56
68C	Manchester Local	1950-52
69C	Bolton & Bury	1950-56
70C	Oldham	1950-52
71C	Cheetham	1950-51
72C	Rochdale	1950-
73C	South Manchester	1950-
74C	Cornbrook	1950-56
74C	Bolton	1956-
1D	Central Newcastle	1950-56
2D	Haymarket	1950-56
3D	Gateshead	1950-54
4D	Stockton	1950-52
4D	Tees-side	1952-56
5D	Middlesbrough	1950-52
6D	Sunderland	1950-55
7D	Quayside	1950-52
8D	Sandyford	1950-54?
9D	Exchange	1950-52
10D	Tyne Tees Parcels	1950-55
20D	York	1950-54
22D	North Leeds	1950-54
23D	South Leeds	1950-54
24D	Central Leeds	1950-52
25D	Central Hull	1950-52
26D	Selby	1950-54
27D	North Hull	1950-54
28D	East Hull	1950-54
29D	Leeds, York & E R Parcels	1950-55
30D	York	1954-56

Appendices

Code	Group Name	Currency
31D	Hull	1954-56
32D	Leeds	1954-55
32D	West Riding General	1955-56
40D	Halifax	1950-54
41D	Ripponden	1950-54
42D	Huddersfield	1950-54
43D	South Bradford	1950-54
44D	Central Bradford	1950-54
45D	Airedale	1950-54
46D	Dewsbury/Batley	1950-54
47D	West Bradford	1950-54
49D	West Riding General	1954-55
50D	West Riding Parcels	1954-55
60D	Central Sheffield	1950-56
61D	Chesterfield	1950-55
62D	Attercliffe	1950-56
63D	Park	1950-56
64D	Doncaster	1950-56
65D	Barnsley	1950-55
66D	Hallam	1950-52
67D	South Yorkshire Parcels	1950-55
68D	Sherwood	1950-55
1E	Bullring	1950-
2E	Coventry	1950-56
3E	Witton	1950-52
4E	Cheapside	1950-56
5E	Aston Cross	1950-56
6E	Tyburn	1950-54
7E	Birmingham Parcels	1950-55
8E	Hockley	1950-
9E	Hay Mills	1950-54
10E	Nuneaton	1950-52
11E	West Bromwich	1950-55
11E	Wolverhampton	1955-56
20E	Wellington	1950-
21E	Walsall	1950-54
22E	Wolverhampton	1950-54
22E	South Staffs	1954-56
23E	Shrewsbury	1950-
24E	Kidderminster	1950-51
25E	West Bromwich	1950-

179

Appendices

Code	Group Name	Currency
26E	Stafford	1950-55
27E	Dudley	1950-56
28E	North Staffs	1950-55
29E	Tunstall	1950-52
30E	Stoke	1950-56
31E	Longton	1950-
40E	North Leicester	1950-52
41E	South Leicester	1950-56
42E	Leicester Parcels	1950-55
43E	Northants Parcels	1950-55
44E	Leicester Tipping	1950-54
45E	Northampton	1950-54
46E	Livestock	1950-54
47E	Luton	1950-52
47E	Luton/Leighton Buzzard	1952-56
48E	Leighton Buzzard	1950-52
60E	Nottingham	1950-55
61E	South Nottingham	1950-54
62E	Derby	1950-56
63E	North Nottingham	1954-56
63E	Nottingham Parcels	1954-56
64E	South Derbyshire	1950-55
65E	Dukeries	1950-56
66E	North Derbyshire	1950-54
80E	Oxford	1950-
81E	Droitwich	1950-
82E	Worcester	1950-
83E	Livestock	1950-
84E	Cowley	1950-
1F	Central Bristol	1950-56
2F	East Bristol	1950-56
3F	South Bristol	1950-56
4F	Bath & Wells	1950-56
5F	Taunton & North Devon	1950-52
6F	South Devon & Cornwall	1950-52
7F	Bristol Parcels	1950-55
8F	South Gloucestershire	1951-54
20F	Poole & Yeovil	1950-56
21F	Parkstone	1950-54
22F	Southampton	1950-56

Code	Group Name	Currency
23F	Portsmouth	1950-56
24F	Exeter	1950-52
25F	Eastleigh Parcels	1950-55
26F	Isle of Wight	1950-56
27F	Railway Cartage	1950-56
28F	Exeter Parcels	1950-52
40F	Reading	1950-56
41F	Swindon & Salisbury	1950-56
42F	Melksham & Frome	1950-56
43F	Guildford	1952-56
60F	East Kent	1952-56
61F	Mid Kent	1952-56
62F	Medway	1952-56
63F	Rother Valley	1952-54
64F	Brighton	1952-56
65F	Guildford	1952-
80F	Exeter	1952-56
81F	Taunton & North Devon	1952-56
82F	South Devon & Cornwall	1952-56
83F	Exeter Parcels	1952-55
1G	Newport	1950-52
1G	Newport District	1952-56
2G	Cardiff	1950-52
2G	Cardiff District	1952-56
20G	Swansea	1950-52
20G	Swansea District	1952-56
21G	West Wales	1950-56
25G	South Wales Pool	1950-55
30G	Wrexham/Welshpool	1950-
31G	Shrewsbury	1950-
31G	Shrewsbury/Central Wales District	1950-56
32G	Wellington	1950-
40G	Forest of Dean	1950-52
41G	Gloucester	1950-52
41G	Gloucester District	1952-56
42G	Hereford	1950-56
43G	South Gloucestershire	1950-
44G	Oxford	1950-52
44G	Oxford District	1952-56
45G	Cowley	1950-52

Appendices

Code	Group Name	Currency	
46G	Worcester	1950-52	
47G	Droitwich	1950-52	
1H	Norwich	1950-56	
2H	Ipswich	1950-54	
3H	North Norfolk	1950-52	& West Norfolk 1952-54
4H	Kings Lynn	1950-	
4H	Stowmarket	1950-54	
5H	Beccles	1950-52	
5H	Beccles & Yarmouth	1952-54	
6H	Yarmouth	1950-52	
7H	Bury St Edmunds	1950-52	
8H	Stowmarket	1950-	
8H	Norfolk & Suffolk Parcels	1952-55	
9H	Bishops Stortford	1950-	
10H	Fordham	1950-	
20H	Huntingdon & Isle of Ely	1950-52	
21H	Peterborough	1950-56	
22H	Wisbech	1950-56	
23H	Cambridge	1950-56	
24H	?	1950-	
24H	Kings Lynn	1950-52	
25H	?	1950	
25H	Bishops Stortford	1950-54	
26H	Leighton Buzzard	1950	
26H	Fordham	1950-54	
27H	South Lincolnshire	1950-54	
40H	Grimsby	1950-51	
40H	Grimsby & Louth	1951-56	
41H	Louth	1950-51	
42H	Gainsborough	1950-51	
43H	Boston	1950-54	
44H	East Lincolnshire	1950-52	
45H	Lincoln City	1950-56	
46H	Scunthorpe	1950-56	
47H	Brigg	1950-54	
?	South Lincolnshire	1950	
60H	Colchester	1950-54	
60H	Ipswich District	1954-56	
Small 'm'	Pickfords (Special Traffics)	1905-56	

APPENDIX B

DISTRICT CODES 1957-1964
BRS LTD AND BRS (CONTRACTS) LTD

Code	District Name	Currency
1A	London	1957-64
2A	Southampton	1957-64
3A	East Anglia	1957-64
4A	Home Counties	1957-64
C5A	London Contracts	1957-64
1B	Southern Scotland	1957-58
1B	Glasgow	1958-64
2B	Northern Scotland	1957-64
3B	Edinburgh	1958-64
1C	Liverpool	1957-64
2C	Manchester	1957-64
3C	Preston	1957-64
1D	Tyne Tees	1957-64
2D	Yorkshire	1957-59
2D	East Yorkshire	1959-64
3D	South Yorks & Lincoln	1957-64
4D	West Yorkshire	1959-64
1E	Birmingham	1959-64
2E	Stoke	1959-64
3E	Leicester	1959-64
4E	Luton	1957-61
5E	Notts & Derby	1957-64
6E	Peterborough	1957-64
C11E	Birmingham Contracts	1958-64

Code	District Name	Currency
1G	Cardiff	1957-64
2G	Swansea	1957-64
3G	Gloucester	1957-64
4G	Oxford	1957-64
5G	Bristol	1957-61
5G	West of England	1961-64
6G	Exeter	1957-61
Large 'M'	Pickfords	1957 onwards
X	Meat Cartage	1957-66

All BRS Districts except 1A, 1C and 3C also operated Contracts vehicles which carried Prefix 'C' in front of the District codes.

APPENDIX C

BRANCH CODES 1955-64
BRS (PARCELS) LTD

Code	Branch Name	Currency
P33A	Metropolitan Smalls	1955-59
P34A	Parcels - City Area	1955-59
P35A	Parcels - South of Thames	1955-59
P36A	Parcels - North of Thames	1955-59
P37A	Shipping	1955-59
P38A	City & Suburban	1959-64
P39A	Shipping	1959-64
P40A	North West London	1959-64
P41A	North East London	1959-64
P42A	South London	1959-64
P6B	Aberdeen	1955-64
P7B	Edinburgh	1957-64
P8B	Glasgow	1957-64
P25B	Dundee	1955
P41B	Edinburgh	1955-57
P61B	Glasgow	1955-57
P4C	Manchester	1957-64
P5C	Liverpool	1957-64
P6C	Lancaster	1957-64
P9C	Liverpool	1955-57
P20C	Lancaster	1955-57
P63C	Manchester	1955-57
P4D	West Riding	1959-64
P10D	Tyne Tees	1955-64
P11D	Middlesbrough	1961-64
P12D	Lincoln	1961-64
P13D	Boston	1961-64
P14D	Hull	1961-64
P15D	York	1962-64
P29D	Leeds, York & E Riding	1955-64
P50D	West Riding	1955-59

Appendices

Code	Branch Name	Currency
P67D	South Yorkshire	1955-64
P7E	Birmingham	1955-64
P8E	Leicester	1957-64
P9E	Northants	1957-64
P10E	Nottingham	1957-64
P12E	Coventry	1961-64
P13E	Stoke	1961-64
P14E	Northampton	1961-64
P15E	Wolverhampton	1961-64
P16E	Derby	1961-64
P17E	Bedford	1961-64
P18E	Luton	1961-64
P42E	Leicester	1955-57
P43E	Northants	1955-57
P60E	Nottingham	1955-57
P7F	Bristol	1955-64
P25F	Eastleigh	1955-57
P63F	Oxford	1957-64
P83F	Exeter	1955-64
P2G	Cardiff, Newport & Cheltenham	1955-57
P20G	Skewen	1955-57
P31G	Welshpool	1955-57
P42G	Hereford	1955-57
P44G	Oxford	1955-57
P60G	Cardiff, Newport & Cheltenham	1957-64
P61G	Skewen	1957-64
P62G	Welshpool & Hereford	1957-64
P63G	Oxford	1957
P8H	Norfolk & Suffolk	1955-64
P25J	Eastleigh	1957-64
P26J	Brighton	1957-64
P27J	Eastbourne	1957-64
P28J	Tunbridge Wells	1957-64
P29J	Margate	1957-63
P30J	Chatham	1957-64
P31J	Canterbury	1957-64

APPENDIX D

TWO-LETTER BRANCH CODES
BRS LTD AND BRS (CONTRACTS) LTD 1964-72
REGIONAL BRS COMPANIES 1972-79

Code	Branch Name	Currency
AA	Mile End	1965-70
AA	Mile End	1971
AA	(Kentish Town Workshop)	1972
AB	(Covent Garden)	1965
AB	(Tilbury)	? - 1972
AB	Dunstable	1973-79
AC	Grays	1965-70
AC	Grays	1971-79
AD	Rochford	1965-70
AD	Rochford	1971-?
AE	Brighton	1965-73
AF	Canterbury	1965-79
AG	(Faversham)	1965
AG	Tufnell Park	1971-?
AG	N London Freight Centre	? - 1979
AH	(Minster)	1965
AH	Kentish Town	1971
AH	Amersham	1972-79
AJ	(Folkestone)	1965
AJ	(Dover)	?
AJ	Drummond Road	1971
AJ	Aylesbury	1972-?
AK	Guildford	1965-79
AL	(Maidsone)	1965
AL	Aylesford	1965-79
AM	Rochester	1965-72
AN	Sheerness	1965-70
AN	Dover	1972-79

Appendices

Code	Branch Name	Currency
AP	(Aylesford)	1965
AP	Mid Kent Contracts	1965-71
AP	Ipswich	1972-79
AQ	Sittingbourne	1965-68
AQ	Felixstowe	1972-79
AR	(Tonbridge)	1965
AS	Southampton	1965-71
AS	Colchester	1972-?
AS	Dagenham	? - 1979
AT	Portsmouth	1965-71
AT	Stowmarket	1972-79
AU	(Camber Quay)	1965
AU	Silvertown	? - 1979
AV	Poole	1965-71
AV	High Wycombe	1972-?
AW	Isle of Wight	1965-71
AW	Elmstead	1972-79
AX	(Cowes)	1965
AX	Brentford	1972-79
AY	Southampton Contracts	1965-71
AY	Enfield	?- 1979
AZ	Drummond Road	1965-70
AZ	(Ipswich Repair Centre)	1972
AZ	Tilbury	?-1979
AO	(S. BRS Head Office)	1972-79
BA	Glasgow	1964-79
BB	Douglas	1964-71
BB	Glasgow Contracts	1971-72
BB	(Forfar R C)	1972
BB	Oban	1977-79
BC	Townhead	1964-67
BC	(Glasgow R C)	1972
BC	Campbeltown	1977-79

188

Appendices

Code	Branch Name	Currency
BD	Paisley	1964-66
BD	(Linlithgow Workshop)	1972
BD	Dunoon	1977-79
BE	Ayr	1964-74
BE	Ardrossan	1974-?
BE	Glasgow Distribution	1977-79
BF	Grangemouth	1964-75
BF	Dumfries	1978-79
BG	Argyll (inc 5 sub-depots)	1964-79
BH	Dunfermline	1964-75
BH	Haslingden	1978-79
BJ	Kirkcaldy	1964-75
BK	Alva	1964-75
BK	Kilmarnock	1978-79
BL	Dundee	1964-75
BL	Campbeltown	1975-77
BL	Lockerbie	1978-79
BM	Forfar	1964-75
BN	Arbroath	1964-75
BN	Newcastle (SRS)	1978-79
BP	Perth	1964-75
BP	(Birmingham)(SRS)	1978-79
BQ	Coupar Angus	1964-67
BQ	Scottish Continental	1974
BR	Aberdeen	1964-75
BS	Inverness	1964-75
BT	Elgin	1964-75
BU	Newington	1964-68
BV	Leith	1964-68
BV	Edinburgh	1968-75
BV	Dunoon	1975-77
BW	Bathgate	1964-75
BW	Oban	1975-77
BX	Haddington	1964-73

Appendices

Code	Branch Name	Currency
BX	Coatbridge	1974-79
BY	Galashiels	1964-75
BZ	Kelso	1964-65
BZ	Tufnell Park	1965-67
BZ	Glasgow Distribution	1973-?
B only	Scottish Contract Spares	1964-72
BO	(SRS Head Office)	1972-79
CA	Liverpool City	1964-72
CA	Liverpool	1972-74
CB	(Liverpool Dock Office)	1964
CB	Dockside Express	1969-75
CC	(Liverpool Fruit Office)	1964
CC	West Cumberland	1972
CD	Warrington	1964-79
CE	St Helens	1964-79
CF	Runcorn	1964-79
CG	Kitt Green	1964-78
CH	North Wales	1964-79
CJ	Widnes	1964
CJ	Hampstead	1965-70
CJ	Stafford	1972-77
CK	Wrexham	1964-79
CL	Greenheys	1964-72
CL	Trafford Park	1972-75
CM	Trafford Park	1964-71
CM	Stoke	1972-75
CN	Salford Dock Office	1964-66
CN	Tunstall	1972-79
CP	Cheetham	1964-79
CQ	Bolton	1964-79
CR	Preston Contracts	1966-72
CR	Sandbach	1972-79
CS	Preston	1964-78

Appendices

Code	Branch Name	Currency
CT	Blackburn	1964-75
CT	Longton	1977-79
CU	Trafford Park Contracts	1964-72
CV	Stalybridge Contracts	1964-72
CV	Stalybridge	1972-74
CW	Stockport Contracts	1964-72
CX	Liverpool Contracts	1964-72
CX	Mancheser R C	1972-79
CY	(Salford Contracts)	1964
CY	Stoke R C	1972-79
CZ	(Contracts Operations, N W Distric Head Office)	1964
CZ	(N W BRS Continental Operations)	1972
CO	N W BRS Head Office	1972-79
DA	York	1964-66
DA	Castle Bros	1970
DA	Sheffield	1971-79
DB	Harrogate	1964-79
DC	Hull	1964-70
DC	Hull (inc Goole)	1970-73
DC	Hull	1973-79
DD	Goole	1964-70
DD	Goole	1973-79
DE	Leeds	1964-79
DF	Castleford	1964-67
DF	Knottingley	1967-79
DG	Bradford	1964-69
DG	Bradford (inc Dewsbury)	1969-74
DG	Bradford	1974-79
DH	Bingley	1964-66
DH	Bingley Contracts	1971-72
DH	Immingham	1972-79
DJ	Dewsbury	1964-69

Appendices

Code	Branch Name	Currency
DJ	Doncaster (inc Worksop)	1971-74
DJ	Doncaster	1974-79
DK	Yorkshire Contracts	1965-70
DK	Northern & Yorkshire Contracts	1970-71
DK	York Contracts	1971-73
DK	York	1973-79
DL	Newcastle	1970-79
DM	Sunderland	1970
DM	Consett	1975-79
DN	Tees-side	1970-79
DP	Darlington	1970-79
DQ	Barnsley	1971-79
DR	Carlisle	1970
DR	Worksop	1974-79
DS	West Cumberland	1970-72
DS	Dewsbury	1974-79
DT	F Crowther	1970
DT	Wakefield	1971-79
DU	Selby Contracts	1970-72
DU	Hull Continental	1978-79
DV	Scunthorpe	1971-79
DW	Leeds Warehousing	1972-79
DX	Newcastle R C	1972-?
DX	Hexham	1977-78
DY	Grimsby	1971
DY	Sheffield R C	1972-?
DZ	Tufnell Park	1965-67
DO	(N E BRS Head Office)	1972
DO	N E BRS Company Pool	1975-79
EA	Cheapside	1964-72
EB	Birmingham	1964-72
EC	Redditch	1964-70
ED	Wolverhampton	1964-71

Appendices

Code	Branch Name	Currency
EE	Walsall	1964-72
EF	Leamington	1964-69
EG	Coventry	1964-69
EH	Tamworth	1964-72
EJ	Oldbury	1974-72
EK	Kidderminster	1964-71
EL	Wellington	1964-72
EM	Worcester	1964-72
EQ	Overnight Express	1969-72
ER	Birmingham Contracts	1964-72
ES	Wolverhampton Contracts	1965-72
ET	Mortons Contracts	1968-?
EU	Rugby	1971-72
EV	Dunstable	1971-72
EW	Northampton	1971-72
EY	Bedford	1971
EZ	Kentish Town	1965-70
E/DS	Birmingham D T S	1969-72
FA	Leicester	1964-70
FA	Liverpool Contracts	1972-79
FB	Rugby	1964-70
FB	(Salford Warehouse)	1972
FB	Fleetwood	1975-77
FB	Burnley	1978-79
FC	Loughborough	1964-70
FC	West Cumberland Contracts	1972
FD	Corby	1964-70
FD	Warrington Contracts	1972-79
FE	Melton Mowbray	1964-70
FE	St Helens Contracts	1972-79
FF	Dunstable	1964-70
FF	Runcorn Contracts	1973-79
FG	Northampton	1964-70

Appendices

Code	Branch Name	Currency
FG	Kitt Green Contracts	1973-79
FH	Bedford	1964-70
FH	North Wales Contracts	1972-79
FJ	Bourne	1965-70
FJ	Stafford Contracts	1975-77
FK	Wrexham Contracts	1972-79
FL	Trafford Park Contracts	1972-79
FM	Stoke Contracts	1972-79
FP	Cheetham Contracts	1974-79
FQ	Bolton Contracts	1975-79
FR	Sandbach Contracts	1972-79
FS	Preston Contracts	1972-79
FT	Blackburn Contracts	1974-75
FT	Longton Contracts	1977-79
FV	Stalybridge Contracts	1972-75
FV	Tameside Contracts	1975-79
FW	Stockport Contracts	1972-79
FZ	Kentish Town	1965-66
FO	(N W BRS Contracts Head Office)	1972
GA	Cardiff	1964-72
GB	Newport	1964-72
GC	Ebbw Vale	1964-72
GD	Pontypool	1964-72
GE	Merthyr Tydfil	1964-67
GF	Hereford	1964-72
GG	Ross-on-Wye	1964-72
GH	Swansea	1964-72
GJ	West Wales	1964-72
GK	Bridgend	1964-72
GL	South Wales Contracts	1964-72
GL	Dundee	1975-79
GM	Margam	1965-72
GM	Forfar	1975-79

Appendices

Code	Branch Name	Currency
GN	British Tissues, Bridgend	1971-72
GN	Arbroath	1975-79
GP	Forest of Dean	1966-72
GP	Perth	1975-79
GQ	Gloucester	1966-72
GR	Newport Timber	1970-72
GR	Aberdeen	1975-79
GS	Cardiff Docks	1970-72
GS	Inverness	1975-79
GT	Sharpness	1971?
GT	Elgin	1975-79
GZ	Tufnell Park	1965
GKW	Bridgend DTS	1968-72
HA	Newcastle	1964-70
HB	Sunderland	1964-70
HB	Glasgow Contracts	1972-75
HC	Tees-side	1964-70
HD	Darlington	1964-70
HE	Carlisle	1964-70
HE	Ayr Contracts	1972-74
HE	Ardrossan Contracts	1974-?
HE	Hawhorn Street Contracts	1977-79
HF	West Cumberland	1964-70
HF	Grangemouth Contracts	1972-75
HF	Dumfries Contracts	1978-79
HH	Haslingden Contracts	1971-72
HJ	Kirkcaldy Contracts	1972-75
HK	Alva Contracts	1972-75
HK	Kilmarnock Contracts	1978-79
HL	Dundee Contracts	1972-75
HL	Lockerbie Contracts	1978-79
HN	Newcastle Contracts (SRS)	1978-79
HO	SRS Contracts Spares	1972-75

Appendices

Code	Branch Name	Currency
HP	Perth Contracts	1972-75
HP	(Birmingham Contracts - SRS)	1978-79
HR	Aberdeen Contracts	1972-75
HS	Inverness Contracts	1972-75
HT	Elgin Contracts	1972-75
HV	Edinburgh Contracts	1972-75
HX	Haddington Contracts	1972-73
HZ	Tufnell Park	1965-67
HZ	Glasgow Contracts	1975-79
H only	Northern District Contracts	1964-70
JA	Sheffield	1964-71
JA	Sheffield Contracts	1972-79
JB	Attercliffe	1964-71
JB	Harrogate Contracts	1972-79
JC	Doncaster	1964-71
JC	Hull Contracts	1972-79
JD	Barnsley	1964-71
JE	Worksop	1964-71
JE	Leeds Contracts	1972-79
JF	Scunthorpe	1964-71
JF	Knottingley Contracts	1972-79
JG	Lincoln	1964-67
JG	Bradford Contracts	1972-79
JH	Grimsby	1964-71
JH	Selby Contracts	1972-79
JJ	Doncaster Contracts	1972-79
JK	York Contracts	1972-79
JL	Newcastle Contracts	1972-79
JM	Consett Contracts	1975-79
JN	Tees-side Contracts	1972-79
JP	Darlington Contracts	1972-79
JQ	Barnsley Contracts	1972-79
JR	Worksop Contracts	1974-79

Code	Branch Name	Currency
JS	Dewsbury Contracts	1974-79
JT	Wakefield Contracts	1977-79
JV	Scunthorpe Contracts	1972-79
JY	Grimsby Contracts	1972-79
JZ	Tufnell Park	1965-67
JO	(N E BRS Contracts Head Office)	1972
KA	Derby	1964-79
KB	Nottingham	1964-71
KB	Kings Lynn	1972-79
KC	Riddings	1964-72
KC	Alfreton	1972
KD	Carfax	1964-71
KD	Norwich	1972-79
KE	Nottingham Contracts	1964-72
KE	Nottingham	1973-79
KF	Burton	1964-79
KG	Chesterfield	1964-75
KG	Nottingham DTS	1977-79
KH	Newark	1964-79
KJ	Stoke	1964-72
KJ	Heath	1975-79
KJ	Chesterfield	1979
KK	Tunstall	1964-72
KK	Brandon	1975-79
KL	Stafford	1964-72
KL	(Stevenage)	1972
KM	Sandbach	1964-72
KN	Leicester	1971-79
KP	Lincoln	1967-70
KP	Lincoln Contracts	1970-72
KP	Lincoln	1973-79
KQ	Bourne	1967-71
KQ	Boston	1972-79

Code	Branch Name	Currency
KR	Loughborough	1971-76
KR	Langar	1979
KS	Corby	1971-79
KT	Melton Mowbray	1971-79
KU	Weldon	1971
KU	Rugby	1972-75
KV	Beccles	1972-79
KW	Northampton	1972-79
KX	Cambridge	1973-79
KY	Peterborough	1972-79
KZ	Kentish Town	1965-66
KZ	Wisbech	1972-79
KO	(E BRS Head office)	1972
KO	Nottingham DTS	1974-77
K only	N Midlands service vehicles	1964-71
K only	E Midlands service vehicles	1971-72
K only	E BRS service vehicles	1972-79
LA	Norwich	1964-72
LB	Kings Lynn	1964-72
LC	Beccles	1964-72
LD	Ipswich	1964-72
LE	Colchester	1964-72
LF	(Chelmsford)	1964
LF	Elmstead	1967-72
LF	Grangemouth	1975-79
LG	Stowmarket	1964-72
LH	Bury St Edmunds	1964-65
LH	Dunfermline	1975-79
LJ	Cambridge	1964-72
LJ	Kirkcaldy	1975-79
LK	Peterborough	1964-72
LK	Alva	1975-78
LL	Whittlesey	1964-69

Appendices

Code	Branch Name	Currency
LM	Wisbech	1964-72
LN	Bourne	1964-65
LP	Stevenage	1964-71
LQ	Boston	1964-72
LR	Felixstowe	1970-72
LS	Thetford	1971-72
LT	Alloa ex R S Forth	1977-79
LV	Edinburgh	1975-79
LW	Bathgate	1975-79
LY	Galashiels	1975-79
MA	Oxford	1964-79
MB	Banbury	1964-79
MC	Reading	1964-72
MC	Middlemore	1974-79
MD	High Wycombe	1964-72
MD	Birmingham Contracts Gen.Service	1974-76
ME	Swindon	1964-79
MF	Aylesbury	1972-74
MF	Birmingham	1964-71
MF	Birmingham Containerbase	1974-79
MG	Chesham	1964-?
MG	Amersham	? - 1972
MH	Tamworth	1973-79
MJ	Oldbury	1972-79
MM	Castle Bromwich	1970-79
MP	Erdington	1971-75
MQ	Ross-on-Wye	1972-75
MR	Cheapside	1972-73
MR	Birmingham Distribution Centre	1973-79
MS	Wolverhampton	1972-79
MT	Worcester	1972-79
MV	Hereford	1972-79
MW	Walsall	1972-73
MX	Forest of Dean	1972-77

Appendices

Code	Branch Name	Currency
MY	Gloucester	1972-79
MZ	Wellington	1972-79
MAX	Reading Workshop	1971-72
MKX	Oxford R C	1971-72
MTS	Oxford DTS	1969-72
MO	(M BRS Head Office)	1972
NA	Tufnell Park	1967-71
NA	(Kentish Town Workshop)	1972-?
NB	Kentish Town	1970-71
NB	(Tilbury Terminal)	1972-?
NC	Hampstead	1970
NC	(Ipswich R C)	1972-?
ND	Mile End	1970-71
ND	Burgess Hill	1972-?
NE	Grays	1970-71
NE	(S BRS, Hull Continental)	1972-?
NF	Drummond Road	1970-71
NF	(Canterbury Workshop)	1972-?
NG	Rochford	1970-71
NG	Bury St Edmunds	1972-79
NH	Dagenham	1970-71
NH	Amersham Ford Distribution	1972-79
NO	S BRS Continental Services	1972-?
NQ	Felixstowe International	1972-?
NT	Bedfont DTS	1972-79
NW	Milton Keynes	1976-?
NX	Staines	1976-79
NZ	(ICS Freight Ltd)	1972-?
OL	Dundee Contracts	1975-79
OP	Perth Contracts	1975-79
OR	Aberdeen Contracts	1975-79
OS	Inverness Contracts	1975-79

Appendices

Code	Branch Name	Currency
OT	Elgin Contracts	1975-79
QN	Overland Iran	1975-?
RA	Bristol	1964-79
RB	(Days Road)	1964
RB	Avonmouth	1969-79
RC	(Avonmouth Office)	1964
RC	Southampton	1970-79
RD	Melksham	1964-79
RE	Wells	1964-79
RF	Exeter	1964-79
RG	Plymouth Bridgwater	1964-79
RH	(Taunton Office) Isle of Wight Newton	1964-79
RJ		1964
RJ	Abbot Reading	1970-79
RK	St Austell	1964
RK	Barnstaple	1964-79
RL	Portsmouth	1972-79
RM	Yeovil	1970-79
RM	Gloucester Sharpness	1964-67
RN	(Western Contracts)	1964-79
RP	H S Morgan	1964-66
RP	Poole	1972-?
RQ	Bristol DTS Reading	1979
RQ	R C Brentford	1977-79
RR	(Brentford)	1970-79
RW	Bristol DTS	1972-?
RY	(W BRS Head Office)	1972-?
RZ		1965-70
RZ		1979
RAW		1970-72
RO		1972

Appendices

Code	Branch Name	Currency
S only	Cartransport (BRS) Ltd	1964-77
SA	Cardiff	1972-79
SB	Newport	1972-79
SC	Ebbw Vale	1972-79
SD	Pontypool	1972-79
SE	Cardiff Docks	1972-74
SF	Newport Timber	1972-74
SH	Swansea	1972-79
SJ	West Wales	1972-79
SK	Bridgend	1972-79
SM	Margam	1972-79
SN	British Tissues	1972-74
SR	(Southampton Contracts)	1972
SW	Bridgend DTS	1972-79
SY	(Cardiff Workshop)	1972
SO	(W BRS Head Office)	1972
TA	(Bromford Mills Property)	1972
TB	Oxford DTS	1972-?
TC	Birmingham DTS	1972-79
TD	Oxford Workshop	1972-?
TE	(Overnight Express)	1972-?
TF	Wolverhampton R C	1972-79
UF	Grangemouth Contracts	1975-79
UJ	Kirkcaldy Contracts	1975-79
UK	Alva Contracts	1975-79
UP	Falkirk Contracts ex BRS Forth	1977-79
UV	Edinburgh Contracts	1975-79
VA	Derby Contracts	1972-79
VB	Kings Lynn contracts	1972-79
VD	Norwich Contracts	1972-79
VE	Nottingham Contracts	1972-79

Appendices

Code	Branch Name	Currency
VF	Burton Contracts	1975-79
VG	Chesterfield Contracts	1972-75
VH	Newark Contracts	1973-79
VJ	(Nottingham Contracts DTS)	1972
VJ	Heath Contracts	1975-79
VK	Brandon Contracts	1975-79
VL	Wellingborough Contracts	1977-79
VN	Leicester Contracts	1972-79
VP	Lincoln Contracts	1972-79
VR	Loughborough Contracts	1972-76
VS	Corby Contracts	1976-79
VT	Melton Mowbray Contracts	1972-79
VU	Rugby Contracts	1972-79
VW	Northampton Contracts	1972-79
VX	Cambridge Contracts	1972-79
VY	Peterborough Contracts	1972-79
VZ	Wisbech Contracts	1972-79
VO	(E BRS Contracts Head Office)	1972
W only	Mortons (BRS) Ltd	1968-81
WA	Oxford Contracts	1972-79
WB	Banbury Contracts	1972-79
WD	Birmingham Contracts	1972-79
WE	Swindon Contracts	1972-79
WF	Birmingham Truck Rental	1975-79
WH	Tamworth Contracts	1972-79
WJ	Oldbury Contracts	1972-79
WM	Castle Bromwich Contracts	1972-79
WN	Redditch Truck Rental	1978-79
WQ	Ross-on-Wye Contracts	1972-75
WS	Wolverhampton Contracts	1972-79
WT	Worcester Contracts	1972-79
WV	Hereford Contracts	1972-79
WX	Forest of Dean Contracts	1972-77

Appendices

Code	Branch Name	Currency
WY	Gloucester Contracts	1972-79
WZ	Wellington Contracts	1972-79
WO	(M BRS Head Office Contracts)	1972
XA	Newington Butts	1965-79
XB	(Cubitt Street)	1965
XB	Colchester Contracts	1972-73
XB	Dover Contracts	? - 1979
XC	(Croydon)	1965
XC	Grays Contracts	1972-79
XD	(Centaur Street)	1965
XD	Rochford Contracts	1972-?
XD	Thamesmead	1975
XD	Welwyn Garden City	1977-79
XE	Victoria Park	1965-79
XF	(Batemans Row)	1965
XF	Canterbury Contracts	1972-79
XG	Brentford Contracts	1965-79
XH	Brentford General Haulage	1972
XH	Ipswich Contracts	1972-79
XJ	(Perivale)	1965
XJ	Aylesford Contracts	1972-?
XJ	Cuckfield	? - 1979
XK	Guildford Contracts	1972-79
XL	Brentford General Haulage	1965-68
XL	London Contracts District	1966-68
XL	Mid Kent Contracts	1971-72
XL	Maidstone Contracts	1972-79
XM	Southampton Contracts	1971-72
XM	Rochester Contracts	1972-?
XM	Croydon	1973-79
XN	Stowmarket Contracts	1972-79
XP	Long Lane	1970-79
XQ	Felixstowe Contracts	1972-79
XR	Tufnell Park Contracts	1972-?

Code	Branch Name	Currency
XR	North London Freight Centre	? - 1973
XS	Burgess Hill	1972-75
XS	Mid Sussex	1975-?
XT	Bedfont	1972-79
XU	High Wycombe Contracts	1972-79
XV	Dunstable Contracts	1972-79
XW	Elmstead Contracts	1972-79
XX	Hainault	1972-75
XX	Sunbury	1974-78
XY	Amersham Contracts	1972-73
XY	North London Freight Centre	1973-79
XZ	Aylesbury Contracts	1972-79
XO	(S BRS Contracts Head Office)	1972
YA	Bristol Contracts	1974-79
YB	Avonmouth Contracts	1974-79
YC	Southampton Contracts	1974-79
YD	Melksham Contracts	1974-79
YE	Wells Contracts	1974-79
YF	Exeter Contracts	1974-79
YG	Plymouth Contracts	1974-79
YH	Bridgwater Contracts	1974-79
YJ	Isle of Wight Contracts	1974-79
YK	Reading Contracts	1974-79
YL	St Austell Contracts	1974-79
YM	Portsmouth Contracts	1974-79
YN	Yeovil Contracts	1974-79
YR	Poole Contracts	1974-79
ZA	Brentford General Haulage	1968-72
ZA	Cardiff Contracts	1974-79
ZB	Newport Contracts	1974-79
ZH	Swansea Contracts	1974-79
ZJ	West Wales Contracts	1974-79
ZK	Bridgend Contracts	1974-79

Appendices

Code	Branch Name	Currency
ZM	Margam Contracts	1974-79

Contracts vehicles carried the letter 'C' either as a prefix to the code or as a suffix to the fleet number, or not at all, between 1964 and 1972

Trailers carried the letter 'T' as a prefix to the Branch Code

No two-letter combinations beginning with the letter 'P' were used as this was still regarded as a Parcels reference

APPENDIX E

BRANCH CODES - 1979 ONWARDS
FIRST TWO LETTERS OF THREE-LETTER CODES

Code	Branch Name	Currency
AA	Dunstable	1988-
AB	?	1988-
AC	Grays	1979
AD	Beccles	1983-
AE	Brandon	1983-89
AF	Kings Lynn	1983-
AG	Norwich	1983-
AH	Amersham	1979-81
AH	Stevenage	1985-
AK	Guildford	1979-
AL	Reading	1983-
AN	Milton Keynes	1988-
AP	Cambridge	1989-
AQ	Felixstowe	1979-81
AS	Dagenham	1979-
AS	Basildon	1991-
AT	Stowmarket	1979-81
AT	Bury St Edmunds	1983-91
AU	Silvertown	1979-
AU	Chadwell Heath	1983-86
AV	?	1988-
AW	Elmstead	1979-91
AW	Colchester	1991-
AX	Kelloggs, Watford	1989-
AY	Enfield	1979-
AZ	Tilbury	1979-86
BA	Glasgow	1979
BB	Oban	1979

Appendices

Code	Branch Name	Currency
BB	Belfast Airfreight	1989-
BC	Campbeltown	1979
BD	Dunoon	1979
BD	Ballymena	1989-
BE	Glasgow Distribution	1979
BF	Dumfries	1979
BF	Craigavon	1989-
BG	Argyll	1979
BG	Glasgow Distribution	1987-
BH	SRS Haslingden	1979
BI	Enniskillen	1989-
BJ	Inverness Distribution	1987-
BK	Kilmarnock	1979
BL	Lockerbie	1979
BL	Renfrew Distribution	1987-
BM	Belfast Distribution	1987-
BN	SRS Newcastle	1979
BP	SRS Birmingham	1979
BP	Falkirk Engineering	1987-
BQ	Belfast, Grosvenor Road	1989-
BR	Rutherglen	1987-
BS	Belfast, Milewater Road	1989-
BV	Edinburgh Engineering	1987-
BX	Coatbridge	1979
BX	Power Services, Aberdeen	1991-
CA	Liverpool	1979-
CB	Burnley	1979-
CD	Warrington	1979-
CE	St Helens	1979-89
CF	Runcorn	1979-91
CF	Widnes	1991-
CG	Kitt Green	1979-82
CG	Chester	1985-
CH	North Wales	1979-83

Appendices

Code	Branch Name	Currency
CH	Rochdale	1991-
CI	N W BRS Company Pool	1981-82
CJ	Stafford Clearing House	1979-83
CK	Wrexham	1979-83
CK	Kelloggs Trafford Park	1987-91
CL	Trafford Park	1979-
CM	Stoke	1979-
CM	Storehouse, Trafford Park	1989
CN	Tunstall	1979-81
CO	N W BRS Head Office	1979-83
CP	Cheetham	1979-89
CQ	Bolton	1979-
CR	Sandbach	1979-82
CR	Mid Cheshire	1983-
CS	Preston	1979-82
CS	Fort Sterling, Bolon	1984-89
CT	Longton	1979-
CU	?	1982-84
CV	Tameside	1979-
CW	Stockport	1979-
CX	Manchester R C	1979-82
CY	Stoke R C	1979-82
CY	Barrow-in-Furness	1991-
CZ	Carlisle	1979-
DA	Sheffield	1979-
DB	Harrogate	1979-85
DB	Chesterfield	1991-
DC	Hull	1979-
DD	Goole	1979-89
DE	Leeds	1979-82
DE	Yorktruck, York	1983-91
DF	Knottingley	1979-91
DG	Bradford	1979-

Appendices

Code	Branch Name	Currency
DH	Selby	1979-85
DH	Huddersfield	1985-89
DI	Hanson Haulage, Pudsey	1983
DJ	Doncaster	1979-87
DJ	Doncaster Engineering	1987-
DK	York	1979-
DL	Newcastle	1979-
DM	Consett	1979-80
DM	Hexthorpe	1981-87
DM	Doncaster	1987-
DN	Tees-side	1979-
DO	N E BRS Head Office & Company Pool	1979-83
DP	Darlington	1979-
DQ	Barnsley	1979-
DR	Worksop	1979-82
DR	Leeds	1982-
DS	Dewsbury	1979-89
DT	Wakefield	1979-82
DT	J Lyons, Barnsley	1987-
DU	Hull Continental	1979-80
DU	Carreras-Rothman, Basildon	1981-86
DV	Scunthorpe	1979-
DW	Leeds Warehousing	1979-82
DW	Carreras-Rothman, Darlington	1983-89
DX	Watsons, Spennymoor	1979-85
DX	Leeds, Bell Hill	1987-89
DY	Grimsby	1979-
FA	Star Bodies	1987-
FC	Central Park	1987-
FE	Kirklees	1990-
FG	Manchester, Oldham Road	1989-
FH	Rochdale	1989-91
FJ	Trafford Park, Barton Dock	1989-

Appendices

Code	Branch Name	Currency
FS	?	1991-
FV	Shearbridge, Bradford	1990-
FZ	Barrow-in-Furness, Council Contract	1990-
GA	Belfast Airfreight	1987-88
GB	Ballymena	1987-88
GC	Craigavon	1987-88
GD	Londonderry	1987-88
GE	Enniskillen	1987-88
GG	Belfast, Grosvenor Road	1987-88
GL	Dundee	1979
GM	Forfar	1979
GM	Belfast, Milewater Road	1987-88
GN	Arbroath	1979
GP	Perth	1979
GR	Aberdeen	1979
GS	Inverness	1979
GT	Elgin	1979
HA	Bridges Transport, Leyland	1982-85
HC *	Campbeltown Contracts	1979
HE	Glasgow, Hawthorn Street, Contracts	1979
HF	Dumfries Contracts	1979
HH	Haslingden Contracts	1979
HK	Kilmarnock Contracts	1979
HL	Lockerbie Contracts	1979
HN	SRS Newcasle Contracts	1979
HP	SRS Birmingham Contracts	1979
HX	Coatbridge Contracts	1979
HZ	Glasgow Contracts & Truck Rental	1979
IA	Rowley Road, Coventry	1981-
IB	(Whitnash)	1981-89

Appendices

Code	Branch Name	Currency
IC	Chipping Warden	1981-83
ID	Pitsea	1981-84
IG	(Baginton)	1981
IH	(Rock Farm)	1981-83
IK	Cheapside	1981-84
IL	(Humber Road, Coventry)	1981
JA	GDS Transport, Glasgow	1981-85
JB	GDS Transport, Lutterworth	1981-82
JB	GDS Transport, Lutterworth	1983-85
JC	GDS Transport, Enfield	1981-82
JC	GDS Transport, Enfield	1983-85
JD	GDS Transport, Yate	1981-82
JD	GDS Transport, Yate	1983-85
JE	GDS Transport, Sheffield	1981-85
JG	GDS Transport, Sheffield Trunk	1981-85
JP	Peaudouce, Hoddesdon	1985
KA	Derby	1979-
KB	Kings Lynn	1979-83
KC	Pinxton	1980-82
KC	Stoke	1983-
KD	Norwich	1979-83
KE	Nottingham, Wells Road	1979-82
KE	Nottingham, two sites	1982-84
KE	Nottingham, Langley Mill	1984-86
KF	Burton	1979
KG	Nottingham DTS	1979-82
KG	(Burnaston)	1984-86
KH	Newark	1979-
KJ	Chesterfield	1979-91
KK	Brandon	1979-83
KL	Wellingborough	1979-85
KN	Leicester	1979-

Code	Branch Name	Currency
KP	Lincoln	1979-
KQ	Boston	1979-
KR	Langar	1979
KR	GDS Transport, Lutterworth	1982
KR	Stafford Clearing House	1983-84
KS	Corby	1979-
KT	Melton Mowbray	1979-
KU	Rugby	1979-80
KV	Beccles	1979-83
KW	Northampton	1979-
KX	Cambridge (including Stevenage)	1979-89
KY	Peterborough	1979-
KZ	Wisbech	1979-
LA	Glasgow, Lister Street	1979-82
LA	Glasgow Power Centre	1984-
LB	Haslingden	1979-86
LB	Kilmarnock	1991-
LC	Elgin	1979-
LD	Dumfries	1979-
LE	Perth	1979-80
LE	Woolworths, Cumbernauld	1982-86
LE	Halls, Edinburgh	1991-
LF	Grangemouth	1979-80
LF	Glasgow R C	1982-86
LF	Glasgow South	1986-89
LF	Stranraer/Kilmarnock R C	1989-
LG	Glasgow Distribution	1979-86
LG	Glasgow North	1986-
LH	Dunfermline	1979-84
LH	East Kilbride	1989-
LI	SRS Birmingham	1979
LI	Edinburgh R C	1982-84
LJ	Kirkcaldy	1979-80

Appendices

Code	Branch Name	Currency
LJ	Kirkcaldy R C	1982-
LK	Kilmarnock	1979-81
LL	Dundee	1979-
LM	Forfar	1979-80
LM	? R C	1982
LM	East Tullos	1983-
LN	Arbroath	1979-
LO	SRS Head Office	1979-
LP	Falkirk	1979-
LQ	SRS Newcastle	1979-82
LQ	Portlethen	1984-
LR	Aberdeen	1979-
LS	Inverness	1979-81
LS	Inverness R C	1982-85
LS	Inverness	1985-
LT	Alloa	1979-85
LU	SRS Company Pool	1981-
LV	Edinburgh R C	1979-
LW	Bathgate	1979-80
LW	Campbeltown	1980-
LX	Coatbridge	1979-86
LX	Co-op, Cumbernauld	1991-
LY	Galashiels	1979-
LZ	Lockerbie	1979-
MA	Oxford	1979-83
MB	Banbury	1979-
MC	Middlemore	1979-83
MD	Birmingham Contracts	1979-86
MD	Birmingham, all services	1986-
ME	Swindon	1978-83
MF	Birmingham Containerbase	1979-86
MH	Tamworth	1979-81
MI	Birmingham DTS	1979-

Code	Branch Name	Currency
MJ	Oldbury	1979-?
MJ	West Bromwich	? -
MK	Oxford (leased to Cartransport)	1979-81
ML	Wolverhampton R C	1979-81
MM	Castle Bromwich	1979-81
MN	Redditch	1979-
MR	Birmingham Distribution Centre	1979-86
MS	Wolverhampton	1979-
MT	Worcester	1979-83
MV	Hereford	1979-83
MW	Walsall Clearing House	1983
MW	Nottingham Castle Meadow	1984-
MY	Gloucester	1979-83
MZ	Wellington	1979-
NB	Harlow	1986-
NC	?	1988-
ND	Ipswich Truck Sales	1986-
NE	Watford Engineering	1986-
NF	Park Royal Engineering	1988-
NG	Bury St Edmunds	1979-83
NH	?	1988-
NJ	?	1988-
NL	BDS, Chiswick	1982-84
NL	Kings Cross Engineering	1986-
NM	Leyton Engineering	1986-
NN	BDS Dunstable	1982-84
NN	?	1988
NP	BDS Hackney	1982-84
NP	Croydon Engineering	1988-
NQ	BDS Kentish Town	1984-85
NS	BDS Hornsey	1982-84
NS	Aldershot	1988-
NT	BDS Hoddesdon	1982-83

Appendices

Code	Branch Name	Currency
NU	BDS Dunstable	1984-85
NV	BDS Lewisham	1982-84
NV	?	1988-
NW	BDS Luton	1982-85
NX	Staines	1979-81
NX	Tonbridge	1988-
NZ	BDS Manor Park	1982-84
NZ	?	1988-
OL *	Dundee Contracts	1979
OM	Forfar Contracts	1979
ON	Arbroath Contracts	1979
OP	Perth Contracts	1979
OR	Aberdeen Contracts	1979
OS	Inverness Contracts	1979
OT	Elgin Contracts	1979
RA	Bristol	1979-
RB	Avonmouth	1979-
RC	Southampton	1979-84
RC	Chandlers Ford	1984-
RD	Melksham	1979-
RE	Wells	1979-91
RF	Exeter	1979-
RG	Plymouth	1979-
RH	Bridgwater	1979-
RJ	Isle of Wight (Islandlink)	1979-
RK	Reading	1979-83
RL	Merthyr Tydfil	1981
RM	Portsmouth	1979-
RN	GDS Transport, Yate	1982-
RN	Yeovil	1989-91
RP	W BRS Company Reserve	1980
RQ	H S Morgan, Eastleigh	1979-84
RR	Poole	1979-

Appendices

Code	Branch Name	Currency
RS	Cardiff	1979-
RT	Newport	1979-
RV	Swansea	1979-
RW	West Wales	1979-
RX	Bridgend	1979-
RY	Margam	1979-80
RY	Par	1989-91
RY	St Austell	1991-
RZ	Bridgend DTS	1979-
SA	Power Western, Bristol	1981-
SD	Power Western, Melksham	1983
SE	Power Western, Wells	1984
SH	Power Western, Bridgwater	1983
TA	Oxford	1983-
TB	Basingstoke	1986-
TC	Birmingham DTS	1979-
TC	Kidderminster	1986-
TD	Abingdon	1989
TE	Swindon	1983-
TF	Wolverhampton R C	1979
TF	Winchester	1989-91
TH	Barnstaple	1989-
TK	Wrexham	1983-
TR	Ross-on-Wye	1989-
TS	Tredegar	1989-91
TT	Worcester	1983-
TV	Hereford	1983-
TY	Gloucester	1983-
UA	Wm Cooper, Prestatyn	1982-83
UF *	Grangemouth Contracts	1979
UH	Dunfermline Contracts	1979
UJ	Kirkcaldy Contracts	1979
UP	Falkirk Contracts	1979
UT	Alloa Contracts	1979
UV	Edinburgh Contracts	1979
UW	Bathgate Contracts	1979
UY	Galashiels Contracts	1979

Appendices

Code	Branch Name	Currency
XA	Newington Butts	1979-
XB	Dover	1979-
XC	Radlett	1984-85
XC	Leyton	1991-
XD	Welwyn Garden City	1979-84
XD	?	1988-
XE	Victoria Park	1979-81
XE	Watford	1983-
XF	Canterbury	1979-
XG	Brentford	1979-
XH	Ipswich	1979-
XJ	Cuckfield	1979-81
XJ	?	1988-
XK	?	1988-
XL	Maidstone	1979-
XM	Croydon	1979-
XN	Newbury	1988
XP	Long Lane	1979-86
XP	Guildford Workshop	1989
XQ	Brighton	1986-
XS	Brentford Clearfreight	1988-
XT	Bedfont	1979-85
XT	Sittingbourne	1991-
XU	High Wycombe	1979-
XV	Dunstable	1979-87?
XW	Dartford	1986
XX	GDS Transport, Enfield	1982
XX	Leyton	1986-
XY	North London Freight	1979-84
XY	Centre Kings Cross	1984-
XZ	Aylesbury	1979-
YN	?	1984-
Unknown:	Yate	1984-85
	Chelmsford	1986-
	Aberdeen Distribution	1986-
	Ashford	1988
	Letchworth	1988
	Andover	1989-
	Greenwich	1991-

Unknown:	Immingham	1991-
	South Killingholme	1991-
	Urmston	1991-
	Ellesmere Port	1991-
	Billingham	1991-
	Broxburn	1991-
	Grangemouth	1991-

* Codes HC-HZ, OL-OT and UF-UY should have become BC-BZ, GL-GT and LF-LY respectively from January 1979 but SRS failed to restore Branches to one code only, plus activity letter, until mid-1979

Trailers continued to carry the letter 'T' as a prefix to the new three-letter codes. The third letter of the three-letter codes are explained elsewhere

A majority of those with indeterminate period of currency were those still in existence in 1991 when the final reorganisation took place. No data is available to say how long they existed beyond this time.

APPENDIX F

BRS PARCELS AND ROADLINE BRANCH CODES 1964-86

Code	Branch Name	Currency
1LN	N W London	1964-66
1LN	Muswell Hill	1966-81
1S	Muswell Hill	1981-
2LN	N E London	1964-66
2LN	Hackney	1966-
3LN	S London	1964-66
3LN	Bermondsey	1966-79
3LNX	Bermondsey	1979-81
3S	Bermondsey	1981-
4LN	City	1964-81
4S	City	1981-
5LN	Shipping	1964-
6LN	Surbiton	1964-81
7LN	Croydon	1964-81
7S	Croydon	1981-
8LN	Eltham	1964-74
8LN	Dartford	1974-81
8S	Dartford	1981-
9LN	Stratford	1964-79
10LN	Tottenham	1964-
11LN	Harrow	1964-72
12LN	Acton	1964-
13LN	High Wycombe	1964-81
13M	High Wycombe	1981-
14LN	Slough	1964-79
15LN	Chelsea	1964-72
16LN	London Airport	?-81
16S	London Airport	1981
17SC	Glasgow	1964-

Appendices

Code	Branch Name	Currency
17SC	SPS Glasgow Anderston	1982-83
17SC	SPS Glasgow	1983-
18SC	Ayr	1964
18SC	SPS Glasgow Distribution	1982-83
19SC	Edinburgh	1964-82
19SC	SPS Edinburgh	1982-87
20SC	Earlston	1964-82
20SC	SPS Earlston	1982-87
21SC	Kirkcaldy	1064-82
21SC	SPS Kirkcaldy	1982
22SC	Dundee	1964-82
22SC	SPS Dundee	1982-87
23SC	Perth	1964-
23SC	SPS Inverness	1982-87
24SC	Aberdeen	1964-82
24SC	SPS Aberdeen	1982-87
25SC	Elgin	1964-
26SC	Inverness	1964-
27NW	Liverpool	1964-77
27N	Liverpool	1977-81
28NW	Colwyn Bay	1964-77
28N	Colwyn Bay	1977-
29NW	Mayfield	1964-71
30NW	White City	1964-75
30NW	Manchester (BartonDock)	1975-77
30N	Manchester (BartonDock)	1977-
31NW	Radium Street	1964-75
32NW	Macclesfield	1964
33NW	Belfast	1964-65
34NW	Burnley	1964-77
34N	Burnley	1977-
35NW	Preston	1964-77
35N	Preston	1977-81
36NW	Lancaster	1964-72

Appendices

Code	Branch Name	Currency
37NW	Carlisle	1964-77
37N	Carlisle	1977-
38	-	not used
39NE	Whitehall Road	1964
40NE	Brown Lane	1964
40NE	Leeds	1964-77
40N	Leeds	1977-79
41NE	York	1964-77
41N	York	1977-
42NE	Hull	1964-77
42N	Hull	1977-
43NE	Bradford	1964-77
43N	Bradford	1977-
44NE	Halifax	1964-67
44NE	Transpennine	1971-75
45NE	Huddersfield	1964-
46NE	Newcastle	1964-67
46N	Newcastle	1977-
47NE	Middlesbrough	1964-77
47N	Middlesbrough	1977-81
48NE	Sheffield	1964-77
48N	Sheffield	1977-
49NE	Lincoln	1964-72
49E	Lincoln	1972-77
49M	Lincoln	1977-81
50NE	Boston	1964-72
50E	Boston	1972-77
50M	Boston	1977-
51M	Nottingham	1964-72
51E	Nottingham	1972-77
51M	Nottingham	1977-81
52M	Derby	1964-72
52E	Derby	1972-77
52M	Derby	1977-

Appendices

Code	Branch Name	Currency
53M	Stoke	1964-72
53NW	Stoke	1972-77
53M	Stoke	1977-
54M	Wolverhampton	1964-72
54NW	Wolverhampton	1972-77
54M	Wolverhampton	1977-
55M	Walter Street	1964-72
55NW	Walter Street	1972-77
55M	Walter Street	1977-81
56M	Vauxhall	1964-66
56M	Droitwich	1968-72
56NW	Droitwich	1972-77
56M	Droitwich	1977-81
57M	South Yardley	1964-68
58M	Coventry	1964-72
58NW	Coventry	1972-77
58M	Coventry	1977-
59M	Belgrave Street, Leicester	1964-68
59M	Western Blvd, Leicester	1968-72
59E	Western Blvd, Leicester	1972-77
59M	Western Blvd, Leicester	1977-81
60M	Gypsy Lane	1964-68
60E	Northampton	1976-77
60M	Northampton	1977-
61M	Great Northern	1964-68
61M	Groby	1968-72
61E	Groby	1972-
62M	Rothwell	1964-
63M	Rushden	1964-
63W ?	Bristol, Feeder Road	1978-
64M	Wellingborough	1964-72
64E	Wellingborough	1972-76
65M	Northampton	1964-72
65E	Northampton	1972-76

223

Appendices

Code	Branch Name	Currency
66M	Bedford	1964-72
66E	Bedford	1972-77
66M	Bedford	1977-
67M	Luton	1964-72
67E	Luton	1972-77
67M	Luton	1977-79
68SW	Oxford	1964-72
68W	Oxford	1972-81
68M	Oxford	1981-91
69SW	Reading	1964-72
69W	Reading	1972-
70SW	Bristol, Albert Street	1964-72
70W	Bristol, Albert Street	1972-81
70S	Bristol, Albert Street	1981-
71SW	Yeovil	1964-72
71W	Yeovil	1972-
72SW	Exeter	1964-72
72W	Exeter	1972-81
72S	Exeter	1981-
73SW	Plymouth	1964-72
73W	Plymouth	1972-81
73S	Plymouth	1981-
74SW	Perranporth	1964-72
74W	Perranporth	1972-81
75SW	Swindon	1964-72
75W	Swindon	1972-81
75S	Swindon	1981-
76W	Welshpool	1964-72
76NW	Welshpool	1972-77
76M	Welshpool	1977-
77W	Cheltenham	1964-
77W	Gloucester	-81
77S	Gloucester	1981
78W	Hereford	1964-81

Appendices

Code	Branch Name	Currency
79W	Newport	1964-79
80W	Cardiff	1964-
81W	Skewen	1964-81
81S	Skewen	1981-
82W	Carmarthen	1964-81
82S	Carmarthen	1981-
83E	Cambridge	1964-77
83M	Cambridge	1977-
84E	Norwich	1964-77
84M	Norwich	1977-
85E	Kings Lynn	1964-77
85M	Kings Lynn	1977-79
86E	Ipswich	1964-77
86M	Ipswich	1977-
87E	Clacton	1964-
88E	Chelmsford	1964-77
88M	Chelmsford	1977-
89E	Southend	1964-77
89M	Southend	1977-
90S	Southampton	1964-
91S	Bournemouth	1974-
92S	Salisbury	1964-70
92S	Basingstoke	1970-
93S	Portsmouth	1964-
94S	Brighton	1964-
95S	Eastbourne	1964-81
96S	Tunbridge Wells	1964-
97S	Chatham	1964-81
98S	Canterbury	1964-
99SW	Bridgwater	1966-72
99W	Bridgwater	1972-81
99S	Bridgwater	1981-

APPENDIX G

LYNX: BRANCH CODES 1993-2005
(FLEET NOT NUMBERED, 1987-1993)

Code	Branch Name
AE	Airdrie
BL	Bristol
BM	Birmingham
BN	Brighton
BS	Body Shop (Leyland?)
BW	Bothwell
BY	Barnsley
CD	Chelmsford
CE	Carlisle
CN	Coulsdon
CY	Colwyn Bay
DD	Dartford
DE	Dundee
DY	Derby
EH	Edinburgh
ER	Exeter
EX	Euro Express (Dartford)
FC	Franchise
GD	Gateshead
GR	Gloucester
HL	Hull
IH	Ipswich
IS	Inverness
JY	Islandlink (Jersey) Ltd
KX	London, Kings Cross
LC	Lincoln
LD	Leyland (Preston)
LN	London, Muswell Hill
LS	Leeds (Pudsey)

Code	Branch Name
MR	Manchester
NH	Norwich
NN	Northampton
NU	Nuneaton
RG	Reading
SA	Swansea (Skewen)
SD	Sheffield
SE	Stoke
SN	Southampton (Eastleigh)
SY	Systems (Birmingham)
WD	Watford
WL	Welshpool

Unknown Codes: Aberdeen
Alfreton
Bournemouth
Dumfries
Earlston
Harlow
Hellaby
Luton
Peterborough DTS
St Neots

Bibliography/Further Reading

Ian Allan booklet 'ABC of British Road Services' published November 1951

Ian Allan booklet 'ABC of British Road Services', second edition published October 1952

Ian Allan booklet 'ABC of British Road Services', third edition published July 1953

Articles, details of Haulage Disposal Units and extracts from Traffic Areas 'Applications and Decisions', published in editions of 'Motor Transport' and 'Commercial Motor' between November 1953 and September 1956.

Ian Allan booklet 'ABC of British Road Services', fourth edition published September 1957

Ian Allan booklet 'ABC of British Road Services', fifth edition published April 1961

Ian Allan booklet 'ABC of British Road Services', sixth edition published August 1963

Article: 'The BRS Story' by G C Johnson, editor of BRS staff magazine, published in TSSA Journal in three parts between October and December 1963

BRS staff magazines up to 1968 and NFC 'Freightway' in-house magazines, 1970-1973

Hardback book 'A Pictorial History of BRS' by Nick Baldwin, published by Frederick Warne in 1982 and since reprinted by Nynehead Books in 2010

Soft back book 'Bristol Goods Vehicles; by Allen Janes and Philip Sposito, produced by Booksprint, Bristol in 1989

Article: 'Restoration of BRS Lorries' by Peter J Davies, published in HCVS magazine of September/October 1992

'Special BRS 50th Anniversary Supplement' by Peter J Davies, published with 'Classic & Vintage Commercials' magazine, November 1998.

Hardback book 'BRS – The Early Years' by Arthur Ingram and Gordon Mustoe, published by Roundoak (Nynehead) in 1999

Hardback book 'BRS Parcels Services' by Mustoe, Ingram and Pearson, published by Roundoak (Nynehead) in 2008

BRS 60 (July 2008), BRS 62 (July 2010) and BRS 64 (July 2012) Programmes by Peter J Davies for events held at Lincoln Farm Truckstop.

Selections of BRS Gazetteers and internal directories, staff magazines and fleet registers made available to us as members of the 'BRSL observers scheme'.

Addendum

Since preparing the schedule of BRS Branch Codes, further details have come to light after study of documents retained by the late Michael Houle. These relate to the period up to 1991. Updates to Codes from 1991 onwards remain shrouded in mystery. *JM, July 2018*

BRS Southern

Previously unknown:
Chelmsford   initially AW as a sub. of Colchester, later revised to AV
Ashford   code XX

Previously unidentified:
XD   Aylesford, for Gateway contract at Maidstone
XK   Leyton, revised from XX
XS   Park Royal, sub. of Brentford
NC   Hitchin Engineering
AB   Letchworth Engineering
XJ   Reading Engineering
NH   Luton Engineering
NJ   Norwich Engineering
NN   Horsham Engineering
NV   Waterloo Engineering
NZ   Hastings Engineering

Additional:
AJ   Lowestoft, for Birds Eye-Wall's contract, sub. of Beccles
NG   Slough Engineering
NK   Willesden Engineering
NT   Brighton Engineering
NW   Folkestone Engineering
NY   Strood Engineering

Most of the Engineering codes related to former NCL Fleetcare sites and were short-lived, becoming merged with existing nearby Branches.

BRS Midlands

One additional Branch introduced:
IF   Walsall, offered Rental and Engineering, 1986-88

BRS Western

Previously unconfirmed:
YN   Yate, for Sainsbury's contract
TD   correct identification 'Milton', for Fleetcare

Additional:
RK   Andover, Truck Rental, 1989-90
      – then RK again, Merthyr Tydfil, for Hoover contract, 1991
TG   Basingstoke, for Boots contract
TM   Middleton Tray Washing Plant, for Sainsbury's
TP   Yate Tray Washing Plant, for Sainsbury's

Scottish Road Services

LE   The second Edinburgh Branch was actually named 'Broxburn'

Milestones in BRS History

1947	Labour Party's Transport Act approves nationalisation of all UK transport
1948	The Road Transport Executive, under the new British Transport Commission (BTC), empowered to take over private hauliers to form British Road Services (BRS)
1949	Road Transport Executive re-named Road Haulage Executive (RHE)
1951	Conservatives get re-elected and promise a return to free enterprise
1953	RHE disbanded and BRS becomes a limited company under the BTC
1953	Road Haulage Disposal Board set up to sell approximately 32,500 BRS vehicles to private companies
1955	BRS (Parcels) Ltd formed as separate operation
1956	Disposals halted. BRS to retain approximately 7,750 general haulage vehicles
1956	BRS (Meat Haulage) Ltd formed
1956	Renationalisation completed. BTC granted armorial bearings and new style door crest with lion 'rampant' introduced
1963	Transport Holding Company (THC) replaces BTC. BRS Federation formed.
1963	Door crest discontinued and a completely new fleet numbering system introduced
1964	Brief period of expansion under Wilson's Labour government including voluntary acquisition of a number of private hauliers
1968	Labour's Transport Act sets out to integrate road and rail services under newly formed National Freight Corporation, which replaces the THC
1969	Freightliners, formed by BR in 1966, transferred from BR Board to NFC
1972	Under the Conservatives, re-elected in1970, BRS is split up into eight regional companies: SBRS, WBRS, NWBRS, EBRS, NEBRS, MBRS, SRS and Morton's BRS
1974	Labour returned to power until the serious economic recession of 1979
1975	BRS Truck Rental launched. BRS (Parcels) Ltd re-named Roadline
1978	Freightliners returned to the control of British Rail
1980	Conservatives reorganise the NFC, renaming it the National Freight Company in readiness for privatization. Employee buyout masterminded by Chief Executive Peter Thompson.
1983	Seven BRS companies pruned down to four: BRS S, BRS W, BRS M, BRS N, plus SRS remaining unaltered.
1987	Lynx parcels service established, replacing Roadline and National Carriers
1995	Transport operations come under Exel Logistics
1998	BRS Truck Rental sold to Volvo trucks
2000	Exel and Ocean Group plc merge to form Exel plc
2005	Exel plc acquired by DHL (Dalsey,Hillblom,Lynn), brand name of Deutsche Post

Printed in Great Britain
by Amazon